The Mountain Bike Book

The
Mountain Bike
Book

Choosing, Riding and Maintaining the Off-Road Bicycle

Third, completely updated and expanded edition

Rob van der Plas

Bicycle Books – San Francisco

Copyright © Rob van der Plas, 1984, 1988, 1993
Third, completely updated and expanded edition
Third printing of this edition, 1994

Printed in the United States of America

Published by:
Bicycle Books, Inc., PO Box 2038, Mill Valley, CA 94942, USA

Distributed to the book trade by:
USA: National Book Network, 4720 Boston Way, Lanham, MD 20706
UK: Chris Lloyd Sales and Marketing Services, 463 Ashley Rd.,
            Poole, Dorset, BHI4 0AX
Canada: Raincoast Book Distribution, 112 E 3rd Avenue,
            Vancouver, BC V5T 1 C8

Cover design by Kent Lytle
Cover photograph by Bob Allen
Frontispiece photograph by Bob Allen

Library of Congress Cataloging in Publication Data:
van der Plas, Robert, 1938 —
The Mountain Bike Book
Choosing, riding and maintaining the off-road bicycle
third edition, 1993
Bibliography: p. Includes index
1. Bicycles and bicycling, manuals, handbooks, etc.
2. Mountains, recreational use
3. Authorship - Handbooks, Manuals, etc.
I. Title

Library of Congress Catalog Card Number 92-85200

ISBN 0-933201-32-X, Paperback original

Acknowledgements

Many people whose names don't appear on the title page contributed to this book. I would like to express my appreciation to those who have helped make this totally revised edition of The Mountain Bike Book what it is. Several readers and experienced mountain bike riders have contributed their comments and suggestions. Others have made their mark through their critical letters or reviews of the first and second editions.

In particular, I would like to thank mountain bike pioneer Gary Fisher for taking the time to go through the manuscript for technical and historic accuracy and to assure it is up to date. Finally, I would like to thank Michele Jones for her thorough editing job and Christina Nau for her contribution in collecting numerous bits of information from various sources, as well as many of the photographs reproduced in this book.

No doubt some deficiencies still remain. The author and his publisher invite readers, riders and reviewers to spare them neither their criticism nor their constructive suggestions. We shall make every effort to incorporate all comments received this way in the next edition.

Rob van der Plas is an internationally recognized expert on bicycle matters. He was also the first one to write a book devoted specifically to the mountain bike. Published March 1984, the first edition of this *Mountain Bike Book* has been the classic book on the subject and has been translated into German, Spanish, French, Italian, Danish, and Dutch.

An engineer and writer by trade, and an experienced off-road cyclist himself, he has spent much of the last 15 years working on bicycle projects. He has written over a dozen books and scores of articles for specialist periodicals on both sides of the Atlantic.

Growing up in Holland and England, he frequently used the bicycle on unpaved roads many years before the idea of the mountain bike matured. When he moved to San Francisco in 1968, he rode his regular bike on the slopes of Mount Tamalpais and the Marin Headlands long before the first fat tire tracks were spotted there. Once they had, he immediately took to this fat-tire bike. Today, he is a full-time writer and lives on the slopes of Mount Tamalpais in California's Marin County, the very place where the mountain bike was born.

Table of Contents

9

Part I
Choosing the Right Equipment

CHAPTER 1

Mountain Biking Today

The mountain bike has come of age. Within the span of a single decade, it has not only taken over as the most popular adult bicycle in the U.S. and most other Western countries, it has helped make cycling more popular than it has ever been before. It is used both for sport and recreation, as well as for utility and touring. Indeed, for the first time since the 1880s, an entirely new type of machine has not only appeared on the market, it has very nearly taken over. Suddenly, fat-tire bikes are everywhere. But by the same token, today's mountain bike is not the same as yesterday's. This book will fill you in on what's current in mountain bikes and the sport of mountain biking.

When first introduced, cyclists quickly fell in love with this rugged bike for all seasons, finding more and more uses for this ultimately practical machine. The industry has not stood still either: Mountain bikes and special components designed for them quickly became big business, and today's machines make the models of only a few years ago look antiquated by comparison. The mountain bike, it seems, has given the industry and the sport a new lease on life.

Indeed, it is hard not to be enthusiastic about this wonderful bicycle. It helps novices become experts in record time, and it allows experienced cyclists to do things they had never thought possible

Dan Gindling photo

before. The mountain bike is not only agile and rugged enough to go anywhere, it is also safer, more reliable and comfortable than any other bike I know.

Although the mountain bike no doubt lends itself better to cycling off the beaten track than any other model, the undeniable fact is that it is also perfectly suitable to be ridden on regular paved roads, whether in the city or the country. While special racing, touring and commuting bikes still have their rightful places, if I could have only one bicycle, I'd probably choose a mountain bike—as most others do these days—because it *is* the most versatile bike available.

About this Book

This book is devoted specifically to the modern mountain bike and the way it is used. All of its uses, not just for riding in mountains. Consequently, you will find quite a lot of advice that will be useful for riding your bike under a variety of circumstances, in addition to specific recommendations for riding off-road.

The book comprises three parts and an Appendix. In Part I (Chapters 1 through 5), you will be shown how to select a bike, its accessories and other equipment, followed by advice on how to set it up initially and what other equipment to take along. Depending on your preferences, your skills and the use to which the machine will be put, certain variants of the mountain bike and other items of

equipment will be more appropriate than others. You will learn how to select the best and adjust it to match your needs.

Part II (Chapters 6 through 13) is devoted to the subject of handling the bike under all conceivable circumstances. Here you will be shown how to get the most out of the equipment you have. These chapters deal with subjects ranging from simple bike handling to safety on and off the road, from steering to gearing, and from cross-country touring to off-road racing.

Part III (Chapters 14 through 22) deals with the technical aspects of the mountain bike. I like to save this for last, since to most of us, this material is not the easiest or most entertaining stuff to read. Although some people will want to know all the technical ins and outs, others will perhaps put the book back on the shelf before things get this technical. However, as a reference, this technical material will be useful to all, as it includes equipment evaluation guidance and repair instructions, which you'll want to have available when the need arises, even if you don't savor it as bedside reading.

New to this edition of the book is a chapter devoted to suspensions, because these systems without a doubt represent the most significant innovations of the last few years. Many systems and components are being offered, and this chapter will help you determine what is useful and what is not—specifically in view of the kind of riding you do.

The Appendix, finally, contains some useful reference material that's too prosaic for general reading. Included are a frame sizing aid and a gearing table designed specifically for the kind of gearing and the wheel size typically found on mountain bikes. In addition, you will find here a troubleshooting guide to help you cure roadside problems, a list of addresses, a bibliography and an extensive alphabetical index.

Compared to the earlier editions of this book (the first edition appeared March 1984 and was indeed the very first book to appear on the subject), the contents of this edition are completely updated. In fact, the book has been entirely rewritten and will be updated for each reprint. All the developments that have taken place since the early days are included in this edition.

Choice of Words

Before continuing, let me settle some points of terminology. In the first place, there is the matter of spelling. Although this book is sold on both sides of the Atlantic, I shall use American spelling as much as my own tolerance for some of the local excesses allows. My British readers will find many words spelled in a slightly unfamiliar way: tire for tyre, aluminum for aluminium, center for centre, and so on. In addition, entirely different words are sometimes in use for the same concept in the two societies. Anticipating the resulting confusion, I have made every effort to explain the meaning of American expressions that differ from those used in Britain by more than the spelling alone whenever a term is used for the first time. Thus you will find that *coaster brake* is American for

Bob Allen photo

13

back-pedalling brake explained in Chapter 1—but you're on your own the next time the term is used: by then, you're expected to know what it means.

Throughout this book, you will encounter references to manufacturers, brands, makes and models of certain products related to the subject. Some of these terms are protected brand names or registered trademarks, though they are not identified as such in the text. Their use here is for informative purposes only, for which reason these terms are not identified by the trademark, copyright or registration symbol.

Finally, on this subject, there is the question of gender. Although my sympathy for sexual equality is as great as may reasonably be expected from any member of the male sex, my tolerance for linguistic concoctions like *he/she* and *man/woman*, or even compounds with *-person*, is very low. And I hold that the meaning of *man* as a general term referring to the entire human race is neither discriminatory nor unreasonable. I find the method of distributing *he* and *she*, *his* and *her* evenly throughout the text, as is sometimes done, so confusing that I'd rather be accused of being anything under the sun than having to read through such material, let alone write it.

Defining the Mountain Bike

To make sure we are all talking about the same thing, let me briefly summarize what to me makes the mountain bike—what distinguishes it from other bicycles. Simply put, fat tires and flat handlebars. But if that were all, the bike I used to ride as a kid in Holland would qualify as a mountain bike, as would the 16-inch wheeled iron monster on which my children first learned to ride. On the other hand, my favorite mountain bike, which is equipped with dropped handlebars, would not qualify. So there must be more to it.

The mountain bike combines some of the best characteristics of several other machines, though it is clearly designed afresh. The fat tires have a tough tread for good traction on dirt, yet they are also light and can be inflated to a relatively high pressure, resulting in significantly less rolling resistance than on other fat-tire bikes. The handlebars are wide enough to offer firm handling and flat enough to allow instant access to the brakes. At the same time, they are ergonomically designed, so they don't force you into a posture that is uncomfortable in the long run.

The frame is rugged, yet reasonably light. The wheels are driven via a gearing system with anything from 18 to 24 speeds that allows you to take most inclines in your stride. And those gears are easy to operate by means of indexed thumb shifters mounted on or below the handlebars. But this intriguing machine won't merely climb, it will go downhill safely, due to its balanced geometry. Finally, with the help of its special brakes, it can be stopped on a dime. Surely, this is a triumph of two-wheel ingenuity.

In subsequent chapters, we shall take a closer look at the characteristic features of the mountain bike and its components. You will learn that there are enough differences within the range of mountain bikes available to make some more suitable for certain purposes than others. Even more suitable, I should say, because basically even a very simple mountain bike will outdo virtually any other type of bicycle for many basic cycling uses.

Perhaps the greatest positive aspect of the mountain bike is the appeal it has to those who have not previously felt very much at ease on a bike. Turned off by the poor performance and discomfort of the old utility bike, yet not at ease with the drop handlebar ten-speed, these are the people whose

bikes if they had them at all stood rusting away in a corner of the garage for many years. Young and old, men and women: all feel at ease on this machine.

Ten-speeds with drop handlebars were fashionable from the early seventies to the mid eighties. Like most experienced cyclists, I still relish mine, which I use preferably on paved roads. But the mountain bike has brought a form of equality to cycling. Now even the less skilled can buy a quality bike that matches their riding habits. Most likely, this is the bike that satisfies your needs, a bike that you can easily learn to handle as well as I can, even if you are a little older or a little less agile or athletically ambitious. At the same time, it is a bike that appeals to the toughest gonzos. Finally fashion has caught up with common sense: here's the bike for everyone.

Renner photo

15

The Mountain Bike's Background

Although the mountain bike is a relatively recent development, it already has a history that deserves to be told. In fact, its roots can be traced back to 1933. Balloon-tired bicycles had been around for about five years at the time, but that was the year Ignaz Schwinn introduced the most successful version in the U.S. It had fat tires, flat handlebars, a relaxed geometry, and an indestructible construction—but few of the other virtues of the modern mountain bike. Heavy and rugged, it soon became the standard for newspaper delivery and other forms of utilitarian cycling. Actually, it was probably meant to be a gag. Emulating the motorized vehicles of adult America, it offered the kids of America the closest approximation to a car possible on two wheels—and muscle-powered, mind you.

Half a century later this curious design was to experience an unexpected revival. Cycling in America had gone through fits and starts, ups and downs. The ten-speed boom had come and gone. At least the ten-speed boom had finally allowed respectable adults to progress self-propelled, which had been unheard of for many years. Meanwhile, the younger generation's BMX bike had become much more than a toy and a means of competition, it had also led to some surprisingly sophisticated technology.

The mountain bike forms a synthesis of the old utility bike, the ten-speed and the BMX bike. Popular lore has it that it all started just North of San Francisco, on the slopes of Mount Tamalpais. Instead, I like to think of 'Mount Tam' as only one of several places where this development took place. What happened there, no doubt also happened elsewhere, and the timing can't have been far off.

As it was, kids such as my now 40-year-old neighbor used their old balloon-tired bikes on the mountain's fire trails for many years before it became fashionable to do so for those who today claim to have invented it. Whatever the official historians of the fat-tire scene claim, these kids were there first. And the idea of modifying their bikes so they climbed and could be stopped better also stems from them. Not until the mid-seventies do we find the beginnings of the official history. Here it is recorded that men and youths made a sport of riding motorcycles down the rough slopes of Marin County's highest mountain, which gave them hair-raising thrills. It was horrible in environmental terms, since it was not only noisy, it caused erosion, which disturbed the natural watershed. When the water district authorities got wind of it, they restricted motorcycles to paved roads. Some of these riders thought of other ways to get their thrills: They copied the kids and took to riding down the same slopes on bicycles—but unlike their examples, they got back up to the top with their bike in a pickup truck.

They must have ruined a lot of bicycles that way, not to mention what they did to the environment, even without a motor. By and by, it became apparent what kind of bike would best stand up to this kind of use: that same fat-tired machine that Schwinn had introduced about 45 years earlier. The Schwinn Excelsior, as it had been built from 1933 until 1941, turned out to be the ultimate bike for this kind of use.

A few problems remained, though. This bike's coaster brake (back-pedalling brake to my British readers) had a way of overheating on the downhill, and the most famous stretch of Tamalpais slope is called Repack in its honor: after one descent, the heat had literally boiled the grease out of the bearings, so you either had to repack the bearings with fresh grease or give up altogether. And then the idea of riding down, only

to hitch a ride back up in a truck, seemed perverse to the true cyclist.

That was not the way Gary Fisher, one of the country's strongest cyclocross bicycle racers, was going to play the game. Instead, he modified his fat-tire bike to take derailleur gearing, thumb shifters, and a seat post quick-release, so he could ride up as well as down. The idea caught on and soon some hillsides were swarming with reckless men and women trying to break their necks going down and busting their backs struggling up again.

Joe Breeze, one of the other named progenitors of the mountain bike according to the California gospel, went a step further. A framebuilder of some expertise, he decided to copy the geometry that seemed to lend the Schwinn Excelsior its superb uphill and downhill qualities onto a frame weighing about 3 pounds less. This was

Mountain biking history: Gary Fisher, the man behind many present-day innovations, showing off what is perhaps the first true mountain bike.

Bob Allen photo

adapted to take the most suitable components available at the time, such as 15-speed derailleur gears, cantilever brakes and moped handlebars and brake levers. Essentially, the mountain bike was born. It just hadn't been discovered yet.

This process was helped along by the next character to appear on the scene. Mike Sinyard is the name, an enterprising bicycle businessman from San Jose, California. Sinyard, through his company called Specialized, had proven in the past to have an excellent feel for what was good and how to sell it. This time, he engaged frame builder Tim Neenan, another member of the California breakneck crowd, to design a mountain bike frame that could be built in series, and specified the components that had proven themselves in actual use. Built in Japan for Specialized, this became the first production mountain bike: the Stumpjumper.

Now everybody with $750 to spare could have a mountain bike to call his own. Sinyard spent a fortune advertising this machine, this way essentially prefinancing the entire mountain bike boom. This is one example of commercial pioneering in mountain bike circles. I suppose the Stumpjumper returned the cost of advertising, but there is even less doubt that the whole mountain bike movement was established in the public mind as a result of this venture. Without it, there is a good chance the mountain bike's light would have remained hidden under the bushel

where many of its slightly off-beat devotees had a way of hiding it.

Not that all the others overlooked the mountain bike's commercial possibilities. For instance, there was the trio of Tom Ritchey. Gary Fisher and Charlie Kelly. Before they went their separate ways as frame builder and component designer, bike businessman, and mountain bike guru, respectively, they set up what was probably the first commercially successful operation dealing only in mountain bikes, *MountainBikes* (which later, as petty punishment for its success, had to be renamed first *Fisher MountainBikes* and then *Gary Fisher Bicycles*). And then there were the many innovative frame builders who were also mountain bike riders, developing one refinement after the other.

Although Specialized clearly had a head start on them, the big American bike manufacturers were not caught napping. They did not waste much time before bringing out their own real or presumed mountain bikes. Some merely continued the junk they had been making for the cash-and-carry market in a form that made it look like a mountain bike. Others went into the business more seriously. But most soon learned to do things right, especially those who had always been concerned with quality. Schwinn was there and even companies like Ross hired competent frame builders to design real mountain bikes that could be mass-produced.

Foreign manufacturers didn't take long to catch on either. First the Japanese and later the Taiwanese soon flooded the market with mountain bikes. As early as 1984, only two years after the introduction of the Stumpjumper, mountain bikes accounted for a third of the adult bicycle sales in the U.S. Today, the mountain bike has taken first place, regularly accounting for more than 75% of all adult bike sales.

Very soon special components, specifically designed with the mountain bike in mind, started to edge out the grab-bag of adapted items from other fields that had served so well in getting the show on the road. Manufacturers like Shimano and SunTour brought out comprehensive ranges of special mountain bike components. Encouraged by Japanese tax incentives, they keep improving their wares from year to year. Just when everybody thought the perfect mountain bike derailleur was here, they introduced indexed derailleurs, and as soon as the gearing had progressed from the original 15-speed to 18- and then 21-speeds, it became all the rage to install 24-speed systems. No sooner had a great brake been found, when the next generation of even better brakes appeared on the market. And just when I thought I was comfortable on the mountain bike, the manufacturers proclaimed that what was needed most was a suspension system to soften the ride. We're still improving and experimenting, but yes, the mountain bike has come of age.

Simultaneously, an entirely new competitive sport has sprouted up. Off-road or mountain bike racing is now not only a popular participation sport, it also very soon became commercialized, with many of the major and minor manufacturers sponsoring their own teams. California and Colorado led the way, but soon enough also other parts of the U.S., Canada and Britain could boast literally dozens of mountain bike competitions and other off-road events each weekend. Europe has its Grundig Challenge cup series of races, and the Mountain Biking World Championships,

Mountain bike framebuilder and designer Tom Ritchey.

David Epperson / Bicycle Sports photograph

which are held alternatingly in North America and Europe, have grown into hotly contested ventures with participants literally from all over the world.

Mountain Bike Periodicals

Nowhere can the rapid development of the mountain bike be more clearly traced than in the remarkable developments in the cycling periodicals press. Back in 1980, Charlie Kelly and Denise Caramagno first brought out their slightly outrageous *Fat Tire Flyer*. Initially, it was no more than a couple of mimeographed sheets of 8½x 11 folded in the middle, filled cover to cover by the sponsors under various pseudonyms. It saw a rapid rise in readership within a very short time, and succeeded in obtaining enough advertising to pay the bills.

Six years later, there were at least four national magazines specifically devoted to the mountain bike in the U.S. alone. Printed on glossy paper, with lots of color photographs, professional layout, phenomenal advertising rates and first class editorial material, they document the vigor of the sport and the industry. The mountain bike press had definitely arrived.

Until Big Brother took over. Rodale Press's *Bicycling* absorbed *Mountain Bike* magazine and integrated it into its own publication. Quite a number of specialized mountain biking periodicals still survive. Not only can you get Mountain Bike separately, so you don't have to read the rest of Bicycling, but on the newsstand you'll also find such titles as *Mountain Bike Action*, *Mountain and City Biking*, and *Mountain Biking*. In Britain and in other European countries they are doing very well too (e.g., the very impressively designed German publication *Bike*). But at the same time, most of the general cycling magazines devote as much of their editorial space to the mountain bike as on all other bicycle types combined.

The advertisers go even farther. Both in bike magazines and elsewhere, they depict healthy adults grinding uphill or speeding down on mountain bikes to sell items that have little bearing on just what kind of machine you ride— or in fact on whether you ride a bike at all. Yes, the mountain bike has come a long way and it is clearly here to stay.

CHAPTER 2

Know Your Mountain Bike

Today, the mountain bike is common enough—it no longer needs a formal introduction. Just the same, it will be useful to investigate the characteristics of the machine, so you will be able to select one smartly when buying a new one. This chapter will also familiarize you with the terminology used in the book.

What's Different About the Mountain Bike

You can look at the mountain bike as though it were an entirely new object, or you can do so as though it is merely a variant on a familiar theme—a different kind of bicycle. The best way to appreciate the machine is by highlighting what distinguishes it from other bicycles, which is what this section is devoted to.

Fig. 2.1 represents a typical mountain bike. Perhaps the fairest way of distinguishing it from the

The mountain bike has come a long way. This one by Trek has front and rear suspension, 24-speed gearing and bar-ends (handlebar extensions).

ten-speed derailleur bike is by adopting the terminology introduced by the editors of the *Fat Tire Flyer*, the long-since defunct mouthpiece of the first California mountain biking gurus. They differentiated between *fat-tired* and *skinny-tired* bikes.

The mountain bike's main components are shown and identified in the illustration. Many of these components themselves comprise a number of distinct minor parts. It takes about 2000 bits and pieces to make up a modern bicycle, although many of these parts are duplicates of one another. Take the chain, for instance: comprising about 600 parts, most chains only have five distinct types of parts—but then over a hundred of each.

Frame and Component Groups

The best way to get to understand the workings of the bike is by looking at the various functional groups of components that make it up. Thus, I like to consider the following categories: frame, steering system, seat, drivetrain, gearing system, wheels, and brakes. These same groups will form the basis for our survey of the technical aspects of the mountain bike in the chapters of Part III. For a quick initial overview of the machine, we'll consider these same groups here, as well as the accessories, to which Chapter 5 will be devoted.

Usually, the frame is the only part actually made by the manufacturer whose name the bike

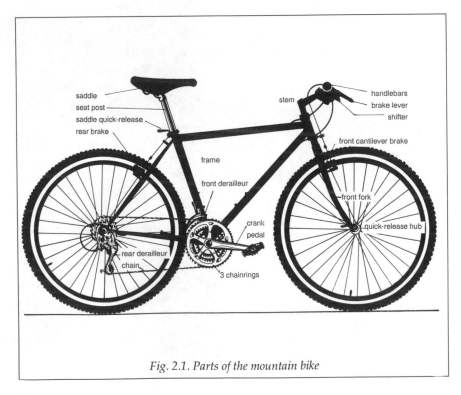

Fig. 2.1. Parts of the mountain bike

bears. All other components are bought from specialist component manufacturers and fitted to the finished frame in the bicycle manufacturer's plant. So, in fact, the bike manufacturer is typically more of an assembler when it comes to the rest of the bike.

The number of frame or bike manufacturers is legion, but the number of component manufacturers is limited. Consequently, you will find the same component selections on many different bikes. The major component manufacturer is Shimano, offering complete so-called gruppos (or groupsets in Britain), comprising just about every conceivable mechanical component used on the bike. They have a whole range of such mountain bike gruppos, ranging from the cheap plastic-coated Exage to the finely polished Deore XTR, matching bikes that range in price (in 1993 dollars) from $500 to $2000. Of course not all that money is in the components, but the cheap components tend to be installed on cheap, slightly cruder and heavier frames, the higher-priced ones on the lighter, more expensive, more carefully built and finished ones.

The Frame

As on any other bicycle, the mountain bike's frame forms its backbone. Most frames are built in large series, but some are hand-built in small numbers, or even to order, by specialized frame build-

ers. These are generally the most exclusive and expensive machines.

The frame itself is made up of metal tubing, generally made of some type of steel, although more and more manufacturers offer aluminum frames these days, while even titanium and carbon fiber are making inroads. The frame's two major parts are the quadrilateral main frame, or forward portion, made up of large diameter tubing, and the double rear triangle, made up of thinner tubes in pairs.

The main frame comprises top tube, downtube, seat tube and head tube, and their respective locations can easily be guessed from these names. The horizontal and vertical tubes of the rear triangle are called chain stays and seat stays, respectively. At the bottom, where down tube, seat tube and chain stays join, is the bottom bracket (sometimes called BB)—the heart of its drivetrain.

The tubes are either connected by means of welded or brazed joints, or they may be held together with lugs, to which they are usually brazed (if steel), welded or bonded (if aluminum or carbon fiber). Technical details of this sort are explained in chapters 14 and 15.

The differences between a typical mountain bike frame and that of a ten-speed is a matter of geometry, i.e. the relationship of the frame's dimensions and angles. Except for the seat tube and head tube, the various tubes tend to be longer on a mountain bike than they are on a ten-speed for the same size rider, and the clearances are more generous, as is the distance of the bottom bracket above the ground. The angles between the horizontal plane and the seat tube and head tube are typically shallower and some of the individual tubes, especially the down tube and the chain stays, should be of slightly greater diameter on the mountain bike. All these features make for a bike that is good natured and less sensitive to the irregularities of the terrain.

The introduction of full suspension bikes has had its effect on the frame, because different frame designs had to be introduced to accommodate the rear suspensions. Even front suspension forks should strictly lead to a different frame geometry, because they raise the head tube up by about 40 mm (1.6 inches), resulting in different angles and an increased height of the frame when the suspension is not compressed.

The Steering System

The bike is steered by a combination of lean and front wheel turn. As will be described in more detail in Chapter 8, the steering system is essential to achieve both. It is comprised of the front fork, in which the front wheel is mounted, the handlebars, with the stem that connects them to the fork, and the headset bearings with which the whole system is pivoted in the frame's head tube.

Clearly, the handlebars are characteristic on these machines: wide and flat, but in recent years they are getting narrower, which works fine with today's nimbler handling characteristics. The stem should be a very sturdy model, to match the high stresses sometimes applied to the handlebars in rough terrain, and typically they raise the handlebars further above the head tube. The fork must be wide enough to accommodate the fatter tires and it had better be very strong. On the other hand, a vertically flexible welded titanium stem, or better yet one with a built-in spring, can add considerably to your comfort by reducing the effect of front end vibrations passed on to the hands.

Interestingly enough, the conventional flat handlebars are gradually being replaced by more versatile designs, and 'bar-ends' or 'bullhorns'—handlebar extensions pointing forward—have become almost standard on sporty mountain bikes.

The design of the steering components has evolved quite a bit in recent years, as will be described in Chapter 16. Most spectacular has been the introduction of suspension systems, which may either take the form of a sprung fork or may be built into the stem. In Chapter 22 we will discuss the benefits of both methods.

The Wheels

Long before the introduction of suspension forks, in fact ever since John Boyd Dunlop first introduced the pneumatic bicycle tire in the year 1887, the wheels have formed the bicycle's major suspension system. On a mountain bike, they perform that task more effectively than on any other kind of machine. They are fat for that very purpose. Keeping them at an adequate pressure will cushion the ride, while at the same time protecting the rims and tires against damage.

The tires, although always fatter than on other bikes, come in several widths, varying from about 1.6 in to 2.2 in, with a nominal diameter of usually 26 in overall on real mountain bikes. On hybrids they tend to be somewhat narrower and usually 28 inches in diameter. The wider tires provide the best real off-road qualities, whereas the less generously dimensioned versions initially were a reflection on a curious excess of economic protectionism. It stems from an excise tax dating back to the thirties, when U.S. bike manufacturers rallied to prevent the importation of cheap bikes with the only size of tires the public wanted at the time: 26 x 1.75 in. Just the same, such relatively narrower tires will do just fine for most kinds of use.

The tires are mounted on aluminum rims. The rims are laced to the wheel hubs in a net of tension-wired spokes, just like any other regular bike wheel. The hubs on your mountain bike may be sealed against dust and water penetration. Earlier models were often attached by means of axle nuts, since that allows the use of solid axles. These are slightly stronger than the hollow axles used for the handy quick-release hub attachments, which are nevertheless used almost universally on mountain bikes as well as on ten-speeds these days. Chapter 17 contains all the detailed information you may ever need about mountain bike's wheels.

The Drivetrain

This is the term for the system of components that carry the rider's pedaling force and motion to the rear wheel. Sometimes the gearing system is included in this group as well, but I prefer to treat the latter separately. So we have the pedals, installed on the cranks, turning in the bottom bracket bearings, with the chainrings attached to the RH crank, the chain, and the freewheel with individual sprockets installed on the rear wheel hub.

Mountain bikes are often equipped with special cranksets, pedals and so on, designed specifically to match the rugged use these machines get and to provide a surer footing. On bottom-line models, the pedals may be of plastic and lack the toeclips familiar from the ten-speed, which are also used on quality mountain bikes and hybrids (as on high-quality road bikes, clipless pedals, similar to ski bindings, are frequently used on quality mountain bikes). The chain and several other components may be identical to those used on other bikes. The bottom bracket may be equipped with supposedly sealed bearings to help keep out the worst dust and moisture.

The Gearing System

Nowadays, mountain bikes have at least 21-speed derailleur gearing. The derailleur gear system is based on the principle that the gear ratio is a function of the relative sizes of front chainring and rear sprocket over which the chain runs. The gearing adaptations are made by shifting the chain sideways while pedaling That's done by means of shifting the front and rear derailleurs, or changers, to engage a particular combination of chainring and sprocket with different numbers of teeth. It's the same principle used on ten-speeds, but it is extended by using a third, and in rare cases even a fourth, chainring in the front, in combination with 6, 7 or 8 sprockets in the rear.

On virtually all mountain bikes, the gears are selected by means of thumb shifters installed on the handlebars within easy reach. Indexed shifting systems have become the standard in mountain bike gearing. These systems move the rear derailleur up and down through the various gears in distinct steps, rather than requiring tricky fine-tuning. Chapters 7 and 19 deal with the practical and technical aspects of the derailleur system.

The Brakes

Mountain bikes need strong and reliable brakes. They are often ridden down steep slopes, and they have to be stopped quickly and surely. Although the cantilever design of the early bikes has in principle survived to this day— relegating presumed improvements of the 80s to the museum— they have evolved quite a bit. The brakes are mounted on pivot bosses that are attached directly to the tubes of fork and frame, for front and rear brakes, respectively. Whatever their type, they must open wide enough to get the wide mountain bike tires through.

The brakes are operated by means of special levers, matching the flat handlebars installed on the mountain bike. These levers are installed within easy reach from the ends of the handlebars. As is the case with the ten-speed and other bicycles with caliper brakes, the levers and mechanisms are connected by means of flexible Bowden cables. Chapter 20 gives all the details.

Saddle and Seatpost

The mountain bike's saddle, or seat, is generally wider than that of the ten-speed bike, and usually more padded. All this to make up for the fact that most mountain bike riders tend to rest a greater portion of their weight on the seat.

The saddle is installed on a seatpost, which is attached in the frame's seat tube by means of a quick-release binder bolt. Loosening this bolt allows adjusting the height of the seat. On some older bikes, an additional quick-release adjustment may be provided to vary the forward position of the saddle relative to the seatpost. These features allow quick response to variations in the terrain.

Accessories

Mountain bikes may be equipped with a number of special accessories. These range from water bottle cages to luggage racks and various other extras that can be hung on any bike to advantage. Generally, they must be designed specifically for mountain bike use, to match their different dimensions, as compared to other bikes. Chapter 5 contains additional information relating to many of the mountain bike accessories available.

Suspension

In recent years, more and more top-quality mountain bikes have been designed around some form of suspension. Generally only the front end is sprung, be it by means of a telescoping fork, a spring-dampened handlebar stem, or some other device. In some cases, the rear end is sprung too, but this tends to require a complete redesign of the frame, which has indeed been done by several manufacturers. Right now, it looks as if front suspension is here to stay, while rear suspension may not be with us indefinitely.

In Chapter 22, you will learn most of what is worth knowing about suspensions, but let it suffice here to say that even the simplest suspension forks make a mountain bike about $200 more expensive than the same bike without, while greater comfort—and better control over the bike—can be obtained with a sprung handlebar stem and perhaps a better choice of saddle. So unless you are willing to pay much more, I can't recommend choosing a suspension bike—for most uses there are more important quality criteria, such as the overall quality of the frame and the moving parts.

Care of the Mountain Bike

Perhaps the best way of becoming better acquainted with your mountain bike is by doing some of your own maintenance. Cleaning, adjusting and lubrication can easily be carried out on a regular basis with a very minimum of special tools and with little initial technical expertise. What you learn while doing this work pays off in terms of increased competence when riding the bike.

Even if you don't do anything else, at least make a habit of cleaning and inspecting your bike regularly. You may decide to let someone else take care of the maintenance, if you are so inclined.

Clean the bike—preferably after every long ride, but at least once a month, more frequently if

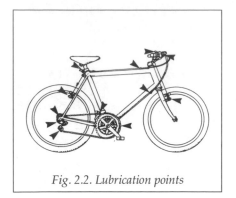

Fig. 2.2. Lubrication points

will remain in place to protect the components against rust. Don't get this mixture into the bearings, since it would dissolve the bearing grease.

3. Next, lubricate the various points in dictated with an arrow in Fig. 2.2, using a spray lubricant. If you don't ride in the rain or over wet terrain, you may select a synthetic oil or a very thin mineral spray lubricant. Otherwise, you'll be better off selecting a waxy lubricant, such as motorcycle chain lube.

4. After cleaning and lubrication, check whether all the mechanisms are adjusted properly: saddle height, handlebars, brakes, gears. Make sure no bolts or nuts are loose or missing and that nothing is bent. Inflate the tires to at least the pressure indicated on the tire sidewall, but use quite low pressures for very soft ground.

you often use it under really dusty or wet conditions. Do this immediately after the ride, rather than waiting until the next time you need the bike, when you may find out too late that it's not in good operating order. Proceed as follows to clean your bike:

1. If the dirt is dry, take it off with a soft brush and a rag. If the dirt is either still wet or caked on, use a damp cloth or clean water to take it off. Just avoid getting lots of water and mud in the vicinity of the bearings, the cables and the chain. After the wet operation, clean it with a dry rag.

2. Using a small brush, or the corner of a rag wrapped around a narrow object, get into all the hidden corners where the dirt is hard to remove. If it is necessary to remove greasy dirt, use a brush soaked in a mixture of ten parts kerosene (paraffin to my British readers) with one part motor oil. When the kerosene evaporates, the oil

You may refer any technical problems you encounter in this inspection to the bike shop. However, if you are more ambitious about maintenance—highly recommended for those who want to become really competent and at ease with their bikes—learn to carry out the adjustments yourself. The chapters of Part III of this book contain practical advice on such maintenance operations. You'll find even more instructions in my book *Mountain Bike Maintenance*.

CHAPTER 3

Selecting the Right Mountain Bike

This chapter will familiarize you with the criteria that establish which particular mountain bike will best serve your needs. Clearly, it will be impossible to simply define what is 'the best mountain bike': it all depends on how you ride, what your needs are, in what kind of terrain you will be riding most often, and how much you can afford to spend.

There are enough differences to make the choice a challenging one. Various makes, models and sizes are available. And there are subtle details that at first escape the attention of even the most careful observer who is not fully prepared. But you *will* be prepared by the

Fisher AL 1 mountain bike with welded aluminum frame.

time you have worked your way through this chapter.

Mountain Bike, Hybrid, and City Bike

For many uses, the real mountain bike may be considered overkill. For those who mainly ride on the road or on relatively firm and

29

smooth trails, the so-called hybrid bike is a perfectly satisfactory alternative. It differs from the real mountain bike in the wheel size, which is typically the French size 700 B, which is a little larger in diameter and with somewhat narrower tires, and by their less rugged design. Consequently it is often also slightly lighter and often less expensive than otherwise equivalent mountain bikes.

Another variant on the mountain bike theme is the city bike, which was actually originally a European derivative of the mountain bike. Again somewhat less rugged, this kind of bike comes equipped with lighting, luggage racks, and fenders. It is a fine all-weather bike, although to date most of the ones I have seen lack the quality features that make a bike last the way I would like it to.

In the discussions below, I will not be making any further distinctions between mountain bike, hybrid, and city bike. The latter two are merely treated as variants of the mountain bike that are otherwise covered adequately.

The Price to Pay

Mountain bikes and machines that look just like them are available in prices that run the gamut from cash-and-carry junk to expensively crafted works of engineering art. Although almost every price has its justification in terms of the work and materials that went into the finished product, it would not be reasonable to suggest that the

most expensive will be the best for every purpose. I know people who have had trouble with the most exclusive equipment they could (or could not really) afford, while others have been perfectly satisfied with bargain basement machines.

My subjective evaluation of the general populace's mountain bike buying habits indicates there are three approaches:

☐ What is the best?

☐ What is the cheapest?

☐ What will be the most suitable?

Those who ask the first question, though probably wealthier, are not really any more sophisticated or smarter than those who try to find the answer to the second. It is my aim in this book to bring as many readers as possible into the category of the informed, those who ask—and attempt to answer—the third question. Only they will be likely to finish up with a bike that is best for them.

It all depends on your needs, the way you want to use the bike, and your priorities. If your priority is conspicuous consumption, then the most expensive will be barely good enough, although you may not benefit one bit from all that expensive sophistication, perhaps even experiencing the drawbacks of such finesse more than its benefits. If you just want to ride around without any competitive intentions or interest in riding in difficult terrain, you may be well served with a cheap to medium-priced machine. If you want to cycle faster than the next person, and have developed your riding skills, you may want the very lightest and sophisticated.

But don't expect miracles from the choice of equipment alone. The fancy bike will allow you to exploit your existing abilities, but you will benefit more from working on your skills before spending all your savings on that ultimate machine. It may take one to three seasons to develop your skills adequately, and if you splurge on that fancy machine now, it may be wrecked before you get a chance

to benefit from its superior qualities.

Most people who buy their first mountain bike, and quite a number of those who have had such machines before, don't do so in order to compete with the gonzos who make a living blazing their trail up and down the steepest mountains. They want a bike they are at ease with. It should be the right size, comfortable enough to ride for hours, light and agile enough to be handled easily, and priced somewhere within their financial possibilities. Yes, it can

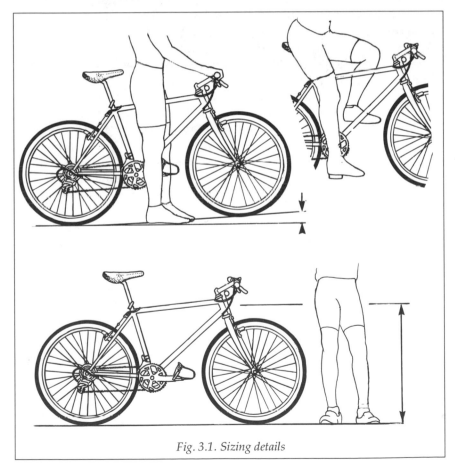

Fig. 3.1. Sizing details

be done, so let's see how to go about it.

The Right Size

Whatever the make, model, type, color, or price, your bike should be of the right size to match your physique. If it's the wrong size, even the highest quality bike is worse to ride than an otherwise inferior model of the right size. Here you will find guidelines for making sure you get a bike that fits.

Bicycle sizes are generally quoted as the length of the seat tube, between the center of the bottom bracket and some point at the top. Yes, some point: Traditionally, in the English-speaking world this upper point has been defined as the top of the seat lug. More and more manufacturers of mountain bikes refer to the more logical location represented by the centerline of the top tube. Some are even smarter, quoting the straddle height, i.e. the distance of the top tube above the ground. The difference between the first two designations may be anywhere from 15 mm to 30 mm (5/8 to 1¼ in), depending on the seat lug detail, while the third size also accounts for the angle of the seat tube and the height of the bottom bracket above the ground. Fig. 3.1 illustrates this and the other critical dimensions of the bike.

The correct frame size will be a function of the length of your legs. As a guideline, you can refer to Table 1 in the Appendix. It gives suggested nominal frame sizes as a function of the inseam leg length, as measured in the illustration.

Obviously, the surest way to find out for yourself is by trying out some bikes. Certainly if you intend to use the mountain bike for its original purpose, namely to ride off-road, the frame should be on the small side, relative to the sizing practice customarily recommended for other bicycle types. Straddle some bikes in the shop and select one on which you retain up to 7.5 cm (3 in) of crotch clearance when your feet are flat on the ground. While straddling the bike, raise the front end. On the right size bike, you should be able to lift the front wheel about 15 cm (6 in) off the ground without discomfort, as illustrated in Fig. 3.1.

In addition to being able to straddle the bike when it is standing still, it should of course fit you when riding it. That is a matter of reaching the pedals from the saddle in the right manner. Fig. 3.1 also shows how you should sit and reach the pedal to try it on for the correct seat height. Don't pedal it that way when riding, though. Instead, keep the ball of the foot, rather than the heel, centered on the pedal.

Once you have established the right saddle height, mark the seat post with an indelible marker at the point where it protrudes from the seat tube. Then undo the quick-release binder bolt and pull it out to check its length. There should be at least 65 mm (2½ in) of the seatpost below the point you just marked. If there isn't, you either need a different bike or a longer seatpost. Insist on it, since a seatpost that is not held in the frame by at least that much is not safe.

Stretched Out or Not

Then there is the length of the bike to consider: how far is the saddle from the handlebars and what is the distance between the wheels. Customarily, the length is quoted as the top tube length, measured between the centerlines of head tube and seat tube. Typically, most manufacturers offer a fixed relationship between seat tube length and top tube length. The critical dimension is also affected by the size of the handlebar stem extension and the relative forward position of the saddle with respect to the seat post.

To find a bike of the right length, start off with the saddle placed in the middle position relative to the seatpost and the handlebars at the same height as the saddle. Seated on the bike, you should be able to sit relaxed, dividing your weight between handlebars and saddle. You should not feel uncomfortably strained. The other extreme, with the hands too close to the body, rarely occurs, since most bikes seem to be rather on the long side these days. Just the same, it's possible, e.g. if your upper body or arms are long relative to your leg length, or when you have progressed to the stretched-out competitive riding posture and are trying out a beginner's bike.

Chainstay Length

Short chainstays—on which the distance between the centerlines of the bottom bracket and the rear wheel is 430 mm (17 in) or less—are reputed to give a bike magic climbing ability. Don't believe it, but the fact is that these short chainstays avoid sway of the rear end when applying force to the pedals. So that's good for people who grind their way up in a gear that is too high. The disadvantage of this design is that it places the rider's weight rather far back, assuming a given angle of the seat tube relative to the horizontal plane. This actually makes it harder to climb very steep inclines sitting down, since the front end will tend to lift off, so you'll need to master the trick of balancing your weight while out of the saddle, as will be described in Chapter 8.

Wheel Size

Virtually all regular mountain bikes are equipped with what is referred to as 26-in wheels. That's the approximate overall outside diameter with inflated tire. There are 26-in tires in numerous different widths. On mountain bikes, they may vary all the way from 42 to 59 mm (1.6 to 2.2 in). Hybrids roll on 700 mm diameter wheels with tires of typically 35–40 mm.

Not everybody needs the widest tires. If you ride on paved roads most of the time, rarely getting into loose dirt, sharp boulders, mud or snow, you may be perfectly happy with 42 mm mountain bike or 40 mm hybrid tires. The wider tires are the solution for really rough terrain or loose dirt, mud and snow. Generally, bikes are designed with a particular tire size in mind, so it is wise to select a bike that is equipped the way you want it, rather than modifying it later.

However, since virtually any tire width can be installed on the same rim, it is often possible to replace the narrow tires with wider models for no more than the cost of the tires. Of course, that only works if the frame clearances are adequate. For more details on tires and wheels, you are referred to Chapter 17.

Evaluate your own physical characteristics critically before buying a bike, so you know what to look out for. Then try out several different models just as critically, and don't rush into buying something before you are sure it fits and suits you.

Your Bike and the Way You Ride

The first mountain bikes were designed to do nothing else quite as well as descending down steep hillsides. That was mainly achieved by keeping the wheelbase, i.e. the distance between the wheel axes, rather long. Since then, different geometries have been introduced by various and sundry manufacturers. Many claim the most curious advantages of certain features, only too often without any substantiation. Here

is a summary of the most important points to consider.

To give you some pretty general rules of thumb, beginners should look for a bike that is built more for comfort than for speed. That means one with relatively shallow frame angles: the head tube should make an angle of 68–71° relative to the horizontal. Due to some geometric relationships, that also means the bike's frame will be a little on the long side. It will not respond as directly to your steering and accelerating efforts. On the other hand, it won't be quite as scary to ride either. Even though these 'comfortable' bikes have a long wheelbase, the rider tends to sit less stretched, due to the selection of a very short and high handlebar stem.

More experienced riders may be well served with a shorter and steeper-angled machine. Frame angles of 72° or more are not unusual in this category. These fast and agile bikes will have a wheelbase of less than 106 cm (42 in), while the better bikes for novices will be longer, say 110 cm (43–44 in). The distance between saddle and handlebars on these machines is increased by means of a handlebar stem design that keeps the handlebars low and far forward.

The shorter and steeper bikes are not only more agile, they are also rather uncomfortable to ride if you are in the habit of resting on the saddle with all your weight. Experienced riders don't: they divide their weight between pedals, handlebars and saddle. You too can get such a 'sporty' bike once you've learned to do that. Some people learn within a single season, while others never catch on.

If you are going to ride in really difficult terrain and make your bike suffer, you'd better get one that stands up to that kind of abuse. Not all mountain bikes are really built to last that way. Many are perfectly good for the kind of use 90 percent of the riders give their bikes, but these probably do not stand up to rough abuse. Such less robust machines are often a little lighter than other bikes in the same price category. Otherwise, lighter bikes tend to be more expensive. Typically, mountain bikes that are really designed for hard riding are built of larger diameter tubing than used for ten-speeds.

Although not as sturdy as bikes with a regular frame, there are some excellent women's bikes with lowered top tube, such as this Kuwahara.

This applies especially to the downtube, the chain stays and the fork.

Taking a look at various models, and asking the right questions in the bike shop, will usually allow you to get a machine that matches your kind of riding. Be fair on your pocketbook: there is no need to get an indestructible expensive machine if you don't really need one. Don't be tempted by what is supposed to be the best. Even the best is relative: you want to choose what is best for *you*.

Mountain Bikes for Him and Her

With respect to the way bicycles fit their riders, there are some differences between the typical female and male physiques to consider. For any given total body height, the woman tends to have proportionally longer legs, shorter

arms, and a shorter torso. Applied to bicycle sizing, that translates into a shorter top tube for the same size frame. I can't tell you what the right top tube length for each frame size for either sex is, since neither men nor women come in standard proportions. Comparing different bikes of the same size, women will generally be happier with a frame that has a shorter top tube. Replacing the handlebar stem with a longer or shorter model, if available, may also do the trick.

There are a number of special components on the market to suit the particular needs of women better than what is standard. These include wider saddles, narrower and smaller diameter handlebars, smaller handgrips, shorter cranks, and shorter-reach brake levers. Smart manufacturers offer special women's versions, or at least proportional component sizing based on the frame size. This is often only done for more exclusive models. At least one (female) manufacturer, Terry, specializes in bicycles designed specifically for women.

Let's keep in mind that people are not standardized into male and female stereotypes. Some men will do better with one or more of the features more typically intended for women, and vice versa. For instance, some men have a pelvis that is as wide as that of some women, and for them the wider women's saddle would be appropriate.

Carrying Luggage

If you will be carrying luggage at some time, whether on long tours, to deliver newspapers, or to do the grocery shopping, you will need a bike that lends itself to that purpose. It should either have racks (carriers, to my British readers) installed, or at least have the appropriate attachment bosses and eyelets, so you can install them at a later time. Most rack manufacturers nowadays copy the standard attachment details pioneered by Jim Blackburn.

If your bike has the bosses front and rear to match those racks, you'll be well prepared to install just about any manufacturer's racks, including Blackburn's own, which are generally acknowledged to be the cream of the crop. If not, all is not lost, since it is possible to attach racks with the aid of provisional clamps and the adaptors.

Gearing Choices

All mountain bikes sold these days have indexed gearing systems. That means there are fixed positions for the various gears, at least on the rear derailleur. That's a nice feature, but there are other things to consider when it comes to gearing as well. In the first place, there is the number of gears. For most riders, I suggest being satisfied with a 21-or even an 18-speed model in preference to one with 24 speeds. This applies in particular if you will be cycling fast in very rough terrain and you do not want to spend a lot of time straightening out your rear wheel, as will be explained in Part III.

Then there are the off-round chainrings, such as the Shimano Biopace, which were the craze for some years. These do provide a better distribution of effort if you pedal at a low pedaling rate and resulting high pedal force. More experienced riders have developed a riding style that is based on spinning fast, while exerting relatively low force. For these riders, the off-round chainrings are of little use. I suggest learning to ride properly, rather than buying the equipment that is designed to compensate for your inefficiency. Interestingly, the manufacturers have meanwhile discovered this too, and the off-round chainrings are now offered only on beginners' models.

Materials and Construction

Many parts of the bike are of aluminum alloy these days. Rims, cranks, chainrings, brakes, hubs and seatpost are generally made of aluminum on a bike of any quality. But more and more, also the bicycle's major component, the frame, is being offered in versions made of aluminum.

Aluminum bikes are generally light and can be of excellent quality—but so can steel bikes be. The major disadvantage is their intangibility: many of the aluminum machines haven't been on the market long enough to assure that they will stand up to the kind of abuse they may get. Although some of the aluminum pioneers such as Charlie Cunningham and Gary Klein produce indestructible aluminum frames, some of the later and cheaper entries have been known to break.

The other, and more practical, disadvantage of aluminum bike frames is the fact that some standard components may not fit on them as easily as they do on a steel frame. The reason lies in the need to use larger diameter tubing, as explained in Chapter 14. Attaching standard components to such an oversize tube may be tricky. Although it would be unfair to call aluminum bikes inferior, amongst moderately priced production bikes, I prefer those with steel frames, if such a subjective opinion is worth anything to you.

Conventional steel frames can be made in one of several ways: lugged or lugless, and lugless either with welded or with brazed joints. Though this will be discussed in more detail in Chapter 15, I should say a few words about it here, since you may be confronted with such a choice when buying a bike. The habit of building without lugs grew out of necessity, since initially no lugs were available to fit the oversize tubing diameters required for an adequately rigid and strong mountain bike frame.

Since those days, lugs in the appropriate sizes have been introduced, yet lugless bikes have not disappeared. At the time of this writing, the best value amongst low-budget bikes from Taiwan seems to be in lugged frames. Finally, some manufacturers use internal lugs, around which the tubes are attached by any one of several different methods, ranging from brazing to bonding with adhesive.

In the eyes of most, lugless brazed frames (smooth joints) are the prettiest. They are also generally the most expensive. They are quite rigid, but not necessarily the lightest, due to the extra weight that goes into the brass fillets.

Suspension

In recent years, many mountain bikes have been introduced with some kind of shock absorption. Generally, that includes a telescoping front fork and sometimes rear suspension as well. Although the tires on your mountain bike are designed to dampen the shocks, there are some advantages to a separate suspension. One of them is the possibility to maintain high tire pressure, and consequently keep the tire's rolling resistance low.

The main advantage is of course the increased comfort. Yet I feel the way I have seen most people ride their comfortably sprung mountain bikes, there is often no justification. Buy one if you really handle rough terrain most of the time, if you can justify the higher cost, and can live with the greater weight. But most people, certainly if they are beginners, simply don't need a bike with suspension for the kind of riding they do.

Conclusion

What's best? If you are interested in being the coolest kid on the block and don't care how much you spend and how long your bike lasts, simply look for the most expensive and lightest bike around. It may have almost any kind of frame: perhaps a lugless, fillet brazed frame, or aluminum, carbon fiber, or even titanium. I must admit it is a delight to ride the lightest possible bike, which feels like an extension of your own body, rather than something with noticeable inertia of its own. On the other hand, my budget forces me to look for things I can afford, and within that range, some of the bikes with welded steel frames are just right for me.

CHAPTER 4

Fitting the Bike to the Rider

In this chapter, you will learn how to set up the equipment you have so that it serves you best. To do this effectively, you should have selected a bike of the right size, as described in Chapter 3. The correct set-up and the initial riding posture will be explained here, which will in turn allow you to reap maximum benefit from the advice contained in the chapters of Part II that are devoted to handling the bike.

Riding Posture

Whereas bicycle racers have long known that in the long run it is most comfortable to maintain a relatively low, crouched position, most beginning cyclists, whatever kind of bike they ride, sit upright. That may be fine for those who make only minor excursions at low speed in easy terrain. However you can learn something about posture from more experienced riders. The fact that you will probably have difficult terrain

Your mountain bike should fit properly. This 15-in Cannondale with downslope top tube is a good choice for small riders.

to handle makes this even more important.

Fig. 4.1 shows the three basic kinds of riding posture for comparison: upright, inclined and fully crouched. If you like the upright position, you may well be convinced this is the only comfortable way to ride a bike. I checked riding postures along a road with a 1% uphill slope for an hour some years ago. In that time, I counted 32 people cycling by in the upright posture. All of them appeared to be working hard—you can tell by the strained expression on their faces, their cramped movements, and their abysmally slow progress. Every now and again another type of cyclist came by. Passing the others at twice their speed, and obviously more relaxed, these rode in either a deep incline or in a fully crouched posi-tion. Some ride racing bikes, others mountain bikes, but what distinguishes them is not their equipment but their posture.

There are, of course, also other reasons why they are going faster and suffering less, but the first and most important step towards this more comfortable style is their different riding posture. In the lower position, the rider's weight is divided more evenly over handlebars, saddle and pedals. Firstly, this reduces the pressure on the buttocks. Secondly, it allows the relaxed fast pedaling technique so essential for long-duration power output, as will be explained in Chapters 8 and 9. Thirdly, it enables you to bring more force to bear on the pedals when needed. Finally, it reduces the air resistance, which is a major factor at speed or against the wind.

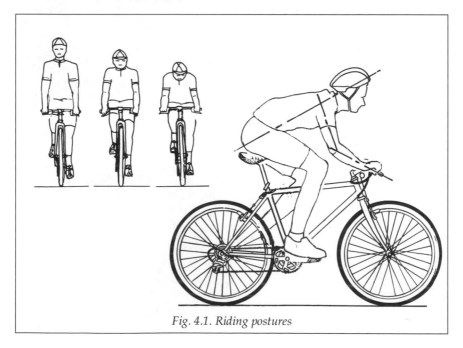

Fig. 4.1. Riding postures

Strangely enough, many people to whom these advantages have been demonstrated nevertheless insist on riding in the upright position. They bring all sorts of arguments, ranging from, "That's only for racing" to, "That is terribly uncomfortable" or "You can't do that on a mountain bike." They are fooling themselves. In reality, they are less comfortable, whatever they think, and have to do more work to cover the same distance or to proceed at the same speed. Get accustomed to the right posture early in your cycling career, and you'll be a more effective cyclist, one who gets less frustration and more pleasure out of the pursuit.

Within the general range of comfortable positions, there are enough variations available to allow you to adapt to different terrain conditions and give you the chance to vary your position from time to time. The latter helps avoid the numbing effect that results when pressure is applied in the same position for a long time.

The following sections describe just how the saddle and the handlebars should be adjusted to achieve the basic relaxed position that is shown in the center illustration. This posture is worth looking into a little closer. Study the proportions. If the bike lacks bar-ends, you cannot provide much variation by holding the handlebars at different points. Instead, you will have to bend or straighten the arms to get lower or higher. This may be required, not just for variation, but also to apply more

force to the pedals, to reduce the wind resistance by lowering the front, or to get a better view by raising the front a little.

Saddle Height

The height of the saddle, or rather the distance of its top relative to the pedals, is the most critical variable for effective cycling. Although it may have to be varied to adapt to the terrain off-road, it should normally be set for cycling on normal roads and relatively level ground. The saddle should be adjusted so that the leg can be almost stretched without straining the knee, which would cause excessive force and rotation at the knee joint. With the pedal in the highest position, the distance between the pedal and the saddle must be such that the knee is not bent excessively. Once this has been set, the correct crank length assures that the latter condition is also satisfied.

I shall describe a simple method of establishing the correct seat height. It is good enough for preliminary set-up and the first several hundred miles of cycling. Your ultimate seat position may require additional fine-tuning, based on your subjective long-term comfort. On the other hand, in the vast majority of cases this technique will lead to a satisfactory seat position in the long run.

The simplest way of finding the correct level-ground seat height is illustrated in Fig. 4.2. It is a trial and error method and is easy to carry out without help. Wear the shoes you will be wearing when cycling. Place the bike next to a wall or post for support when you sit on it. On of the cranks should be pointing down in line with the seat tube. Adjust the seat up or down, following the adjustment procedure below, until you can rest the heel of your shoe on the lower pedal with your knee nearly straight but not strained.

☐ Sit on the bike and place your heels on the pedals. If you have pedals with toeclips they will be dangling down.

☐ Pedal backwards this way, making sure you do not have to rock from side to side to stay in touch with the pedals.

☐ Now lower the saddle by whatever is the difference in height between heels and soles.

☐ Tighten the saddle in this position.

The heels-on-pedals style only applies to adjusting the seat height, not to riding the bike: When cycling, the ball of the foot (the second joint of the big toe) should be over the center of the pedal axle, with the heel raised so that the knee is never fully straightened.

You may have to do some fine-tuning to achieve long-term comfort. Riders with disproportionately small feet may want to place the saddle a little lower, those with big feet perhaps slightly higher. There is no need to get carried away though: raise or lower the

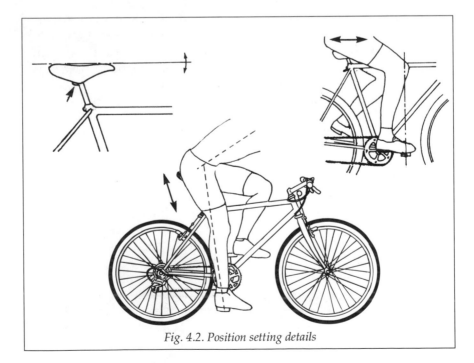

Fig. 4.2. Position setting details

seat in steps of 6 mm (¼ in) at a time. Then try to get used to that position by riding perhaps a hundred miles, several days, before attempting any change, which again must be about 6 mm to make any real difference.

Saddle Position and Angle

The normal saddle position is such that the seat post is roughly in the middle of the saddle. For optimum pedaling efficiency, adjust the saddle forward or backwards after it has been set to the correct height.

☐ On any regular mountain bike, sitting on the bike with the front of the foot on the pedal and the crank placed horizontally, the center of the knee joint should be vertically aligned with the spindle of the forward pedal.

☐ You can locate the center of the knee joint at the bony protrusion just behind the knee cap.

☐ The angle of the saddle relative to the horizontal plane should initially be set so as to keep the line that connects the highest points at the front and the back level.

It may be necessary to modify this angle to prevent slipping forward or backwards once the handlebars have been set to the correct height. This may not become apparent until after some miles of cycling. Adjusting procedures for both forward position and angle are outlined below.

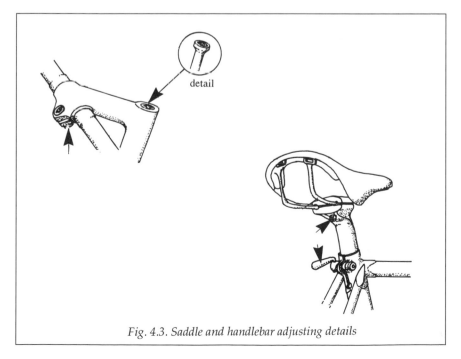

Fig. 4.3. Saddle and handlebar adjusting details

Saddle Adjustments

To carry out the actual mechanical adjustment on the saddle, first take a close look at the way it is installed on the bike, comparing it with the illustration. The saddle height is easy to adjust on a typical mountain bike:

☐ Loosen the quick-release binder bolt behind the seat lug; raise or lower the saddle with the attached seat post in a twisting motion, and tighten the quick-release again when the saddle is at the right height, making sure it is aligned straight.

If your bike is equipped with a height adjusting spring device, such as the Hite-Rite, you will be able to adjust the seat within an adequate range very conveniently. Just apply the right amount of downward force to let the spring adjuster raise or lower the seat to the desired position. If the presently set range should be exceeded, which is rarely the case but may occur when adjusting a bike for a different rider or when it is first installed, refer to Chapter 21 for the appropriate instructions.

☐ To change the saddle's forward position, undo the adjustment bolt (two bolts on some models) on the seat post. This bolt is usually accessible from below or the side, but sometimes from under the saddle cover.

☐ Some older mountain bike seat posts also have a quick-release here. Once loosened, push the saddle forward or backward until the desired position is reached, then tighten the bolts, making sure the saddle is held under the desired angle relative to the horizontal plane.

Handlebar Height and Position

Even on a mountain bike, the highest point of the handlebars should be no higher than the top of the saddle to ride efficiently. Just how low is the right position will be determined by the shape of the handlebars and the rider's physiognomy. This depends on the relative distribution of body weight and height, as well as the upper and lower arm length.

Only by experimenting can you determine what will work best for you. Here I shall simply tell you how to determine the initial position for a frame size check, followed by the adjustment for a relaxed initial riding style. After a few weeks of riding, you should have developed enough sensitivity to fine-tune the handlebar height and stem length to match your needs perfectly. To set the handlebars for a relaxed riding posture, proceed as follows:

☐ First set the top of the bars about 3 cm (1¼ in) lower than the saddle. Sit on the bike and reach forward for the handgrips, as though ready to grab the brake handles.

☐ In this position your shoulders should be about midway between seat and hands, as shown in Fig. 4.1 at the beginning of this chapter. The arms should feel neither stretched nor heavily loaded and should not project sideways from the shoulder width too much.

If your hands are much further apart than the shoulders, the handlebars are too wide. They can either be replaced or cut off at the ends. I have never yet seen the opposite phenomenon on any mountain bike, namely that the handlebars were too narrow. Typical, bikes with a sporty geometry tend to be too stretched-out between saddle and handlebars if you are new to the sport. You may have to twist the handlebars a little in the stem, or replace the stem by a shorter model, to find the most comfortable position; the latter adjustment is also outlined below.

If you should have a particularly short combination of arms and torso in relation to your leg length, you may not be comfortable even with a short stem. In that case, a smaller frame, which generally also has a shorter top tube, may be in order with an overlong seatpost installed. If no bike can be found with the right top tube length, you may need a custom-built frame with the desired dimensions of seat tube and top tube. This would be the ultimate solution, although it is probably not so critical that you can't make do with a stock frame.

Most high-end mountain bikes nowadays are equipped with bar-ends, which allow a greater variety of hand placements for long-term comfort.

Handlebar Adjustments

You are referred to the accompanying illustration. To vary the height of the handlebars, proceed as follows:

☐ Straddle the front wheel, clamping it between your legs.

☐ Undo the expander bolt, which is recessed in the top of the stem.

☐ If the stem does not come loose immediately, you may have to lift the handlebars to raise the wheel off the ground, then tap on the head of the expander bolt with a hammer. This will loosen the internal clamping device.

☐ Now raise or lower the handlebar stem as required. Tighten the expander bolt again, while holding the handlebars straight in the desired position.

If you want to change the angle of the handlebar ends with respect to the horizontal plane, here is how that is done:

☐ Undo the binder bolt that clamps the handlebars in the front of the stem.

☐ Twist the handlebars until they are under the desired angle, and then tighten the binder bolt again, holding the bars centered.

Older mountain bikes may have a stem with a V-shaped reach, equipped with two or even four binder bolts holding the handle-bars. To install a longer stem or a different bar design, you are referred to the instructions in Chapter 16 or to your friendly bike store.

The correct handlebar position often puts more strain on the hands than beginning cyclists find comfortable, especially when rough surfaces cause vibrations. Minimize this problem by keeping the arms slightly bent, never holding them in a cramped position. If you still experience discomfort, replace the handgrips with cushioned foam models. Wearing gloves will also releave the strain.

Once you start riding off-road, especially in mountainous terrain, you may want to lower the saddle or move it further back to cycle down a steep incline. Since the variations in geometry from one make and model to the next are quite significant, you may have to do a bit of experimenting to find the best positions for such special uses.

Getting On and Off

Once saddle and handlebars are adjusted correctly, it will be time to start riding your bike. In case you are not yet familiar with the bicycle, here is a suggestion for getting on and off the bike. All other riding and handling techniques involve prolonged learning processes that will be treated in Part II of the book. However the simple act of starting the bike should be mastered immediately. Easy though this may seem, it is worth practicing, if only to avoid embarrassing or dangerous mishaps. You will learn more advanced methods, appropriate to regular and specific off-road riding practice, respectively, in Chapters 8 and 9.

Since even mountain bikes are ridden on regular roads where there is traffic to worry about much of the time, I shall include references to your safety involving considerations for other vehicles. To some extent, these apply on the trail as well, where you may get in the way of other trail users, including other cyclists. Of course, most cyclists are not entirely new to the game: you too may feel you've been cycling long enough to do

without any additional advice or practice. It still does not hurt to follow the procedures described below. Do it consciously, so you become more efficient at handling the bike when riding off- road as well.

☐ Before starting off, make sure your shoe laces are tied and tucked in, or are short enough not to run the risk of getting caught in the chain.

☐ Select a low gear, with the chain on the middle chainring and an intermediate or big sprocket.

☐ Start off at the side of the road, after having checked to make

One of the greatest small riders, mountain bike racer Cindy Devine, demonstrating excellent high-speed downhill posture.

Bob Allen photo

47

sure no traffic is following closely behind.

☐ Straddle the top tube by swinging the appropriate leg either over the handlebars, the top tube, or the saddle.

☐ Hold the handlebars with both hands and place one foot on the corresponding pedal, the other on the ground.

☐ Look behind you to make sure the road is clear, then check ahead to establish which course you want to follow.

☐ Place your weight on the pedal, leaning lightly on the handlebars, and start forward. Put the other foot on the other pedal when it is in the top position.

To slow down, whether just to stop or to get off the bike, first look behind you, to make sure you are not getting in the way of following cyclists or motorists. Aim for the place where you want to stop. Change into a lower gear, appropriate for starting off again later. Slow down by braking gently, using mainly the front brake to stop. Just before you have come to a standstill, lean in the direction you want to dismount. Place the foot on the ground, while moving forward off the saddle to straddle the seat tube. Now you are in the right position to dismount or start again.

If you want to get off the bike at this point, lift the other leg over, balancing away from the bike. However, under most circumstances, especially when loaded with luggage, you will find that the machine is most easily controlled when you remain on the bike, straddling the top tube. Consequently, only dismount completely if it is really necessary.

CHAPTER 5

What to Take Along

To enjoy mountain biking at its best, you will need more than just a bike. In addition, you'd do well to get some of the accessories that will be introduced in this chapter. This other equipment is of two kinds: things to install on the bike, and things to wear or take along that have nothing to do with the bike as such.

Mountain Bike Accessories

While you are at the bike shop buying your mountain bike, consider a few other essentials. They will run up the price of your purchase quite a bit, but you won't regret it, since they will help you get more use out of your machine. Not all the things mentioned here must be bought right away, but it's good to know what's available. We'll take the essentials first, followed by optional equipment.

Many of these regular accessories, such as racks, bags, and fenders, are available in special versions for mountain bike use. This is not excessive diversification, since the dimensions, characteristics of design, and the different way the machine is used, dictate distinct dimensions, designs and materials for the accessories as well.

Dressed to kill. For the ultimate in style and comfort, you can buy special mountain biking clothing, as this lady did,

Bob Allen photo

49

The Lock

Sadly enough, bicycles are a lot harder to hold on to than they are to ride. The best lock is barely good enough to keep up with the determination of those who make a living by taking what belongs to others. Since society at large has not caught on to the high price of quality bikes, the act of stealing one is regarded merely as petty theft, and thus relatively riskless to the perpetrator.

Lock your bike whenever you're not riding it, in any place, including your own basement and the backwoods, which are actually not much safer than city streets when it comes to bike theft. And don't just lock it by itself but to something strong and firmly embedded. The best locks available are the large U-locks, such as those made by Kryptonite. For your mountain bike, the largest model is about the right size. Lock at least the frame and one wheel to a firmly embedded object over which the lock can't be lifted; preferably also remove the other wheel and lock it up too.

The Pump

Don't rely on the air supplied at gas stations. You'll save a lot of time, trouble and frustration if you carry your own pump. Check the pressure before you set out on a ride and inflate the tires if necessary: at least 4 bar (60 psi) if you travel mainly on paved roads, about 3 bar (45 psi) if you ride on rough and rocky terrain, and about 1.7 bar (25 psi) if you travel mainly on soft, loose or muddy ground. This assumes a rider of average weight: the pressure should be up to five psi higher or lower if you're particularly heavy or light, respectively.

The tire inflation pressure greatly affects the bike's rolling resistance. Harder tires roll better, assuming a hard, smooth surface. Higher pressures also protect both tires and rims against damage from protrusions on rough surfaces. On soft ground or snow, the pressure should be quite low, so the wheels don't get bogged down.

Pumps come in several types. For home use, the big stand pump with integral pressure gauge is best, but on the bike you need a more portable model. Either type should have a connector or head to match the tire valves, which in turn come in two types. The Schrader valve is the same thing found on car tires and is easily inflated at the gas station, but not with the portable pump: It has an internal spring that makes it hard to pump up by hand. The Presta valve has a little screw that must be undone before inflating, and tightened again afterwards.

Make sure your pump matches the valves on your bike. When not in use, install it along one of the frame tubes. In addition to a pump, I suggest you get a pressure gauge. It will take the guesswork out of inflating to the right pressure.

Water Bottle

Certainly for longer rides in hot weather, a water bottle, held in a frame-mounted cage, is an essential accessory. Make sure there are bosses to mount at least one bottle cage on the bike. The way you use the bottle has to be learned too: pull the tip out while it is still in its cage. Then remove the bottle and squeeze it to squirt a jet of water into the mouth—you're not supposed to suck but to squirt.

With the mountain bike, much larger bottles than were formerly available have been introduced, and you may need them to avoid running dry far away from any water source. I particularly like the Swiss aluminum bottles made by Sigg, in which your drinks do not take on the flavor of either plastic or of whatever you had in them last. These are not squeezed, but their spigot is designed to provide an adequate squirt when held upside down and seal perfectly when closed. They are even available in an insulated version to maintain the temperature of the drink.

Fenders and Other Guards

To protect your equipment, it is not a bad idea to install some devices that may or may not be offered as standard accessories on some bikes.

Fenders, called mudguards in England, help keep dirt and moisture off your bike and your body.

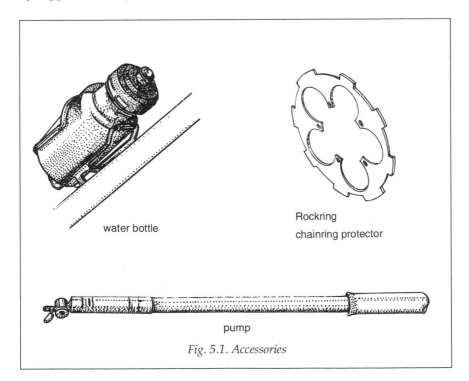

water bottle

Rockring
chainring protector

pump

Fig. 5.1. Accessories

Whatever they're called, most inhabitants of the U.S. wouldn't be seen dead with them on their bike. Yet fenders are useful in rainy weather or whenever the ground is wet or muddy, so it makes sense to install them if that is often the case in your part of the world. Get a model with a mud flap (or add your own) at the bottom of the front fender which stops the rain from splashing right into your shoes. Fenders can be a problem in particularly muddy terrain on a bike with insufficient wheel clearance, since the mud builds up inside them, eventually hindering more than they help.

Luggage Carrying Equipment

Make sure your mountain bike can be equipped with racks (luggage carriers), i.e. that it has at least the eyelets and lugs to which a rack can be installed, as mentioned in Chapter 3. If you go touring with a lot of gear, you'll want racks both front and rear. Otherwise, a rear rack will generally be adequate.

You may also carry your gear in some kind of bag, attached either to the bike or the rider. I prefer the saddle bag, which is very popular in Britain, while most Americans seem to prefer the handlebar bag. Handlebar bags negatively affect your bikes handling and make it hard to mount most headlights. They are handy for relatively light items to which you want ready access, such as a map, sunglasses and perhaps a camera. Make sure the handlebar bag is firmly supported from the top and restrained at the bottom by means of elastic shock cords run to the ends of the front fork.

Quite useful is a protective guard for the rear derailleur—a kind of sturdy metal wire cage with a mounting plate that goes between the derailleur and the RH drop-out. Unfortunately these things are not considered cool and are consequently mainly found on low-end bikes, but if you're more interested in protecting your equipment than your image, you can put one on any bike.

If you ride in really rough terrain, with large boulders and fallen treetrunks to ride over, you may want to install a Rockring. This is a stainless steel ring that fits over the chainrings to protect them against bending and chipping when the ground clearance is inadequate.

Tools

Buy the essential tools right away. If nothing else, at least get a tire patch kit, a set of three tire levers, a small screwdriver to adjust the derailleurs, and a crank tool to tighten the crank. I usually carry a more complete tool set, which also includes various wrenches and a chain tool. You may also take along a tube of waterless hand cleaner and a rag to wipe your hands off when you've finished fixing the bike.

Certainly for longer tours, it will be wise to carry some additional tools and spares to match the various parts on your bike. Wrap the tools in a rag and keep them all together with an elastic band, or sew a pouch to keep them together and organized. Ask at the bike shop when you buy the bike which tools you are likely to need, or establish that yourself.

Clothing

Even if you don't intend to dress up like a bicycle racer, there are a few items of bicycle wear that may benefit everybody. Besides, there are some considerations in the selection of clothing that should be applied whatever kind of clothing you wear when riding your bike.

Fig. 5. shows some of the typical things cyclists wear, although one of the most essential, the hel-

met, is depicted separately in Fig. 5.3. These items are all designed with the motion and exposure typical for cycling in mind. Thus, all garments are flexible and light, covering the areas of contact between bike and rider with some form of protection, and are made of materials that absorb perspiration. Keep these points in mind when buying clothing to wear when riding your mountain bike.

Consider the risk of falling off the bike. For that reason, I suggest you wear long-sleeved tops and long-legged pants, rather than T-shirts and shorts. It will be even better to wear two (thin) garments over the top of one another since in case of a spill the two layers will slip over one another rather than taking chunks out of your skin. The hands could use the protection of a pair of gloves.

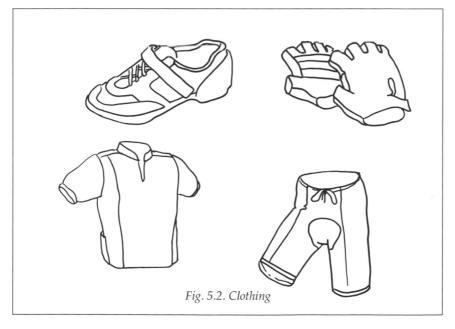

Fig. 5.2. Clothing

Helmets

A bicycle helmet is the first and probably most important item of bicycle wear to get. Today's cycling helmets are a far cry from the old padded hairnets. They are real energy absorbing models, usually referred to as hard shell helmets. In Chapter 6, you will get some of the background information about the need for head protection. For the time being, it should suffice to know you will be better prepared if you wear one. Don't just put it on top of your head, but buckle it up, if you want it to do you any good.

Before you get carried away on the safety issue, though, be aware that the helmet is no universal cure, and millions of people in the world feel quite safe without. I for one know one situation where I regularly take my helmet off: In hot and humid weather it becomes unbearable to cycle up steep inclines wearing one for me. I perspire a lot under these circumstances, and as long as the perspiration on your head gets a chance to evaporate, you may feel quite comfortable. But since you'll be going at a low speed, even the most intricately designed helmet ventilation system will not carry off your perspiration from under that helmet. You may also want to take the helmet off under those circumstances—and put it back where it belongs as soon as you reach the top, to protect you on the more dangerous downhill.

Unfortunately, there is a trend toward excessive helmet pressure

in the U.S. these days, with publications banning photos of 'topless' cyclists and cycling organizations calling for mandatory helmet wearing laws.

Let's stay realistic: 99.9% of the world's cyclists, many of whom ride on roads no less dangerous than our roads and trails, ride without a helmet. In fact, the fatality rate amongst cyclists in the U.S. since the introduction of helmets has neither dropped noticeably since the introduction of the helmet, nor is it perceptively lower than it is in other countries where cyclists habitually go without. And I feel it is every person's own responsibility to decide whether or not to take any particular precaution, without coercion from others. After all, motorists and pedestrians who get seriously or fatally injured in accidents (and there are many more of those than of cyclists) also typically do so as a

Fig. 5.3. Bike helmet

result of head-impact, and I hope we're not about to propagate universal helmet use for those groups.

Whatever their protective potential, it is not true that cyclists without helmets are endangering either society at large or even the reputation of 'serious cyclists' (a curious term used in the U.S. to describe those who ride for fun). Publications that refuse to print articles or review books with illustrations showing cyclists without helmets, and organizations that propagate restricting the rights of their own ranks, are getting scarily close to being fascist, and I shall have nothing to do with this approach.

Yes, I think wearing a helmet is wise, but no, I don't believe anyone has the right to pressure anybody else into it. And it is outright stupid to claim that without a helmet you are a bad example and you can't be a 'serious cyclist'— whatever that means—since it obviously excludes the 5 million Dutch bicycle commuters who use their bikes more than just about any American.

Shoes

Good cycling shoes have a stiff sole, to better divide the pedaling force over the entire foot and deliver it to the pedal. Models intended for mountain bike use should have slightly flexible soles with a grippy profile, since you will probably have to get off and walk occasionally.

Nowadays, many people use clipless pedals on their mountain bikes. Although some of the ones specifically designed for mountain bike use can be ridden with regular shoes, they obviously don't hold the feet in place unless you get the matching shoes. At the time of this writing, Shimano's SPD system is easily the most convenient on the market, and their special shoes with recessed clips are highly recommended. These shoes are fine for walking, but this *is* a rather expensive solution.

Cold Weather Wear

Mountain bikes are great machines for riding even when the weather is a little cooler. Wear something akin to the gear depicted in Fig. 5.4. Several thin and flexible layers, preferably of materials such as knitted polypropylene or wool, are preferable to one layer of a thicker fabric. Watch out in particular for wind protection: the outer layer should be very closely woven, especially in the areas that face forward.

Rain Gear

In many parts of the U.S., most cyclists never venture out when it rains. I don't relish rain either, but think it is smarter to prepare for the possibility of rain than to stop riding altogether when there is only the slightest chance of rain. In areas like Britain and the Pacific Northwest, nobody would get

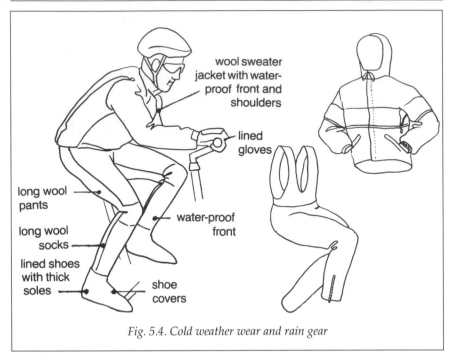

Fig. 5.4. Cold weather wear and rain gear

much cycling done if they didn't accept the possibility of getting wet. Cyclists there take the necessary clothing to fend it off, and so should you if there is a chance of rain, wherever you live.

The problem with most rain garments is that if they are really waterproof enough to keep the rain out, they also trap perspiration in. Avoid this problem by selecting rain gear made from the kind of fabric that keeps rain out but allows water vapor through. Examples of such fabrics are Gore-Tex and Tenson, though there are others.

For the top, I suggest using a cape, although you may prefer a jacket. If your helmet has cut-outs and air scoops, you may also need a helmet cover. If you don't wear a helmets you may keep your head dry by means of a sou'wester which also keeps the rain from running down your neck by means of a large back flap. It does not limit your vision like a hood.

To keep the legs dry, I prefer spats to full rain pants or leggings. Spats are covers for the front of the legs. At the bottom, they should continue to cover the top of the shoes. To keep your feet dry, you may either use pedal covers or you may wear plastic overshoes. Personally, I find the most effective way to keep comfortable is by putting thin polyethylene bags over the socks. That may not seem very elegant, but it works well. In really muddy terrain, I go one step further and wear light rubber boots, cut off just above the ankles to allow adequate freedom of movement.

Part II
Getting the Most out of Your Mountain Bike

CHAPTER 6

Safe Mountain Biking

Riding a bike—whether done on the road, on trails or cross- country—is not an entirely riskless undertaking. Neither are many other pursuits: accidents and other health hazards are very real risks everywhere. In this chapter you will be shown how to minimize the risks you are exposed to when riding your mountain bike.

Presumably, mountain biking is done off-road, and that would seem to remove the risk of traffic accidents. However, even here, the risk is not reduced to zero: running into a ranger's truck can be just as deadly as running into any other motor vehicle and there are many hazards that have nothing to do with motor vehicles. If you

Bob Allen photo

follow the advice in this chapter, you can learn to avoid most of the dangers, minimize injuries and stay healthy riding your bike.

Considering the various hazards, ranging from those to your own body and equipment to the harm or loss you may cause others, it may be smart to take out some kind of insurance. Personal liability insurance is perhaps the most important. In the U.S., where the concept of national health insurance is still regarded as some dangerous communist threat, rather than a public necessity as it is in all other western countries, you may want to make sure you have adequate health insurance to cover the danger of falls or collisions.

It would be a good idea to learn how to deal with accidents, injuries, sickness and other health related emergencies while cycling or touring. Do you really know what to do when you are bleeding, when you think you may have broken something, when one of your companions faints or is seriously hurt? Take a first aid course to be prepared for dealing with the unanticipated. That is a lot smarter than shutting your eyes, hoping nothing serious will happen. Even if you are spared yourself, you may be able to save someone else's life. If you can't take a first aid course, at least read up on the subject—appropriate literature is included in the Bibliography.

A lot of research has been done in recent years on the subject of bicycle accidents and injuries. To summarize the available evidence

in a nutshell, the majority of bicycle accidents are attributable to a very limited number of typical mistakes, most of which can be avoided or counteracted by intelligent cycling techniques—whether the cyclist is legally considered at fault or not. That's known as defensive riding, and even off-road, it's a good idea to practice it.

Off-road Dangers

What may astonish most people at first is that the risk of being involved in an accident is greater on trails and paths than on roads with motor traffic. Many of the very characteristics that make cross-country cycling so enjoyable are also responsible for the increased risk.

Whereas roads are designed for wheeled vehicles travelling at speed, the back country is not—fortunately, in a way. Realize this when cycling, so you are prepared at all times to react to the unevenness of the surface, soft or slippery sections, ridges and various other obstacles. Anticipate emerging wildlife, hikers, rangers or cyclists, who may suddenly appear from around the next bend or from behind a bush or rocky outcrop. Practice the control of your bike as outlined in the preceding chapters, so you can react to the unexpected and regain control over your bike even under difficult conditions. Braking, steering, yes even falling gracefully, can all be practiced and perfected.

Protective Gear

The need for protective gear should be just as obvious in off-road cycling as it is while riding in traffic. Despite my reservations about excessive expectations and peer pressure expressed in Chapter 5, it is smart to wear a helmet, gloves and perhaps long-sleeved and long-legged garments, preferably double layers (the two layers sliding relative to each other in a crash will spare your skin). Helmets are not some magic cure against motorists running into you, as some cyclists seem to think, but they serve to stop you from cracking your skull or damaging its contents when you

fall off the bike, and even if you are an accomplished rider, you'll still be likely to fall off your bike more than once when travelling in the outback.

If you fall on your head, the impact tends to smash the brain against the inside of the skull, followed by the reverse action as it rebounds. The human brain can usually withstand this kind of treatment without lasting damage if the resulting deceleration does not exceed about 300 G, or 3000 m/sec^2. And when hitting any object, the deceleration is enormous, unless protected by an impact-absorbing medium. Assume the head falls to the ground from a height of 1.5 m (5 ft). This results

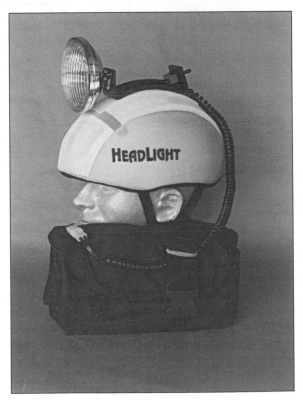

Whether off road or in traffic, to ride at night, you'll need good lighting. This curious looking helmet-mounted headlight does the job, although you'll probably find handlebar-mounted lights more convenient.

in a speed of 5 m/sec^2 at the time of impact. To keep the deceleration down below 3000 m/sec^2, this speed must be reduced to zero in no less than 0.002 sec.

Neither your skull nor (probably) the object with which you collide will deform gradually enough to reduce the deceleration to such a low value. That's why energy-absorbing helmets with thick crushable foam shells were developed. Neither a soft, flexible nor a hard material will do the trick by itself. It's not a bad idea to have a hard outer shell cover to distribute the effect of the impact, and it is nice to get some comfort inside from a soft, flexible liner, but it's the crushing of about ¾ inch of seemingly brittle foam that absorbs the shock. The minimum requirements for a safe helmet are those specified in the American standard ANSI Z-90.4, while an even tougher standard is that of the Snell Foundation. The label inside the helmet will specify which standards it meets.

Risk Evaluation

Perhaps the most important lesson to learn from the investigations dealing with the safety of touring cyclists is the correlation between risk and trip length found. Put simply, the likelihood of getting hurt—be it as a result of an accident or a fall—increases dramatically after you get tired. This applies especially to cyclists carrying luggage and handling difficult terrain, and most dramatically to in-experienced riders. Hence the following advice: if you are new to cycling, keep your daily distance down to no more than 60 road miles or 4 hours off-road to minimize the risk.

Another significant finding is that more experienced cyclists have markedly fewer accidents, and can go longer distances than beginners. This is one good argument for gaining experience and learning the necessary skills as quickly as possible. Following the advice contained in the following chapters will not only increase the joy, satisfaction and effectiveness of cycling, it will also minimize the hazards.

Finally on the subject of risk evaluation, I should mention the theory of risk compensation, which may well apply to mountain biking. This theory holds that people tend to adjust their willingness to take risks in proportion to their perceived or real protection. The little quantitative evidence available does suggest that people who use helmets and other safety gear tend to accept greater risks and consequently still finish up with about the same proportion of injuries as before they started using the safety gear. This puts the helmet discussion in a different light: Perhaps many riders accept a higher risk because they are wearing a helmet, while others get the same injury risk not wearing one.

The ones will argue they get more thrills wearing a helmet because they can do things they would not otherwise risk. But the other standpoint, namely that some people simply enjoy riding without encumbrances more, is no less valid. Within reasonable limits set by the overall cost to society, I feel it is imperative to retain the right for every person to decide for him or herself whether to accept a certain risk or not. In the name of civil liberties, I feel the pressure that is put on cyclists in the U.S. —particularly by their own organizations and press—is highly improper.

Falls and Collisions

In bicycle falls and collisions, virtually every injury to the cyclist results from the impact when the cyclist falls off the bike. He either hits the surface, an object on or along his path, another person or vehicle, or his own bike. Four types of falls and collisions can be distinguished: stopping, diverting, skidding and loss of control. I shall describe each of these categories, followed by a few hints about preventing and treating the typical injuries that may result.

Stopping Accidents

In a stopping accident, the bicycle runs into an obstacle that halts its progress. Depending on the cyclist's speed, the impact can be very serious. As the bicycle itself is stopped, inertia keeps the rider going forward, throwing him against or over the handlebars. The kinetic energy of the moving

mass will be dissipated very suddenly, often in an unfortunate location. Your genitals may hit the handlebar stem or your skull may hit the ground or the object with which the bike collided.

The way to guard yourself against these accidents is to look and think ahead, so you don't run into any obstacles. If necessary, control your speed to allow handling the unexpected when a potential danger may be looming up around the next corner. Learn to apply the diverting technique described in the preceding chapter. The way to minimize the impact of the most serious form of stopping accident is to wear an energy absorbing helmet.

Diverting Accidents

A diverting accident occurs when the front wheel is pushed sideways by an external force, while the rider is not leaning in the same direction to regain balance. Typical causes off-road are rocky ridges, while on roads the same effects are caused by railway tracks, cracks in the road surface, the edge of the road, and by touching another rider's rear wheel with your front wheel. The result is that you fall sideways and hit the ground or some obstacle by the side of your path. Depending how unexpectedly it happens, you may be able to break the fall by stretching out an arm, which seems to be an automatic reflex in this situation.

Characteristic injuries range from abrasions and lacerations of the hands and the sides of arms and legs to bruised hips and sprained or broken wrists. More serious cases, usually incurred at higher speeds, may involve broken collarbones and injuries to the face or the side of the skull. The impact of lesser injuries can be minimized by wearing padded gloves and double layers of clothing with long sleeves and pants. Wearing a helmet will minimize damage to the side of the head.

Diverting accidents can often be avoided if the cyclist is both careful and alert. Keep an eye out for the typical danger situations. Don't overlap wheels with other riders, don't approach surface ridges under a shallow angle. A last second diversion can often be made along the lines of the diverting technique described in Chapter 9. In the case of a ridge in the surface, use the technique of sideways jumping, also described there. When your front wheel touches the rear wheel of the rider in front of you, or if your handlebars are pushed over by an outside force, you may sometimes save the day if you react by immediately leaning in the direction you were diverted, and then steering to regain control.

Skidding Accidents

When the bicycle keeps going, or moves off in an unintended direction, despite your efforts to brake or steer, it will be due to skidding between the tires and the road surface. This happens more frequently when the surface is loose or wet, but may also be caused by moisture, frost, loose sand, or fallen leaves. Under these conditions, sudden diversions or movements, hard braking, and excessive lean when cornering may all cause skidding either forward or sideways.

Skidding accidents often cause the cyclist to fall sideways, resulting in abrasions, lacerations or more rarely, fractures. Avoid skidding by checking the surface ahead and avoiding sudden steering or braking maneuvers and excessive leaning in curves. Cross slick patches, ranging from loose gravel and wet rocks off-road to railway tracks, sand, leaves or even white road markings on regular roads, with the bicycle upright. Carry out the requisite steering and balancing actions before you reach such danger spots. If you can not avoid it, once you feel you are entering a skid, try to move your weight towards the back of the bike as much as possible, sliding back on the saddle and stretching the arms. Follow the bike, rather than trying to force it back. Finally, don't do what seems an obvious reaction to the less experienced, namely getting off the saddle to straddle the top tube with one leg dangling. As with so many cycling techniques, skidding can be practiced in a relatively safe environment such as an empty parking lot.

Loss of Control Accidents

At higher speeds, especially in a steep descent, loss of control accidents sometimes occur. In this case, you can't steer the bike the way you intend to go. This happens when you find yourself having to steer in one direction when you are leaning the other way, or when speed control braking initiates unexpected oscillations. This situation often develops into a fall or collision along the lines of one of the two accident types described above.

Prevention is only possible with experience: don't go faster than the speed at which you feel in control. The more you ride under various situations, the more you will develop a feel for what is a safe speed, when to brake and how to steer to maintain control over the bike. Once the situation sets in, try to keep your cool. Don't panic. Follow the bike, rather than forcing it over. The worst thing you can do is to tense up and get off the saddle. Stay in touch with handlebars, seat and pedals, steering in the direction of your lean. This way, you may get out of it without falling or colliding, though your nerves may have suffered.

Traffic Hazards

In this section we shall discuss in detail what most upset at least one reviewer about the first edition of this book: the fact that I treat bicycle traffic safety in a mountain bike book. Paradoxical though it may seem at first, it *is* justified, since most mountain bikes are ridden as much in traffic as they are off-road. Besides, it's the danger of cycling in traffic that scares off most beginners from the sport. Cycling on regular roads does not have to be as dangerous as it seems. You can learn to handle it, since traffic is nothing but people moving. Since you are human yourself and probably smart enough to understand the basic laws of physics and mechanics, you can learn to avoid the risks associated with such an environment on your bike as much as in your car.

Usually, fatal accidents are the only ones that get public attention. Yet these constitute only a tiny percentage of all injuries, and numerous other serious accidents do occur.

Although the majority of all injured cyclists are themselves to blame for their injuries, there will always be some accidents that are directly attributable to bullying and inconsiderate motorists. Unfortunately, this type of accident forms a high proportion of those that experienced cyclists encounter. These riders have learned to handle their machines rationally and safely in traffic, virtually eliminating their risk concerning the more common kind of accidents to which the incompetent are exposed. But they are just as vulnerable to the remaining irrational dangers of the road.

The only defense against inconsiderate road users is not to

provoke them. Give in, even if it seems highly unfair. It's an unequal battle and sometimes its smarter not to insist on justice. You will encounter fewer of these particular risks if you avoid the situations where they are most likely: Sunday afternoons and late evenings, when many boisterous drunks are on the road. Oddly enough, these accidents are also more likely on lightly travelled roads near small towns than in heavy traffic near a big city. Although I realize that the latter condition does not make the ideal cycling environment, try to avoid the quiet roads near small towns at high-risk times.

Most accidents, of course, are not of this type. They simply happen when two people each make a mistake: one initiates a wrong move, and the other fails to react in such a way that a collision is avoided. Keep that in mind when cycling. Remain alert for possible mistakes others may make, and try to avoid taking unexpected or inconsiderate actions yourself as much as humanly possible. Anticipate not only the predictable, but also the unexpected: the motorist looming behind the next corner or intersection, the dog appearing from a driveway, or the cyclist suddenly crossing your path in the dark without lights.

The latter subject deserves special attention. The only way to arm yourself is to make sure you do not cycle out after dark without lights, so at least *you* can be seen and your light will help you see the other rider. Proper

lighting on the bike is needed in addition to the curiously ineffective array of reflectors that is increasingly prescribed by law in most countries. The gravest danger of reflectors lies in the inappropriate impression they give of making you highly visible. In reality, several of them only make you visible to those who do not endanger you anyway. A bright light in the front and a big rear light or reflector facing back are essential, while all the other reflective devices don't do a thing that the former wouldn't do more effectively.

Most accidents occur in daylight, even though the relative risk is greater at night. Whether by day or night, cycle with all your senses alert. In general, ride your bike as you would drive your car, always verifying whether the road ahead of you is clear and taking particular care to select your path wisely at junctions and intersections. As a relatively slow vehicle, you must look behind you, to ascertain that nobody is following closely, before you move over into another traffic lane or away from your previous path.

Forget anything you ever heard about bikes being different from motor vehicles. As a wheeled vehicle, your bike answers to the same laws of physics as does your car. Adhere to the most basic rules of traffic you learned to handle a car and you'll be safe on a bike. No doubt the worst advice ever given to cyclists in many parts of the U.S. is to ride on the side *facing* traffic. Although that may be correct for pedestrians, on a bike, you *are* the traffic, and you belong on the same side as all other vehicles travelling the same way.

The rules of the road as applied to motor vehicles are based on a system that has evolved gradually and logically. This system works the way it does because it is logical. If it is dangerous for motorists to do certain things, then it will be at least as dangerous on a bike. This applies equally when travelling abroad, although it will be smart to prepare for the peculiar kind of laws that have been instituted in some societies which relegate cyclists to a bike path or any inferior (and invariably more dangerous) place on the road.

Don't hug the curb but claim your place on the road. Your place is somewhere to the right of the centerline of the path normally taken by cars on a wide road (assuming RH traffic). Keep at least 90 cm (3 ft) away from the inside edge, even if the road is too narrow to stay clear to the right of the normal path of motor vehicles. Don't dart in and out around parked vehicles and other obstructions along the side of the road. When making a turn, choose your lane early but only after checking behind you to make sure that it is safe to move over. Thus, to go straight at an intersection, make sure you will not be overtaken by vehicles turning right. To turn right, get close to the RH edge. To turn left, choose a path near the center of the road or the middle of a traffic lane marked for that direction well before the actual intersec-

tion, after having established that you will not be cutting across the path of vehicles following closely behind.

Excessive attention is often paid to hand signals in traffic education for cyclists. Yes, when cycling on the road, you should signal your intention before you do things like diverting, turning off or slowing down. That applies particularly when cycling with others in a group, where the first person should also point out and audibly identify obstacles or hazards in the road. But avoid the dangerous habit of assuming a hand signal will ward off danger. Your hand is not a magic wand, and if somebody is following so closely that you can signal your intention of turning across his path to him, you should not do it. Instead, wait until your maneuver does not interfere with vehicles following closely behind.

The most feared type of bicycle accident is the one that involves being hit from behind. These accidents are surprisingly rare but almost invariably very serious. Although there is hardly any possible defense to ward them off, it is worth considering that they are characterized by a number of common factors. They invariably occur on otherwise deserted roads, where the attention of motorist and cyclist alike are at a low, since both feel perfectly secure.

Inconspicuous clothing, a low sun, blinding one or both participants, and a lack of the cyclist's awareness, due to tiredness at the end of a long day, are also common features. It may be smart to increase your conspicuity. Wearing light and bright colors, such as white, yellow, pink, or orange, may well help others spot you in time to avoid this type of accident.

Treating Injuries

In this and the following sections, you will be shown how to treat or limit the effect of several typical bicycle injuries. The most common type of injuries are abrasions, referred to in cycling circles as road rash, even when incurred off-road. They usually heal relatively fast, although they can be quite painful. Wash out the wound with water and soap, and remove any particles of road dirt to prevent infection. There may be a risk of tetanus if the wound draws blood. Even if you have been immunized against tetanus before, get a tetanus shot within 24 hours if the last one was over two years ago.

If you have never been immunized before, get a full immunization, consisting of two (different) shots within 24 hours, followed by two more after two weeks and six months, respectively. Apply a dressing only if the location is covered by clothing, since the wound will heal faster when exposed to air. Avoid the formation of a scab by treating the wound with an antibacterial salve. See a doctor if any signs of infection occur, such as swelling, itching or fever.

Sprained Limbs

In case of a fall, your tendency to stick out an arm to break the impact may result in a sprained or even a fractured wrist. In other accident situations this can also happen to the knee or the ankle. Spraining is really nothing but damage to the ligaments that surround and hold the various parts of a joint together. Typical symptoms are a local sensation of heat, itching and swelling.

Whenever possible, keep the area cold with an ice bag. Get professional medical advice if you feel a stinging pain or if fever develops, because it may actually be a fracture that was at first incorrectly diagnosed as a sprain. This may be the case when the fracture takes the form of a simple 'clean' crack without superficially visible deformation of the bone.

Fractures

Typical cycling fractures are those of the wrist and the collarbone, both caused when falling: the one when extending the arm to break the fall, the other when you don't have time to do that. You or medical personnel may not at first notice a 'clean' fracture as described above: there may not be any outward sign.

If there is a stinging pain when the part is moved or touched, I suggest you get an X-ray to make sure, even if a fracture is not immediately obvious. You'll need medical help to set and bandage the fracture, and you must give up cycling until it is healed, which will take about five weeks. Sad if that happens during a bicycle tour but better than continuing in agony.

Other Health Problems

The remaining part of this chapter will be devoted to the health hazards of cycling that have nothing to do with falling off the bike. We will look at the most common complaints and discuss some methods of prevention, as well as possible cures. This brief description can not cover the entire field. Nor should most of the issues discussed here be generalized too lightly. The same symptoms may have different causes in different cases; conversely, the same cure may not work for two superficially similar problems. Yet in most cases the following remarks will apply.

Saddle Sores

Although beginning cyclists may at first feel uncomfortable on the bike saddle, you probably have no idea what kind of agony real seat problems can bring. As soon as any pressure is applied—i.e. when you sit on the saddle—things will get worse. Avoid the most serious seat problems by taking it easy for one or two days after symptoms start to develop. During the hours you spend in the saddle, the combined effect of perspiration, pressure and chafing may cause cracks in the skin, where dirt and bacteria can enter. The result can be any-

He's just having fun, although he looks pretty scared, and well he should be taking risks without a lid.

photo courtesy Titanal

thing from a mild inflammation to the most painful boils.

There is of course little chance of healing as long as you continue riding vigorously. Prevention and early relief are the methods to combat saddle sores. The clue to both is hygiene. Wash and dry both your crotch and your cycling shorts after every day's ride. Many cyclists also treat the affected areas with rubbing alcohol, which both disinfects and increases the skin's resistance to chafing, or with talcum powder, which prevents further damage.

You'll need at least two pairs of cycling shorts if you ride at all regularly, so you can always rely on a clean, dry pair when you start out. Wash them out, taking particular care to get the chamois clean, and hang them out to dry thoroughly, preferably outside, where the sun's ultraviolet rays act to kill any remaining bacteria. Treat the chamois with either talcum powder or a special treatment for that purpose, I prefer to use a water-soluble cream, such as Noxema, since it is relatively easy to wash out.

The quality of your saddle and your riding position also affect the development of crotch problems. If early symptoms appear in the form of redness or soreness, consider getting a softer saddle, sitting further to the back of your saddle, or lowering the handlebars a little to reduce the pressure on the seat. If the problem gets out of hand, take a rest from cycling until the sores have fully healed.

Knee Problems

Because the cycling movement does not apply the high impacting shock load on the legs that is associated with running, it's surprising that knee problems are so prevalent amongst bikers. They are concentrated mainly with two groups of riders: beginners and very strong, muscular riders. In both cases, the cause seems to be pushing too high a gear. This strains the knee joint, resulting in damage to the membranes that separate the moving portions of the joint and the ligaments holding the bits and pieces of the joint together. The problems get aggravated in cold weather , so it will be wise to wear long pants whenever the temperature is below 18 °C (65 °F), especially if fast descents are involved.

Prevent excessive forces on the knee joint by gearing so low that you can spin lightly under all conditions. Avoid climbing in the saddle with pedaling speeds below 60 RPM. Equip your bicycle with the kind of gear ratios that allow you to do that, and choose a lower gear whenever necessary. Once the problem has developed, you can aid the healing process by either giving up cycling or riding loosely in low gears, avoiding steep climbs. I suggest you continue cycling in very low gears, spinning freely. That will probably prepare you to get back into shape, while forcing you to avoid the high gears that caused the problem in the first place.

Tendinitis

Tendinitis is an inflamation of the Achilles tendon, which attaches the big muscle of the lower leg, the gastrocnemius, to the heel bone. It is an important tendon in cycling, since it transmits the pedaling force to the foot. It sometimes gets damaged or torn under the same kind of circumstances as described above for knee injuries: cycling with too much force in too high a gear. The problem is ag gravated by low temperatures, which explains why it generally develops in the early season.

To avoid tendinitis, wear long woolen socks whenever the temperature is below 18 °C (65 °F). It may also help to wear shoes that come up quite high, maximizing the support they provide. Get used to riding with a supple movement in a low gear, which is the clue to preventing many cycling complaints. Healing requires rest, followed by a return to cycling with minimum pedal force in a low gear.

Numbness

Beginning cyclists, not used to riding long distances, sometimes develop a loss of feeling in certain areas of contact with the bike. The most typical location is the hands, but it also occurs in the feet and the crotch. The numb feeling is caused by excessive and unvaried prolonged pressure on the nerves and blood vessels. The effects are usually relieved with rest, al-though they have at times been felt for several days.

Once the problem develops, get relief by changing your position frequently, moving the hands from one part of the handlebars to another or moving from one area of the seat to the other if the crotch is affected. To prevent numbness in the various locations, use well padded gloves, foam hand grips, a soft saddle in a slightly higher position, or thick soled shoes with cushioned inner soles. Lace your shoes loosely at the bottom but tightly higher up, so the foot does not slip forward to push the toe against the front of the shoe.

Back Ache

Many riders complain of aches in the back, the lower neck and the shoulders, especially early in the season. These are probably attributable to insufficient training of the muscles. It is largely the result of unfamiliar isometric muscle work, keeping still in a forward bent position. This condition is also aggravated by low temperatures, so it is wise to wear warm bicycle clothing in cool weather.

To avoid the early-season reconditioning complaints, the best remedy is not to stop cycling in winter. Two rides a week at a moderate pace, or extended use of a home trainer with a proper low riding position, will do the trick. Alternately, you may start off in the new season with a slightly higher handlebar position and once more low gearing. Sleeping on a firm mattress and keeping warm also help either alleviate or prevent the problem.

Sinus and Bronchial Complaints

In the cooler periods, many cyclists develop breathing problems, originating either in the sinuses or the bronchi. The same may happen if you are used to cycling at sea level and suddenly get into the mountains, where the cold air in a fast descent can be very unsettling. It's generally attributable to undercooling, the only solution being to dress warmer and to cycle slowly enough to allow breathing through the nose.

After a demanding climb in cooler weather, do not strip off warm clothing, open your shirt or drink excessive quantities of cold liquids, even if you sweat profusely. All these things may cause more rapid cooling than your body can handle. You will cool off gradually and without impairing your health if you merely reduce your output and allow the sweat

to evaporate naturally through the fibers of your clothing. This works best if you wear clothing that contains a high percentage of wool.

Sunburn

On a clear day, especially in high-lying areas, the exposure to ultra-violet rays caused by a couple of hours of riding may well be more than is good for you. Unless you have a naturally high resistance to UV-rays, you will need some extra protection. Clothing is the most effective shield, because—unlike any form of lotion—it does not get washed and wiped away by your own perspiration and your efforts to remove it. A long-sleeved jersey, a helmet or cap with a visor, perhaps even long pants, can all help you prevent painful and potentially dangerous exposure.

There is no known treatment for sunburn. Although there are sprays and ointments that reduce the burning sensation, they only tackle the symptoms, not the cause. Prevention is the name of the game.

CHAPTER 7

Understanding and Using the Gears

Your mountain bike is equipped with a sophisticated derailleur system for multiple gearing. To change gears, the chain is shifted onto another combination of chainring and sprocket with the aid of two derailleur mechanisms. Nowadays, systems with 21 or 24 gears are generally used, though some 15- and 18-speed mountain bikes are still around. The more common 21- and 24-speed systems have three chainrings combined with 7 and 8 sprockets respectively, while older bikes may have three chainrings with 6 or sometimes only 5 sprockets, giving 18 and 15 speeds respectively—probably quite enough for most people.

The derailleur method of gearing allows minute adjustments of the gear ratio to the cyclist's potential on the one hand, and the terrain, wind resistance and surface conditions on the other. All this is mere theory for most riders, because the majority of people, including most beginning mountain bike riders, plod along in the wrong gear for the work load. Indeed, learning to

Today's typical gearing for mountain bike use: 3 chainrings and 8 sprockets.

photo courtesy Diamond Back

select the right gear may well provide the biggest single step towards improved cycling speed and endurance. That's the subject of the present chapter.

There is a sound theory behind the principle of gear selection, based on the optimum pedaling rate, which I have covered in several of my other books, such as *The Bicycle Racing Guide* and *Bicycle Technology*. Interesting though this theory is, you can apply the technique without a thorough theoretical background. That's why I shall limit the discussion here to what you absolutely have to know to select your gears correctly.

Parts of the System

Fig. 7.1 shows and names the mechanical components of the derailleur system as used on the mountain bike. The chain runs over (usually) three chainrings mounted on the RH crank, and any one of (usually) 7 or 8 sprock-

ets mounted on a freewheel. Providing you are pedaling forward, the chain can be moved from one chainring to the other by means of the front derailleur or changer, and from one sprocket to another by means of the rear derailleur.

The various chainrings and sprockets have different numbers of teeth. Consequently, the ratio between pedaling speed and the speed with which the rear wheel is driven changes whenever a different combination is selected. As illustrated in Fig. 7.2, bigger chainrings in the front and smaller sprockets in the rear result in higher gears, whereas smaller chainrings and bigger sprockets give lower gears. Higher gears are selected when the cycling is easy, so the available output allows a high riding speed. Select a lower

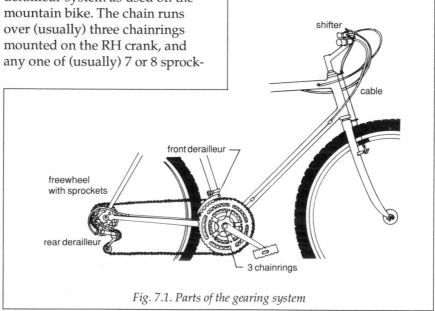

Fig. 7.1. Parts of the gearing system

gear when higher resistances must be overcome, such as riding uphill or against a head wind, when riding on soft ground, or when starting off from a standstill.

On the mountain bike, each derailleur is controlled by means of a shift lever that is mounted on the handlebars, within easy reach without taking the hands off the grips. Beginners' bikes tend to have double-lever (push-push) shifters mounted under the handlebars, while bikes intended for more experienced riders have single-lever shifters mounted on top of the handlebars, and some models are equipped with a twist grip or twist ring.

The front derailleur, or changer, simply shoves the cage through which the chain runs to the right or the left, placing the chain onto a larger or smaller chainring, respectively. On single-lever shifters, pulling the lever back engages a larger chainring for a higher gear range; pushing it forward engages a smaller chainring, obtaining a lower gearing range. On under-the-bar double lever shifters, pushing the big lower lever shifts to a bigger chainring, pushing in the small upper one engages a smaller chainring.

The rear derailleur is a little more complicated with a set of little wheels over which the chain runs, but it has the same effect: you move the chain on a larger sprocket (lower gear) or smaller one (higher gear) as you move the shifter.

Most shifts are made with the rear derailleur, while the front changer is primarily used to move from one general range of gears to another. With the usual set-up, all the gears in the high range are reached by shifting the rear derailleur while the front derailleur remains on the largest chainring; all intermediate gears are reached while the front derailleur is set to engage the intermediate chainring; and the gears in the low range are selected with the front changer in the position to put the chain on the smallest chainring.

The rear derailleur is controlled by means of the RH shifter. For under-the-bar shifters, you shift in single steps to the next higher gear, repeating several times if you want to skip intermediate gears. One lever is used to shift down, the other to shift up. In the case of over-the-bar shifters, move the lever clockwise to shift up, or counterclockwise to shift down. Whatever type of shifter is installed, the one mounted on the RH side always controls the rear derailleur (used for most shifts), the one on the LH side the front changer.

Older models may not be indexed (meaning you don't shift in steps but have to fine-tune the position of the lever). Some of us actually prefer that solution, since it is not so sensitive to wear-related adjustment changes. Believe it or not, it is quite possible to shift these so-called friction levers just as accurately as indexed ones: it just takes more practice and sensitivity.

Gearing Theory

Gearing enables you to pedal at an efficient rate with comfortable force under a wide range of conditions and riding speeds. If the combination of chainring and sprocket size were fixed, as it is on the single-speed bicycle, any given pedaling speed would invariably correspond to a certain riding speed. The rear wheel would be turning at a speed that can be simply calculated by multiplying the pedaling rate with the quotient of chainring and sprocket sizes (expressed in terms of their respective numbers of teeth):

$$v_{wheel} = v_{pedal} \times T_{front} / T_{rear}$$

where:

v_{wheel} = wheel rotating speed (RPM)

v_{pedal} = pedaling rate (RPM)

T_{front} = number of teeth on chainring

T_{rear} = number of teeth on sprocket

The actual riding speed depends on this wheel rotating speed and the effective wheel diameter. The effective diameter of a nominal 26 inch wheel is about 650 mm. This results in a riding speed in MPH that can be determined by multiplying the wheel speed in RPM by 0.075. These two calculations can be combined to find the riding speed in MPH directly from the pedaling rate and the chainring and sprocket sizes as follows:

$$MPH = 0.075 \times v_{pedal} \times T_{front} / T_{rear}$$

where:

MPH = riding speed in MPH and the other symbols are as defined above. To express riding speed in km/h, use the following formula instead:

$$km/h = 0.12 \times v_{pedal} \times T_{front} / T_{rear}$$

To give an example, assume you are pedaling at a rate of 80 RPM on a bike geared with a 42-tooth chainring and a 21-tooth rear sprocket. Your riding speed, expressed in MPH and km/h respectively, will be:

$$0.075 \times 80 \times 42 / 21 = 12 \text{ MPH}$$

$$0.12 \times 80 \times 42 / 21 = 19 \text{ km/h}$$

Depending on the prevailing terrain conditions, this may be too easy or too hard for optimum endurance performance. If you are riding up a steep incline, this speed may require a very high pedal force, which may be too exhausting and damaging to muscles, joints and tendons. On a level road, the same speed will be reached so easily that you don't feel any significant resistance.

The derailleur gearing system allows you to choose the combination of chainring and sprocket sizes that enables you to operate effectively at your chosen pedaling speed with optimum performance. You may of course also vary the pedaling rate, which would appear to have the same effect as selecting another gear. Indeed, with any given gear, pedaling slower reduces riding speed and therefore demands less power, whereas a higher pedaling rate increases road speed, requiring more power.

However, power output is not the sole, nor indeed the most important, criterion. Performing at the same power output may tax the body differently, depending on the associated force and speed of movement. It has been found that to cycle long distances effectively, without tiring or hurting excessively, the pedal force must be kept down by pedaling at a rate well above what seems natural to the beginning cyclist.

Whereas the beginner tends to plod along at 40–60 RPM, efficient long duration cycling requires a pedaling rate of 80 RPM or more. Racers generally pedal even faster whether riding off-road or not. This skill doesn't come overnight, the cyclist first has to learn to move his legs that fast, but it is an essential requirement for efficient bicycling. Much of your early cycling practice should therefore be aimed at mastering the art of fast pedaling, referred to as spinning.

Gearing Practice

Once you know that high gears mean big chainrings and small sprockets, it's time to get some practice riding in high and low gears. First do it 'dry': the bike upside down or supported with the rear wheel off the ground. Turn the cranks by hand and use the shift levers to change up and down, front and rear until you have developed a good idea of the combinations reached in all conceivable shift lever positions.

Under-the-bar shifters: Best solution for beginners, and any rider with weak hands.

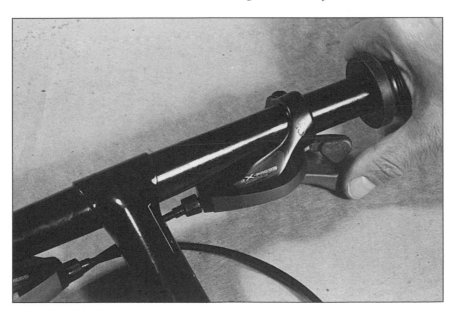

photo courtesy SunTour

Listen for rubbing and crunching noises as you shift, realizing that the shift has not been executed properly until the noises have subdued. Generally, noises come from the front, since the indexing takes care of such problems in the rear. You may have to move the shifter for the front derailleur if you discern a noise after a rear derailleur shift, since the chain—now running under a different angle—may be rubbing against the front derailleur.

Now take to the road or any other level terrain. Select a place where you can experiment with your gears without the risk of being run over by a closely following vehicle or getting in the way of other cyclists. Start off in a low gear and shift the rear derailleur up in steps. Then shift to another chainring and change down through the gears with the rear derailleur followed by the same changes with the chain on the third chainring.

When shifting, reduce the pedal force, still pedaling forward. The front derailleur in particular will not shift as smoothly as it did when the cranks were turned by hand. You will notice that the noises become more severe and that shifts don't take place as you intended. To execute a correct front change with a non-indexed above-the-bar shifter (or an indexed one that is switched to the friction mode), you may have to overshift slightly first: push the lever a little beyond the correct position to affect a definite change, then back up until the chain is quiet again. Practice shifting until it goes smoothly.

All this can be learned if you give it some time and attention. Some people never learn, quite simply because they don't take the trouble to practice conscientiously. Others take that trouble and learn to shift predictably and smoothly within a week. All it takes to become an expert very quickly is half an hour of intensive practice each day during one week, and the continued attention required to do it right during regular riding afterwards.

Gear Designation

Just how high or low any given gear is, may be expressed by giving the respective chainring and sprocket size engaged in the particular gear. However, this is not a very good measure. It may not be immediately clear that a combination designated 42 X 16 (really meaning 42 / 16) has the same effect as one designated 52 X 21, as can be verified mathematically.

To allow a direct comparison between the gearing effects of different gears and bikes, two methods are in use, referred to as gear number and development, respectively, as illustrated in Fig. 7.2. The gear number is determined by multiplying the quotient of chainring and sprocket sizes with the wheel diameter in inches:

$$gear = D_{wheel} \times T_{front} / T_{rear}$$

where:

gear = gear number in inches

D_{wheel} = wheel diameter in inches

T_{front} = number of teeth, chainring

T_{rear} = number of teeth, sprocket

Returning to the example of a bike with 26-in wheels with a 42-tooth chainring and a 21-tooth sprocket, the gear would be:

26 x 42 / 21 = 52 in

This is the customary, though rather quaint, method used in the English speaking world to define bicycle gearing. The rest of the world expresses gears in terms of development. This is the distance in meters covered by the bike with one crank revolution. Development can be calculated as follows:

Dev. = 3.14 x D_{wheel} x T_{front} / T_{rear}

where:

Dev. = development in meters

D_{wheel} = wheel diameter in m

T_{front} = number of teeth on chainring

T_{rear} = number of teeth on sprocket

The development for the same example would be:

Dev = 3.14 x 0.650 x 42121 = 4.10 m

In practice, you are not expected to figure this out yourself. Instead, you may refer to the tables in the Appendix. Just remember that a high gear is expressed by a high gear number or a long development. For off-road purposes, gear ranges tend to be lower than they are on other bikes. Low gears in terms of gear number are in the low to mid twenties (around 1.90–2.20 m in terms of development). The highest gears are those above 80 in (development of more than 7.40 m).

Gear Selection

Possibly the biggest problem for the beginning cyclist is to select the right gear out of the bewildering array available. Simply put,

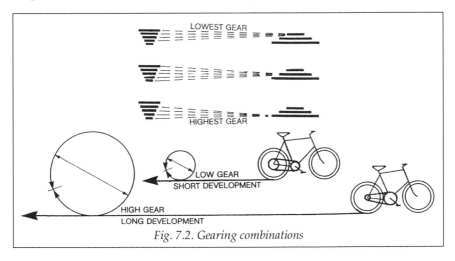

Fig. 7.2. Gearing combinations

choose whichever gear allows you to maximize your pedaling rate without diminishing your capacity to work effectively.

Perhaps you are initially able to pedal no faster than 60 RPM. Until you learn to spin faster, the right gear is the one in which you can reach that rate at any time, preferably exceeding it. Use either an electronic speedometer with an RPM function or count it out with the aid of a wrist watch until you develop a feel for your pedaling speed. If you find yourself pedaling slower, change into a slightly lower gear to increase the pedaling rate at the same riding speed. If you're pedaling faster, keep it up until you feel you are indeed spinning too lightly, and then change to a slightly higher gear to increase road speed while maintaining the same pedaling rate.

Gradually, you will develop the capacity to pedal faster. As this happens, increase the pedaling rate along with your ability, moving up from 60 to 70, 80 and eventually even higher. When riding with others, don't be guided by theothers' gear selection, since they may be stronger or weaker or may have developed their pedaling speed more or less well than you have.

It should not take long before you can judge the right gear in advance, without the need to count out the pedal revolutions. You'll know when to change down into a lower gear as the direction of the road changes, exposing you to a head wind, or when you reach an incline. You will also learn to judge just how far to change down and up again when the conditions become more favorable. Change gears consciously and frequently in small steps, and you will soon master the trick.

Derailleur Care and Adjustment

For optimum operation of the derailleur system, several things should be regularly checked and corrected if necessary. The derailleurs themselves, as well as the chain and the various sprockets, chainrings and shifters, must be kept clean and lightly lubricated. Cables for index shifting systems should be kept clean, but not lubricated. The cables must be just taut when the shift levers are pushed forward and the derailleurs engage the appropriate gear. The tension screws on over-the-bar shift levers must be kept tightened to give positive shifting without excessive tightness or slack.

When the chain is shifted beyond the biggest or smallest chainring or sprocket, or when certain combinations cannot be reached, the derailleurs themselves must be adjusted, which is described in Chapter 19.

CHAPTER 8

Elementary Bike Handling

Basically, riding a mountain bike is like riding any other bike—only more so. The combination of rough surfaces and high downhill speeds may prove tricky if you are not properly prepared. On the other hand, you have the right machine to do some things easily that would otherwise be difficult. To competently and confidently ride off-road, you have to be in complete command of your machine. In this chapter and the one that follows, we will take a closer look at these skills, and you will be shown how to achieve the necessary mastery.

The present chapter deals with increasing your basic competence at handling the beast, with proper control over the steering and braking mechanisms. This will help you cycle with minimal effort and maximum confidence, whether on the road or off-road. In the next chapter, you will be introduced to the peculiarities of effective riding techniques that are specific to off-road use. Although an understanding of the theoretical background is helpful, I shall concentrate as much as possible on the practical aspects, telling you

Dan Gindling photo

how to put into practice what you've learned.

The Steering Principle

The bicycle is not steered most effectively by merely turning the handlebars and following the front wheel, as is the case for any two-track vehicle, such as a car. Although bicycles and other single-track vehicles indeed follow the front wheel, they also require the rider to lean his vehicle into the curve to balance it at the same time, so it doesn't topple over to the outside of the curve due to the centrifugal force.

If you were to merely turn the handlebars, the lower part of the bike would start running away from its previous course in the direction in which the front wheel is pointed. Meanwhile, the mass of the rider, perched high up on the bike, would continue following the original course due to inertia. Thus, the center of gravity would not be in line with the point of contact between the bike and the ground, and consequently the rider would come crashing to the ground. Due to the effect of centrifugal force, the tendency to throw the rider off towards the outside of the curve increases with higher speeds, requiring a more pronounced lean into the curve the faster you are going.

It is possible to steer by turning the handlebars, and then correct lean and steering to regain balance afterwards. In fact, many older people, especially women, seem to

do it that way, succeeding quite well at low speeds. As soon as imbalance becomes imminent, they have to make a correction in the other direction. After some more cramped and anxious movements, they finally get around the corner. This accounts for the tense and impulsive riding style typical of such riders. They have ridden this way so long that they don't realize their movements are awkward and their balance is precarious.

The more effective technique for riding a curve at speed is to place the bike at the appropriate angle under which the centrifugal force is offset by a shift of your weight to the inside, *before* turning. Two methods may be used, depending on the time and space available to carry out the maneuver. I refer to these two methods as the natural and the forced turn, respectively. To understand these techniques, we should first take a look at the intricacies of balancing the bike when riding a straight line, after which the differences between the two methods of turning can be explained.

Bicycle Balance

What keeps a bicycle or any other single-track vehicle going without falling over is the inertia of its moving mass. Rolling a narrow hoop, such as a bicycle rim, will show that it has an unstable balance: once the thing starts to lean either left or right, it will go further and further down, until it hits the ground. This is because the mass is no longer supported vertically in line with the force. Try it with a bicycle wheel if you like. If the bike's front wheel could not be steered, and the rider couldn't move sideways, he'd very soon come down the same way.

On the bicycle, you notice when the vehicle starts to lean over. Theoretically, there are two ways out of the predicament: either move your body back over the center of the bike, or move the bike back under your body. In practice, the latter method is used most effectively, especially at higher speeds. When the bike begins leaning to the side, over-steer the front wheel a little in the same direction, which restores the balance. In fact, this point will be passed, so the bike starts leaning the other way, and so on *ad infinitum*.

This entire sequence of movements is easiest to observe when you are cycling slowly. When you try to stand still, the balancing motions become so extreme that only a highly skilled cyclist can keep control. The faster the bicycle, the less perceptible (though equally important and therefore harder to master) are the steering corrections required to retain balance. To get an understanding of this whole process, I suggest you practice riding a straight line at a low speed. Then do it at a higher speed, and see whether you agree with the explanation.

Clearly, both riding a straight line and staying upright with the bike are merely illusions. In reality, the bike is always in disequilibrium, following a more or less curved track. Bike and rider lean alternately one way or the other. At higher speeds the curves are longer and gentler while the

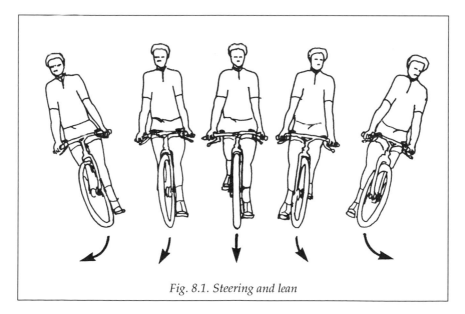

Fig. 8.1. Steering and lean

amount of lean can be perceptible; at lower speeds the curves are shorter and sharper, with a less pronounced lean angle for any given deviation.

The Natural Turn

Under normal circumstances, you'll know well ahead of time where to turn, and there is enough room to follow a wide curve. This is the situation in a natural turn, illustrated in Fig. 8.3, comparing the two types of turning action. This method makes use of the lean that results from your balancing moves during normal straight-path riding. To turn to the right, you simply wait until the bike is leaning that way, while the left turn is initiated when the bike is leaning to the left.

Instead of turning the handlebars to that same side, as you would do to get back in balance when trying to ride a straight line, you leave the handlebars alone. This causes the bike to lean further and further in the direction of the turn. Only when the lean is quite significant, do you steer in the same direction, but not as abruptly as you would to straighten up. Instead, you fine-tune the ratio of lean and steering to ride the curve out.

You will still be leaning in the same direction when the turn is completed, and you would ride a circle without some corrective action on your part. To get back on a straight course, you steer further into the curve than the amount of lean demanded to maintain your balance. This allows you to resume the slightly curving course with which you approximate the straight line.

Unconsciously, you probably learned to do this when you were a kid, but never realized what was going on. You could perhaps continue to ride a bicycle forever without understanding the theory. However, to keep control over the bike in demanding situations encountered while riding off-road, you will be better off if you have the theoretical knowledge and have learned to ride a calculated course, making use of this information. Get a feel for it by riding around an empty parking lot or any other level area many times, leaning this way and that, following straight lines and making turns, until it is second nature on the one hand, but also something you understand consciously.

While you are practicing this technique, as well as when riding at other times, note that speed, curve radius, and lean are all closely correlated. A sharper turn requires more lean at any given speed. At a higher speed, any given curve requires greater lean angles than the same curve radius at a lower speed. As you practice this technique, learn to judge which are the appropriate combinations and limitations under different circumstances.

The Forced Turn

Especially off-road, you will often be confronted with situations in which you can't wait until you are leaning the right way to make a natural turn. Irregularities in the surface, an obstacle or another trail user may force you into a narrow predetermined path, with only a few inches to spare. Or you may have to get around a curve that is too sharp to be taken naturally at your riding speed.

These situations require the second method of turning, which I call the forced turn, also illustrated in Fig. 8.2. In this case, the turn must be initiated quickly, regardless of which way the bike happens to be leaning at the time. You have to coerce the bike to lean in the appropriate direction and at an adequate angle just at the right time. And it has to be done quickly.

Do that by sharply steering *away* from the turn just before you get there. You and the bike will immediately start to lean in the direction of the turn. You would risk a disastrous crash, as your bike moves away from the mass center, if you were to continue in a straight line. You have quickly achieved a considerable lean angle in the direction of the turn. Compensate for this by steering abruptly in the same direction. Since this is the direction of the turn, you are set up just right to make a sharp turn. Once completed, steer into the turn a little further to regain the approximately straight course, as explained for the natural turn.

The forced turn technique must be practiced intensively and consciously, since it by no means comes naturally. The beginning cyclists has to overcome all sorts of reasonable inhibitions and practice a lot before he can initiate a *left*

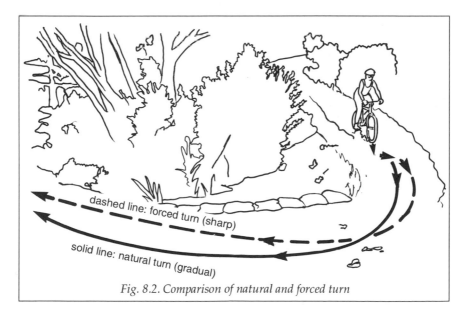

Fig. 8.2. Comparison of natural and forced turn

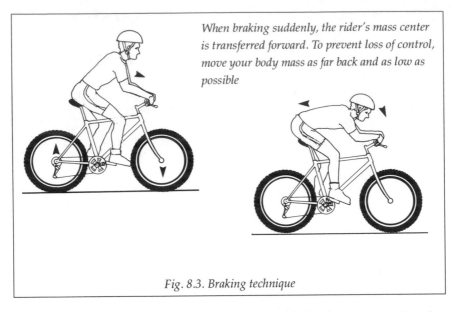

When braking suddenly, the rider's mass center is transferred forward. To prevent loss of control, move your body mass as far back and as low as possible

Fig. 8.3. Braking technique

turn by steering *right*. Take your bike to a level, grassy area or an empty parking lot a few days in a row, wearing protective clothing in case you fall: helmet, gloves, jacket and long pants.

Practice and experiment until you've mastered the trick, and refresh your skill from time to time, until this instant-turning technique has become second nature. In Chapter 9, you will be shown how to apply the forced turn technique to the difficult task of avoiding a suddenly emerging obstacle.

Braking Technique

When out mountain biking, you often have to use the brakes, though not always to make a panic stop. In fact, once you have become a skilled and sensitive cyclist, you'll hardly ever have to brake to a standstill. Instead, you will use the brakes to control and regulate your speed. Effective braking means that you can ride up fast close to the turn or the obstacle that requires the reduced speed, brake to reach the lower speed quickly, and accelerate immediately afterwards.

You will be using the brakes to get down in speed from 20 to 10 MPH to take a turn, or from 20 to 18 MPH to avoid running into the person ahead of you. Or you may have to get down from 30 to 10 MPH to handle a switchback or avoid a tree or a rock on a steep descent. To do this effectively without risk requires an understanding of braking physics. Although at times you may have to reduce your speed quickly, you should also develop a feel for gradual speed reduction to prevent skidding and loss of control. In fact, most cyclists are more often in danger due to braking too vigorously than due to insufficient stopping power.

Applying the brakes results in deceleration or speed reduction, which can only take place more or less gradually. The rate of deceleration can be measured and is expressed in m/sec^2. A deceleration of $1\ m/sec^2$ means that after each second of braking the travelling speed is 1 m/sec less than it was at the beginning of that second. A speed of 30 MPH corresponds to 13 m/sec. Getting down to standstill would take 13 sec if the deceleration is $1\ m/sec^2$; it would take 4 seconds to reach 9 m/sec or 20 MPH. At a higher rate of deceleration it would take less time (and a shorter distance) to get down to the desired speed.

The modern mountain bike has remarkably effective brakes—providing it's not raining. A modest force on the brake handle can cause a deceleration of 4–5 m/sec^2 with just one brake. Applying both brakes, the effect is even more dramatic, enabling you to slow down from 30 to 15 MPH within one second. There are some limitations to braking that have to be considered though.

In the first place, moisture has a negative effect on the rim brake's performance, as the build-up of water on the rims reduces the friction between brake block and rim drastically. This applies especially

A fine demonstration of the correct posture for steep downhill braking.

Bob Allen photo

if ordinary rubber brake blocks are used. I have measured a deterioration from 4.5 to 1.5 m/sec^2 for a given hand lever force for rubber brake blocks on aluminum rims (and only about 0.7 m/sec^2 for bicycles with chrome-plated steel rims). Lately, special brake block materials have been introduced that are less sensitive to rain. Several manufacturers now offer the sintered material first used for the Modolo D-1000 racing brake blocks. These are now also available in versions to match the typical mountain bike brake.

The second limitation is associated with a change in the distribution of weight between the wheels as a result of braking. Because the mass center of the rider is quite high above the ground, and its horizontal distance to the front wheel axle comparatively small, the bicycle has a tendency to tip forward in response to deceleration. Weight is transferred from the rear to the front of the bike, as illustrated in Fig. 8.3. When the deceleration reaches about 3.5 m/sec^2, the weight on the rear wheel is no longer enough to provide traction. Trying to brake harder than that with the rear brake makes the rear wheel skid, resulting in loss of control— not in faster stopping.

In a typical riding posture, the rear wheel is unloaded so far the bike actually starts to tip forward when a deceleration of about 6.5 m/sec^2 is reached. Consequently, no conventional bicycle can ever be controlled when trying to brake harder than this, regardless of the type, number and quality of the brakes used. This is a very high deceleration, which you should not often reach, but it is good to realize there is such a limit and that it cannot be avoided by using the rear brake alone or in addition to the front brake, but only by braking less vigorously. During a sudden speed reduction, or panic stop, such high deceleration may be reached. The effect will be even more pronounced on a down-slope, since it raises the rider even higher relative to the front wheel. In all such cases, you can reduce the toppling-over effect by shifting your body weight back and down as much as possible: sit far back and hold the upper body horizontally.

Since twice as great a deceleration is possible with the front brake as with the rear, the former should be used under most conditions. In most circumstances short of a panic stop, you can brake very effectively by using the front brake alone. When both brakes are used simultaneously, the one in the front can be applied quite a bit harder than the one in the rear. If you notice the rear brake is less effective when pressed equally far, it will be time to check it, and if necessary adjust, lubricate or replace the brake cable.

All the above is fine as long as you are riding a more or less straight line. When riding off-road, you may have to brake in a curve. Under these conditions, all my smart advice about using the front brake may be of little use: since the bike will not be directly in line with the path of travel, it will slip sideways when you apply the brake in a curve. Consequently, distinguish strictly between straight line and curved path braking. In the latter case, use mainly the rear brake. Better yet, try to brake before you get to the curve, using primarily the front brake.

Most braking is not done abruptly. Gradual braking must also be practiced. Gradual deceleration, particularly when the road is slick, in curves or when others are following closely behind, is vitally important. You must be able to control the braking force within narrow limits. Practice all the various forms and conditions of braking. Pay the utmost attention to the complex relationship between initial speed, curve radius, brake lever force and deceleration, to become fully competent at handling the bike when slowing down under all conceivable circumstances.

On a steep downhill, the slope not only increases the tendency to tip you forward, it also induces an accelerating effect, which must be overcome by the brakes merely to keep the speed constant. A 20% slope, which is not a rare phenomenon off-road, results in an acceleration of about 2 m/sec². Obviously, you will encounter big problems in wet weather on such a downhill stretch if you don't keep your speed down from the start. Reduce the speed by gradual, intermittent braking. This will help wipe most of the water from the rims, retaining braking ef-

ficiency a little better. This way, the brakes are not overtaxed when you do have to reduce speed suddenly, as may be required to handle an unexpected obstacle or a sharp turn.

Practice effective braking to achieve complete control of the bicycle under normal and difficult cycling conditions. The dramatic difference between the bike's behavior when braking on the straight and in a curve must be experienced to be appreciated. Again, this is a matter for practice in a place without traffic. Include braking in your regular exercises during the first weeks of cycling preparation. Even after you have been riding for some time, you will be well advised to repeat from time to time the practice sessions for steering and braking control.

Other Riding Techniques

Riding a mountain bike with total confidence requires hands-on experience. Most of the associated skills can be learned faster and more thoroughly when you understand the underlying principles. Building up on the information about posture, gearing, steering and braking provided in the preceding sections, you will be shown here what to do under various typical riding situations. The many miles of experience will come soon enough when you start riding. However the handling practice is gained more effectively when applying these techniques.

Getting up to Speed

Though you may not be into cycling for speed alone, you should
learn to reach an acceptable speed
quickly. You have already been
shown how to get on the bike and
start off smoothly. The next trick is
to reach the ultimate riding speed
quickly and efficiently. The idea is
to waste as little time and energy
as possible during this process of
getting up to speed. Tricky, because acceleration demands disproportionately high levels of
power output. And the faster it's
done, the more demanding it is.

Clearly, you have to strike a
balance. Accelerating faster than
necessary wastes energy that will
be sorely needed later. Done too
slowly, it may become a plodding
affair, especially if your speed
remains inadequate to overcome
steep sections or soft ground. You
will have to find the right balance
between speed and effort, but the
way to reach it is easy to describe:
start in a low gear and increase
speed gradually but rapidly.

There are two methods: either
pedal faster and faster in the low
gear changing up only as you
reach a significant speed, or be
prepared for a surge of hard work,
standing on the pedals, throwing
your weight from one side to the
other. As soon as speed is reached,
sit on the saddle and select a good
gear for spinning at a comfortable
but high pedaling rate. Once you
are going at the desired speed, try
to maintain it constantly, to save
you the effort of accelerating after
every slow-down.

Accelerating

However efficient a constant
speed may be, sometimes you
want to accelerate to a higher
speed. This may be necessary to
catch up with other riders, or to
avoid getting left behind. In traffic, you may have to accelerate to
get across an intersection before
the light changes, to avoid running into another vehicle on the
road, or to escape a pursuing dog
without a leash.

As for getting up to speed in
the first place, it is most efficient to
increase the speed as gradually as
possible. Unless you are already
spinning at your highest possible
rate, you will find accelerating by
increasing pedaling speed more effective than by increasing pedal
force in a higher gear. In other
words, as long as you can spin
faster it is best to shift down into a
slightly lower gear and increase
the pedaling rate vigorously. Once
you gather momentum and are approaching your maximum spinning speed, shift up and continue
to gain speed in the slightly higher
gear.

Riding Against the Wind

At higher speeds or whenever
there is a strong head wind, the effect of air drag on the power
needed to cycle is quite noticeable.
This may not always seem very
significant off-road, but certainly
when travelling on regular roads
and whenever you are in open,
level terrain this matters quite a

bit. Economize your efforts by minimizing the wind resistance as much as possible.

To achieve that, keep your profile low when cycling against the wind. When riding alone, try to seek out the sheltered parts of the road wherever possible, using ridiculously low gears when the terrain doesn't call for it. Refer to Chapter 7 for advice on selecting the right gears.

Hill Climbing

With some conscious effort, everybody's climbing skills can be improved up to a point, even though some riders are born climbers, while others may have to go uphill slowly all their lives. It is an ability that can be learned and developed well enough by the average rider to handle all the hills he encounters.

A regular pedaling motion is most efficient, and that is best mastered by staying seated in a low gear. Mountain bikes are invariably equipped with gears that are low enough to allow you to get up almost any incline while staying in the saddle. What's lacking is a true understanding of gear selection by many riders. Only too often do I see people plodding up at very low pedaling rates in too high a gear, or using an unnecessarily tiring technique, requiring long muscle work phases and short recovery periods.

Climbing Out of the Saddle

On very steep sections, where even the lowest available gear is too high to allow a smoothly spin-

If it gets too steep, there is nothing wrong with climbing in a '2-foot' gear.

Renner photo

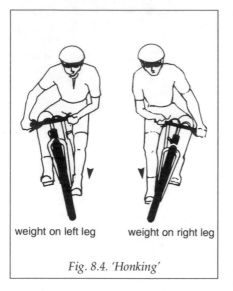

weight on left leg   weight on right leg

Fig. 8.4. 'Honking'

although few people know they're using an old-fashioned technique, which makes use of the rider's body weight to push down the pedals.

The weight of the whole body is pulled up after each stroke very quickly. In this mode, the muscle work is done each time the body is raised, rather than when pushing the pedal down and around. To do it effectively, you can either take quick snappy steps, or throw your weight from side to side in a swinging motion, as illustrated in Fig. 8.4 . I suggest you practice honking as well as spinning: the one in a relatively high gear at pedaling speeds below 55 RPM, the other in a considerably lower gear at 65 RPM or more. Avoid pedaling rates of 55–65 RPM by choosing your gears so as to stay within either one range or the other.

ning leg motion, it is time to apply another technique, standing up while riding. This is known as honking in England and used to be almost unknown in the U.S. until the advent of mountain biking. Now it's cool to stand up,

CHAPTER 9

Advanced Off-Road Riding Techniques

This chapter will expand on the material introduced in the preceding chapter to develop specific off-road riding skills. Although the underlying techniques are the same, the particular applications and their circumstances are different enough to justify special treatment. Just the same, we'll start with what may seem to be the simplest feat possible, gradually expanding our practice to some of the really gonzo tricks that only experienced off-road cyclists have learned to master.

The Running Start

Since the mountain bike is tough enough to be handled less gingerly than a fragile racer, you can actually jump on board when mounting. There are two good ways to do it: with or without a running start.

Off-road, the situation is complicated by the unpredictable traction of the unpaved path and the effect of any incline. On level firm ground it's easy enough: To mount without a running start, select a low or intermediate gear. Place the left crank in the horizontal forward position, holding the

David Favello photo

91

bike by the ends of the handlebars. Place the left foot on the pedal and push off with the other leg swinging it over the saddle before losing momentum.

Once you're moving along, find the RH pedal and keep pedaling, shifting to a higher gear when you've gained speed. To do a running start, begin in a higher gear, walk or run by the side of the bike until you've gained enough speed, jump up, swing your leg over and hop in the saddle.

Whatever way you boarded, the first thing to do is find a balance between traction and stability. Stay out of the saddle and distribute your weight so that handlebars and pedals are both loaded adequately to keep traction on the rear wheel and to allow reliable steering. If the rear wheel slips, move back a little, if the front wheel starts to lift off, move forward a little. On slick surfaces (ice, snow, wet rock), unload the front end especially when steering.

Walking the Bike

Although your mountain bike is meant to be ridden, it may occasionally have to be walked or even carried. It may not seem difficult to walk, whether with or without your bike; yet there is a distinct skill that allows you to do it effectively. In off-road situations, you may have to dismount suddenly to walk or even carry the bike part of the way, over obstacles or through a muddy or sandy patch.

Once you have traversed the difficult section, you should be able to get back on without undue loss of time and energy. Doing this skillfully is particularly important in off-road racing, but can also help you enjoy recreational off-road riding. Estimate ahead of time where you will have to get off and shift down to a low gear. Move forward off the saddle and transfer your weight to the pedal on the side on which you want to get off—usually the left.

Slow down as appropriate for the situation and swing the leg on the side opposite to where you'll be getting off over when you get to a modest speed, holding it just behind the other leg. Fix your eyes on the point where you are going to stop and slow down to a trotting speed when you are ready to dismount. Swing the free leg through, between the other leg and the bike and take a sizeable step forward, moving away from the bike sideways, just enough to avoid the pedal from overtaking you in a painful manner. Keep trotting or slow down to a walking pace, holding the bike either by the handlebar ends or by handlebars and saddle.

Now you can either walk or carry the bike. In case you have to carry it to overcome serious obstacles, let the hand on the far side slide down from the handlebars along the down tube, grabbing it a little below the middle, while still trotting or walking. At this point, raise the bike up on your shoulder, letting it slip into place at the point where seat tube and top tube come together. In-stalling a padded strap there will help protect your shoulder. Grab the handlebars near the middle with the arm that goes through the frame, keeping the other hand free.

After you have carried the bike over the obstacle, you may either want to walk by the side of the bike or get back on. Either way, lower the bike off the shoulder and grab the handlebars at both ends. To walk the bike, just con-tinue this way. To get back on quickly, keep trotting and remount as described above.

Avoiding Obstacles

Off-road, you will often be con-fronted with some kind of obstacle that would be small enough to avoid—if it were not right in your path. This may be anything from a pothole or a broken branch to a

crashed cyclist just in front of you. Depending how much time and space you have available, use either the natural or the forced turn technique described in Chap-ter 8. Since at speed it is hard to go anywhere except where you are ac-tually looking, don't look at the obstacle but at the point where you want to pass it, steering to do so in a natural way.

To cycle around an obstacle that appears suddenly, you can develop a technique based on the forced turn. This maneuver is il-lustrated in Fig. 9.1. As soon as you perceive the obstacle ahead of you, decide whether to pass it to the left or the right. Ride straight up to it and then, before you reach it, briefly but decisively steer in the direction opposite to the obstacle (to the right if you want to pass it on the left). This makes the bike lean over towards the other side. Now steer in that direc-

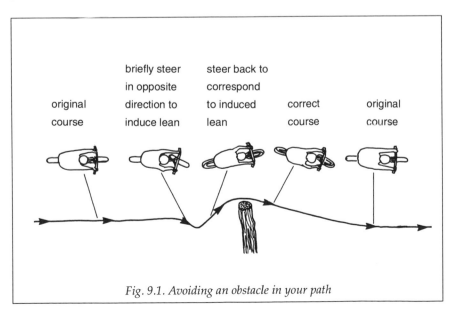

Fig. 9.1. Avoiding an obstacle in your path

tion just as quickly, which will result in a very sharp forced turn. As soon as you've passed the obstacle, oversteer a little more, causing a lean that helps put the bike back on its proper course.

This technique can also be practiced on an empty parking lot or any other level area, wearing a helmet and two long sleeved shirts. Mark phoney obstacles with chalk or put down foam pads or sponges. Practice passing them gradually and abruptly on both sides, until you've mastered the trick. Only then should you try doing the same in more difficult terrain.

Off-Road Braking

Using the brakes to come to a complete standstill, or more typically to reduce your speed to a controllable level on a fast downhill stretch, is a tricky matter under off-road conditions. Firstly, the slope may be so steep that you tend to topple forward easily, while at the same time you have to deal with the inevitable accelerating effect caused by the downslope. Secondly, the less predictable road surface may greatly reduce the traction between the tires and the ground. Finally, you may have to brake while at the same time avoiding an obstacle.

Before going downhill, get ready for it. Put your seat low down, which is easily done if you have a Hite-Rite saddle height adjusting spring. Sit far back on the seat and hold back, keeping a low profile, the pedals horizontal. The single most frequently made mistake amongst novices is to let one or even both legs dangle, with the pedals either spinning freely or in top and bottom position.

Get a feel for how much braking force is enough. While going straight down, you can use both brakes, but on a very long slope you may want to use them intermittently, to keep both of them effective. As long as the slope is not too steep, you can probably get by applying only one brake. That may be the front brake as long as you are going straight. When deviating one way or the other, try to brake just enough before you get to the curve, so you don't need to do so while leaning. If you do have to brake while leaning in a curve, only apply the one in the rear—gently.

Try to stay relaxed, rather than tensing up in a cramped position, so you follow the bike and its movements. This way you will soon learn to balance the amount of braking necessary with the accompanying weight shifts needed to keep control over the bike. Don't feel you have to be braking all the time: just keep down to a speed that is low enough to give you control in critical locations. That may mean braking rather vigorously on certain sections, where the surface is good and the route straight, letting the bike gather momentum again up to the next controllable stretch.

Downhill Switchbacks

Often in off-road situations, you will have to somehow get down slopes that seem too steep and too rough to ride straight down. For the time being they probably are, but there are ways around this problem. Instead of roaring straight down the shortest way, you can use the same technique applied in downhill skiing where you shift your weight from side to side, following what is essentially a switchback course.

The same can be done on a bike. You ride along the contour of the grade, dropping elevation only slightly, deviating from your eventual destination. Then you shift your weight in a very sharp forced turn towards the opposite side and go down the same way in the new direction. This way, you never reach the murderous speed induced by a straight downhill course. Instead, you stay within a reasonable speed. This maneuver is tricky, so you'd better practice it. As your confidence develops, you will be able to handle higher and higher speeds, requiring fewer and fewer turns to get down the hill.

Start this kind of practice on a relatively wide open downhill stretch, where you have plenty of room to deviate one way or the other. Point your bike down only slightly at an angle, so you are riding along the side of the hill, rather than straight down. Sometime before your speed gets too high, but while still going straight, apply the front and rear brakes together briefly, immediately followed by the steering action and the necessary shift of weight to the downhill side, to induce a forced turn.

Hard to do: the front wheelie

Bob Allen photo

95

Repeat this maneuver in the opposite direction, again shifting your weight to the uphill side. This way, you make another sharp turn, back the same direction as at first. Continue crisscrossing down the hillside until you get down. It will take you a long time, compared to what it would have taken to roll straight down, and perhaps you picked a slope you could have handled straight down. However, you'll have gained a lot of practice, and once you can do it down a gentle slope, you will feel confident trying it down a steeper one. With a few days' deliberate practice, you'll have learned to do this so well that you can get down quite steep slopes.

Off-Road Climbing

In Chapter 8, you have learned how to cycle uphill one of two ways: spinning fast in a relatively low gear for the slope, and standing on the pedals, 'honking' uphill

Fig. 9.2. Using tire cushioning to jump up.

in a relatively high gear for that slope. When cycling off-road, another factor has to be considered: in addition to otherwise unheard-of grades, you have to get used to riding on loose soil, rather than smooth asphalt or other surfaces that offer high and consistent traction.

Although your mountain bike probably has the kind of rubber on its wheels that provides as much traction as you can get, the conditions riding up steep slopes are a little tricky. This is due to the combined effect of loose or unpredictable surfaces and the extreme steepness of the grade. As you go uphill, your center of gravity shifts back on the bike. While this does improve traction by increasing the load on the rear wheel, it also reduces the load on the front wheel to such an extent that your steering becomes less predictable.

When you stand on the pedals on a steep uphill stretch, your weight is relatively far back, and that may unload the front wheel so much that the bike gets out of control, beginning to lift off or

shift sideways. With the first trace of this, lean a little further forward, bending the arms a little to lean on the handlebars. Not too far though, keeping enough weight on the rear wheel to ensure traction. It all becomes a subtle play, balancing your weight by minute forward and backward shifts to keep the front wheel on the ground, while retaining traction in the back.

Jumping the Bike

Another weird but useful act for off-road cycling situations is making first the front, then the rear wheel jump over an obstacle. You may have to do this when there is an unavoidable obstacle ahead of you. It's a matter of shifting your weight back and forth to lift the appropriate wheel off the ground. To jump up, first throw your weight backwards, while pulling up on the handlebars to lift the front wheel. At the same time accelerate vigorously, by pushing hard on the forward pedal.

Some obstacles can be overcome by lifting bike and rider over them while riding along. That's the way it feels when you can do it: to the observer it seems more like flying.

To do this, you'll be using the energy stored in the compressed air in the tires. The basic requirement is a tire pressure that's just high enough to protect the tube yet low enough for your weight when it comes hard down on the rear wheel to go down by about ¾—1 inch. The energy released when this much air is compressed is enough to lift bike and rider up several feet.

Start practicing on a hard level surface (it won't work at all on soft ground because the energy, rather than being stored by the compressed air in the tire, goes into deforming the soil, which isn't going to spring back). Balance the bike standing still with the cranks horizontal—you just learned how to do that, so I hope you've been practicing. Pounce down with all your weight towards the rear of the bike to

compress the rear tire in a short, snappy movement, and then just as snappily transfer your weight back forward. If all is well, the rear wheel comes off the ground.

The first few times you do this, it may seem like a pretty unspectacular performance. Keep doing it, interrupted by some riding to release the tension that is built up in your nerves more than in the tires. A couple of fifteen minute practice sessions two or three days in a row should pay off with quite spectacular results: you have mastered one third of the trick and it is time to get on with the next third, raising the front wheel off the ground.

To raise the front wheel is normally referred to as doing a wheelie. And it is just as normal to do that by merely shifting your weight back quickly to unload the front wheel and briefly bring your mass center behind the rear wheel on account of the momentum of the body moving back. That's worth practicing, because it will be used in other stunts too. From a low speed or even standing still, balancing the bike now that you can do that, first keep your weight low and forward. Then throw it back with a decisive jolt, loading the rear wheel and releasing the front while pulling the handlebars up with you. Again, it may take some practice to perfect it, but this particular one is quite easy to learn.

To get both wheels off the ground, you want to do things a little more sophisticated than this, though. Since you have to com-

bine it with the raising of the rear wheel eventually, the thing to do is to put an explosive charge under the front wheel, again in the form of tire compression, just as was done to get the rear wheel coming up. So don't just throw your weight back, but first pounce on the front end of the bike: quickly push down with your body weight on the handlebars, then immediately release it and throw your weight back as in a conventional wheelie.

Finally, it will be time to combine the two movements of lifting the front and the rear wheel. Your first step will be to achieve it consecutively, first the front and then the rear. Balancing while standing still, push down hard on the front end and immediately release it, transferring the weight to the rear, compressing the rear tire quickly; then immediately release it by shifting your weight forward again. That should be one continuous movement that cannot be broken up into steps. Do it as though you're reading and following the sentence as fast as possible.

Suddenly, after a few days with two or three short practice sessions each, you can do it, and you'll wonder why it ever seemed so difficult. Notice how you graduated from putting one wheel up after the other to getting both of them up at the same time, without my telling you how it's done? It's nothing but the logical extension of what you were doing, and as you got better at it, those wheels started spending more time up in the air together simultaneously.

There are people — and I am not one of them myself — who can get both wheels to lift off at the same time. That's done by distributing the body weight over the front and the rear of the bike while pouncing down and at the same time compressing the body like a spring. When you raise the body just as suddenly by straightening your legs, arms and back, the whole unit of bike and rider starts to defy gravity and comes straight up. So they say, but if you are at all hesitant, you'll want to make sure nobody is watching as you clown around frustrated without getting any air. On the other hand, if you are more agile, coordinated and determined than I am, you will probably master this trick pretty soon too.

Jumping over Obstacles

The hopping routine described in the preceding section is as much a lesson in general bike handling as a practical device in itself. In the fine art of observed trials competition, it is an absolute prerequisite, but in everyday use you'll benefit more from the sense of bike control and balance derived from it than from the actual skill itself. In the real world things happen when you're moving forward, not when you're standing still.

David Arbogast demonstrating some of the unique skills of mountain biking in an observed trials event.

David Favello photo

99

In your reality there will be the occasional (or sometimes frequent) obstacle in your path, ranging from ditches across the trail to potholes in city streets, from boulders and fallen trees to curbstones and railway tracks. It's consoling to know that the same techniques that are so useful in the boondocks also can be put to good use in the more prosaic circumstances of urban riding, as well as out on the trail.

The first step is to learn to go up a step, even if only to practice for bigger and better things. Find an area with a step in it that is between six inches and one foot high and learn to approach it, lift the front wheel just before you get there, then hop onto it with the rear wheel, and keep riding. Perhaps you even want to practice it on an imaginary ridge: a chalk line drawn on an empty parking lot.

Next, try to do the same thing but now approach the ridge riding parallel to it and then hopping onto it sideways. That's actually

Fig. 9.3. How to jump over an obstacle.

the more typical situation in real life, where many obstacles are almost parallel to your path rather than straight across. This is done by first briefly steering away from the ridge, and then immediately and snappily correcting the lean by steering back, so you shoot across the ridge with the front wheel almost perpendicular to it very briefly, before continuing in your original direction.

Whether jumping up a perpendicular or parallel ridge, once the front wheel is over, you have to unload the back by shifting your weight back to the front end of the bike and lifting the rear wheel. You'll be surprised how easily it follows.

Your next step towards obstacle-running mastery will be jumping across things like tree trunks. Start off with something a little smaller, like a broomstick. You'll really notice it if you don't clear it with either wheel, but it is less intimidating and easier to place just where and how you want it. Front wheel up, rear wheel up and go. Practiced during

a few fifteen-minute sessions, and quite soon, you will feel like graduating to tree trunks, boulders and the likes. As soon as you can do it, start applying each skill in your everyday riding so you reach perfect mastery gradually while enjoying what you do, rather than as a conscious exercise.

Riding Through a Ditch

Actually, this can be any hole in the ground. Ditches can be seen as inverted obstacles. Only very wide ones can be ridden through, while smaller ones must be handled by trying to jump over them.

To ride through a wide ditch, select your path so that it is as gradual as possible, often going through it at an angle. Shift your weight as you go through, so you don't get bogged down at the bottom of the pit. Just before you reach the lowest point, transfer your weight back so the front wheel gets unloaded. This way you gain badly needed traction on the way up and protect your bike

as well as yourself (you might go over the handlebars if the bike suddenly comes to a stop as it bogs down). Transfer the weight back towards the front again as you climb out.

Now to clear a narrow trench or hole in the ground you have to do very much the same as to clear an obstacle projecting from the ground. The reason is that, unless you lift the wheels to make the bike go up at least a little, they'll just fall into the hole. So gain some speed and then, just before you get there, lift the front wheel as you've learned to do in the last section. As soon as the front wheel has come off the ground, transfer the weight back to get the rear wheel off the ground and start heading for safe ground with the front wheel, keeping the weight forward until the rear wheel has also cleared the ditch.

Practice this technique as you go on your regular rides and you'll be surprised how much easier it will become. In effect, once you get this far, you'll find you spend much less time in the

Bob Allen photo

saddle than you ever thought you would want to. And even if you are in the saddle, you are always alert and always have your weight well distributed over pedals, handlebars and seat, with your limbs slightly bent but tense enough to act as shock absorbers at all times. This way, obstacles are easy to overcome. It'll just be a matter of raising one part of your body relative to the other in a natural flow of movement.

Getting air is perhaps the most exciting to do on your mountain bike. Not a very practical skill, but fun just the same.

CHAPTER 10

Where to Ride Your Mountain Bike

Perhaps it seems curious to devote a whole chapter to a question that shouldn't really have to be asked. After all, the mountain bike is supposed to go anywhere. Still, like most riders, you will probably benefit from a little advice about how to find the kind of terrain where it can display its strengths most impressively, especially if you don't live in the middle of a renowned mountain biking mecca.

It's most fun to ride off-road. However, to get places, mountain bike or not, any bicycle is most efficient, and therefore most enjoyable, ridden on hard, dry, smooth and level ground. That may contradict what you've heard about the mountain bike before, but it's useful to keep in mind when deciding where to ride.

Getting Out There

Don't feel that a mountain bike must be transported to the trailhead in the back of a pickup truck or on the roof of your car. Any bike, including your fat-tired machine, is a means of transportation. It is intended to get you from A to B. The mountain bike can do

James Cassimus photo

this off roads as well as on the road, but there's no need to shun using the machine to get from your house to some point in the woods, nor to use it for shopping, commuting and any of the other potential uses.

What's nice about riding off-road is not a function of the roughness, the dirt, or any of the other characteristics of the terrain. Instead, what you'll relish most is the remoteness, the solitude, the experience of nature and the lack of traffic. Without these, even a mountain bike is not more enjoyable on rough roads than on smooth ones. So, unless you go for the challenge, select the most direct, smoothest, hardest, driest and most level surface that can be used to get you from A to B.

Keeping that in mind, we can now concentrate on the kind of terrain for which your mountain bike is more suitable than any other machine known to man. The argument that you may put in 80 percent of your mileage or more on paved roads should not necessarily discourage you from getting the kind of equipment that is best suited to rough riding. After all, that enjoyable remaining 20% was probably the reason for getting this particular kind of bike in the first place. The thickest tires and the strongest forks don't detract from your riding pleasure on paved roads as much as they benefit you off-road.

Exploit the advantages and other characteristics of your mountain bike wherever you can, so you get the full benefit and maxi-

mum enjoyment out of your equipment. If I were to select just one bike for all uses, I would probably select a mountain bike. That's because it is the most universal machine. It does anything my other bikes can do, most things almost as well, some better and some that the other bikes can't do at all. What other bikes can't do as well as the mountain bike will be the subject of the remainder of this chapter.

Uphill-Downhill Riding

In most parts of the U.S. and Canada, and perhaps even more so in the rest of the world, there is suitable terrain for real off-road riding within easy cycling reach, wherever you live. So you can ride there and back. This will give you considerably more cycling experience than you would otherwise get. Besides, it's a lot simpler than dealing with loading and unloading bikes and returning to the place where you parked your car.

Open hillsides or those with rough trails dropping down steeply can be found in many areas. The mountain bike's characteristics definitely lend it superbly to this kind of use. In fact, that's how the mountain bike was born. The first mountain bike riders did little more (or less) with their machines than ride them down steep, unpaved hillsides at a murderous pace, only to struggle their way up again to start all over.

This kind of uphill-downhill riding is most enjoyable as a

group activity. Having tried it by myself, I must admit it is about as boring as counting sheep, whereas the company, the mutual encouragement, the fun of it all, makes it more exciting when in the company of others. In addition, it is more educational: you may never learn the proper control over your bike and its movements, unless you can gauge your own progress with that of others.

Consider the environmental impact and the legality of what you are doing, though. If there is an ordinance against it, chances are it's not merely to spoil your fun, but rather to prevent you from doing damage to the natural environment. What some of this riding does to the watershed characteristics of the terrain can be quite serious. Although I don't believe mountain biking is the direct cause of the California mud slides of recent years, it may well have been a contributing factor in some cases.

If you are new to the sport, the best places to do downhill riding are probably known to others who ride mountain bikes. If nobody can put you on the right track for uphill-downhill riding, find your own site. You'll be surprised in what unlikely places you can find quite acceptable slopes. I even found several places within cycling range from my parents' home in Holland, which is a

A familiar sight, but to my mind also usually an unnecessary one. You will get more out of your mountain bike if you ride it to your destination, rather than polluting the air and adding to the congestion on the road. Try to become part of the solution, rather than of the problem.

photo courtesy Cannondale

105

proverbially flat country. It needn't be a thousand-foot drop: riding down the embankment of a high bridge ramp or a pile of soil next to a building site may do the trick for fun and practice.

Although you won't find another Repack, that famous Northern California slope that drops 1300 feet in less than two miles, you might discover quite a respectable little slope. After all, some of the most challenging and enjoyable slopes in off-road cycling are only one or two hundred feet high. You're not looking for the ultimate challenge all the time, you're just out to do your thing.

Trail Riding

A lot of mountain bike riding has nothing to do with racing down steep hills. For those who are more into peace and solitude, cycling on unpaved roads and trails is the more mind-expanding experience. This is my kind of riding, largely because I'm a cautious old cat, who has taken all the unnecessary risks in his day and wants to live to tell others about it. Not only because I'm a coward: there is a distinct thrill to relaxed riding where there is no bustle and roar of cars to interrupt the tranquility, where all the obstacles are of God's creation, rather than man's.

Although I prefer to cycle alone or with only one companion, this activity is not the exclusive domain of recluses and hermits. In fact, some of the major organized off-road events, with hundreds of par-

ticipants, are of this kind. To find the right terrain for non-organized trail biking, there isn't a better tool than the topographical map, referred to as Geological Survey map in the U.S., Ordnance Survey in Britain.

This kind of map shows all trails, paths and roads, while the road map will show you which of these are paved and used for motor traffic. The difference is your exclusive domain, apart from any right-of-way restrictions you may have to contend with. In fact, access and right-of-way are the two intangibles in trail cycling these days. The sport is getting too popular too fast, and in defense, or out of fear, authorities have banned cyclists from many potentially suitable areas.

You will probably use forest service or fire roads and trails intended for hikers most of the time. Don't stray off these trails, since this may cause damage, both to the environment and to our reputation. As long as you stay on the trails and do it with a modicum of consideration for others, you have nothing to fear and should not risk being banned from them by public agencies.

In many areas a distinction is made between single-track trails and wider ones. Single tracks are often considered off-limits to mountain bikers, although in most cases they are perfectly suitable and there are not enough hikers and other trail users to worry about potential conflicts. In fact, single trails naturally limit the biker's speed to an acceptable level.

Shared Use

The problems of shared use just don't seem to go away, and today there is unfortunately as much animosity between different users of nature as there has ever been. I have indeed witnessed some horrible examples of authorities and hikers manipulating or circumventing facts to find justification for attempts to deny cyclists access.

In the first edition of this book, I had included a couple of envious remarks about the relative success of equestrians at gaining access as compared to mountain bikers, claiming the latter do more harm than we do. This provoked some harsh responses from fellow cyclists who are also equestrians. Of course, in reality mountain bikers and equestrians have some of the same problems, and fear or misunderstanding is the driving force behind the restriction of either

sport. It would seem wise to cooperate in efforts to share the trails and to keep it legal for both groups.

The same applies to hikers. Those on foot have a justified claim to the most comprehensive access, and cyclists would do well to do all they can to defer to them. I have witnessed both ridiculous pedestrian fear of anything on wheels or hooves, and totally brutal disregard of the right of those on foot on the part of some mountain bikers. Be considerate, and team up with others to sway both the public and the authorities against instituting or enforcing unwarranted restrictive access rules.

Government authorities and public representatives at all levels are supposed to be accountable to all the people, including you and your mountain biking friends. If you have the right arguments and present them reasonably, chances

David Epperson / Bicycle Sport photo

are pretty good you'll be able to secure or retain access in most cases where you and your bike don't represent a serious threat to the environment.

Join forces with other potential users of the same terrain, such as hikers and equestrians. Try to emphasize that mountain bike riders are normal, responsible, mature adults who eat lots of apple pie and watch fireworks, rather than some weird bunch of near outlaws. It also helps to be a member of some recognized, dignified outdoor or conservation organization, and pointing this out whenever you present your case in public. Yes, I know that right now many of these organizations are not well disposed towards bikers, but if you can't beat them, you have every right to join them: Become active on your own behalf in their organizations, as long as you feel their charter is not intrinsically contradictory to your aims.

Access

As regards access, a particularly touchy issue is that of National Wilderness Areas and the even more obscure so-called National Wilderness Study Areas in the U.S. The latter are regions that are under consideration for future designation as Wilderness Areas. This makes them off-limits at a slight of hand, without the Government's obligation to do anything to protect or develop the area. Although the sign at the trailhead may explicitly prohibit only

'motor vehicles', you may soon run into some ranger who'll lay down the law.

That's because the 1964 Wilderness Act prohibits the use of 'motor vehicles and other forms of mechanical transport,' while specifically permitting horseback riding. You or I may not think of the mountain bike as providing 'mechanical transport,' but your friendly ranger probably does. It's a stupid regulation, clothed in very imprecise wording, so help get it changed: ask your favorite member of Congress to raise the issue and do something about it.

Unfortunately, there are many vested interests trying to push cyclists back off the public lands, and no methods seem to be shunned. I participated in hearings about access to the Golden Gate National Recreation Area, that should have put all reasonable thinking officials to shame if there had been any. A staff member had been ordered to make a report on the effect of mountain biking on erosion. But what she presented, and what was accepted by the officials, was a presentation on erosion. Then it was observed that mountain bikers used some of the trails where there was erosion, and she jumped to the conclusion that the bikers had actually caused the erosion. That was patently unrealistic, because the erosion traces shown were simply the result of run-off along trails and not the result of mountain bike use.

Fringe Areas

Not everybody has a National Wildlife Area, State Forest or National Forest on his doorstep, and in other English-speaking countries these terms might as well be the names of holy places in Sanskrit. Lacking such facilities, as well as the peculiar problems associated with securing access to them, you may be satisfied to remember that you can ride on any kind of open terrain and unpaved road, without worrying about such controversial terrain.

On the fringes of just about every city and suburb, there are areas where paved roads are anything from sparse to non-existent.

Such areas may not always be the most idyllic, but they are usually quite suitable for your kind of use. If they don't give you the solitude of nature, instead constantly reminding you of man's encroaching action upon God's work, at least they offer a superb training ground for more romantic rides when you do get the chance to ride out in the woods.

Their advantage is that such areas are invariably easily accessible, both in terms of distance and in the way the paved roads allow you to get out there in little time. Use the maps proposed in this chapter and make the most of the information that can be obtained from them. Consult Chapter 11 for

Going the rocky road. Very often you will find terrain like this, or other suitable terrain, even in the vicinity of big cities.

Dan Gindling photo

Andreas Schlueter photo

an explanation of the most effective ways of using the maps.

The ultimate way to find good off-road cycling terrain goes well beyond the use of the map. It's out there, riding your bike, that you will find the best places to do it. Don't be bashful about going beyond where you know the way or are sure you can find your way back. Personally, I am punished with a particularly poor sense of orientation. That has the advantage that I often stumble into —to me—totally new areas. Despite my handicap, I have always managed to return home alive, even satisfied, often finding really nice and different routes there and back. You should be able to do it too.

It is not necessary to travel a long way for challenging terrain: This is a demonstration of impromptu downhill racing at the local gravel pit

With your mountain bike, you can take on the hills, going up and going down, or you can go around them. You can go where other road users would not care to travel. These are the advantages of your particular mode of transport. Exploit them. Making the most of these advantages, fearing neither sweat nor agony, the true mountain bike rider quickly discovers enjoyable, scenic, sometimes even spectacular, routes away from regular roads. Get out there and enjoy it to the full. Your mountain bike is waiting to get out there.

CHAPTER 11

Touring with Your Mountain Bike

Bicycle touring has made a remarkable comeback in recent years. I don't mean bicycle touring defined as just any kind of riding that is not strictly for competition or utility. Although trips of several hours or so qualify as touring in the eyes of some, I am mainly referring here to longer rides, generally with at least one overnight stay, either all off-road or partly on regular roads.

The mountain bike lends itself superbly to the purpose. In this chapter we will look at the things to consider when touring with your mountain bike. You will find very comprehensive advice on general bicycle touring in Kameel Nasr's *Bicycle Touring International* and my *Bicycle Touring Manual*. The present chapter covers those touring aspects that are most relevant for mountain bike riders.

Perhaps the best way to start out touring is gradually, finding out on shorter trips whether the whole thing appeals to you. This way you can make sure that you can really handle every situation you are likely to encounter on a longer tour. Gradually progress

Dan Gindling photo

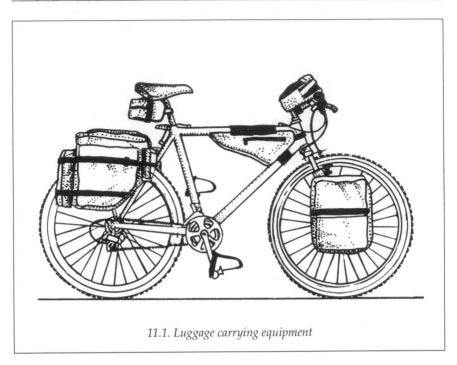

11.1. Luggage carrying equipment

from day rides to overnight trips to long tours.

Even though you use a mountain bike, there is no need to limit your touring experience to off-road cycling. There are several different approaches. For instance, you may go on a longer trip along regular roads, only to take an excursion at some point into the outback. Or you may combine a longer off-road trip with approach and return rides along the regular road. Finally, you may actually stay off-road for the entire trip, or at least a major portion of it.

Depending on your starting point and your destination, each one of these approaches to touring may be appropriate. In general, I suggest starting off without taking on really big challenges. For your first tours, select moderate distan-

ces, riding mainly on regular roads. Later you can progress to longer ones, gradually adding longer sections of off-road work. Finally, proceed to real off-road tours, camping out in the wilderness for several days in a row, and carrying in food for a longer period, if needed.

Carrying Luggage

For short tours, you can ride the bike the way it probably was when you bought it: bare. That's the way most Americans ride any bike. If you are serious about touring, you should install some accessories that enable you to handle more situations. Thus, I suggest mounting or taking lights in case your trip takes you out until after dark, even if you didn't plan on it, and mount fenders when there is the slightest chance of rain.

For carrying luggage, install at least a rack in the back and some kind of bag, even for a short trip, more for a longer one. As a permanent bag on the bike for any kind of use, I prefer a saddle bag. The latter is a relic from my life in Britain and is highly recommended as a luggage carrying device. As illustrated in Fig. 11.1, it attaches to the saddle, which may have to be equipped with an adaptor if it doesn't have eyelets for the necessary straps. The saddle bag puts the weight of anything you carry very close to the most neutral point of the bike, thus interfering least with its handling characteristics.

The other alternatives for carrying modest amounts of luggage are the handlebar bag, a small backpack and the belt bag, more usually referred to as fanny pack in the U.S. Be my guest if you prefer one of these, but they are definitely less comfortable and don't hold as much luggage as the saddle bag. The handlebar bag affects the bike's steering response and is of necessity modestly sized. Make sure it is at least supported by means of a bracket that keeps it in shape at the top, and is restrained by means of two shock cords running from the bottom at both sides to the tip of the front fork. The handlebar bag is quite handy for items that require easy access along the way, including map, wallet, and something to eat.

The frameless backpack has the advantage that it stays with you, even when you leave the bike somewhere. Though handlebar bags can also be equipped with carrying straps, the chances of you losing your valuables are minimized by carrying them on your

Kimberlee Caledonia photo

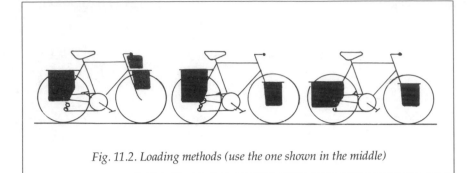

Fig. 11.2. Loading methods (use the one shown in the middle)

body at all times. Select a model with wide and preferably padded shoulder straps and a waist strap to stop it from swaying sideways. To keep it in shape, and to protect your back from the discomfort caused by irregularly shaped items carried inside, place a piece of fiber board the size of the back panel inside the bag, or select a model with an integral stiffener frame inside the bag.

Take the right clothing and at least the essential tools and spares when touring. You may refer to Chapter 5 for some suggestions on clothing and the other absolute essentials. Even on a one-day trip, it is smart to be on the generous side. Realize that you may be riding in the cool early hours, the heat of the afternoon and in the evening. You may be far from the nearest source of food or supplies. Help may be hard to get once you are a long way from home.

For trips of several days, certainly if you are camping, quite a lot of luggage will be necessary. I suggest using pannier bags both front and rear. When packing, remember that the bike must remain stable. That means the weight must be divided relatively evenly between front and rear. In the front, the weight should be

Fig. 11.3.
Checking the stability of the load. Holding the bike from the handlebars, shake it and make sure the load does not start swaying the bike and the bags don't flop about. Sometimes it actually helps to have the load a little unevenly distributed, e.g. more weight on the one side than on the other.

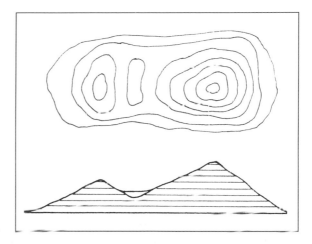

Fig. 11.4
The meaning of contour lines: each contour line connects all points at a certain elevation above sea level. The closer together they are, the steeper a particular route. The more you cross, the greater the overall elevation difference.

centered close to the front wheel axle, while in the back it should be as far forward as possible within the restraints of adequate heel clearance. Bags should all be attached firmly both at the top and pulled down and against the bike at the bottom.

Of the various ways to distribute the load, the method shown in the middle of Fig. 11.2 is the one that least affects the steering and balancing process. Make sure the racks are solidly attached to the bike and the bags are properly mounted. To test the effectiveness of your packing operation, take the loaded bike from the front by the handlebars and shake it sideways, as shown in Fig. 11.3. Sway along the axis shown there should be minimal if it is loaded correctly.

The luggage racks themselves should be very strong and rigid. Their attachment to the bike is crucial. Special designs for mountain bike use are most suitable, since those are dimensioned to accommodate the greater clearances typi-

cal for mountain bikes. The front rack should preferably be of the so-called low rider design, which centers the weight near the front wheel axle. The one in the rear will carry most of the weight. I suggest using pannier bags that are of modest size and complementing them with a rectangular rigid case on top of the rear luggage rack. For attachment of this case, non- stretching straps or belts are more suitable than bungee cords, since the former don't allow the load to shift or sway.

When it comes to packing the bags themselves, try to roll up the various items so that they form relatively long and regularly shaped packs or rolls, corresponding to the width of the bag in which they will be packed. Put the things you will need first or most suddenly at the top of the bag. This way, you don't spend a long time digging for things when you set up camp, nor will everything get wet while looking for the items to keep you dry in a storm. Maintain a certain logic, packing items that obviously belong together in the same bag, and small things in the outside pockets, similarly logically arranged.

Maps and Orientation

In all touring situations, you should get familiar with the use of the map and other aids to orientation. You may get some more detailed advice on this subject from the books just mentioned. However, for most trips, it may suffice to get familiar with the map and its use. Try to visualize the situation out in the terrain before you set out, referring frequently to the map along the way, to make sure you always know where you are.

Familiarize yourself with the various characteristics of the particular map you use, including the very helpful aid to elevation provided in the form of contour lines on most Geological Survey (in Britain, Ordnance Survey) maps of an acceptable scale. This, I would suggest, is about 1:100,000 for day rides on roads, 1:50,000 for touring difficult terrain, 1 : 25,000 for real off-road work, and perhaps 1:200,000 for long tours of several days mainly on roads.

Fig. 11.4 shows the meaning of contour lines: each contour line connects all points at a certain elevation above sea level. The closer together they are, the steeper a particular route. The more you cross, the greater the overall elevation difference. If needed, also use other aids and clues to establishing the most suitable route. Even though your bike is called a mountain bike, for longer trips and tours the advantage of riding on level terrain is so overwhelming, that you'll be actively in search of it as much as possible within the scope of your route.

Once you are familiar with the use of the map itself, also learn to orient yourself in the field. Remain conscious of the landmarks along the way. Consider what you see immediately along your path and what you can recognize at some distance on the horizon. Make a point of knowing when you are going in one direction or the other whether the road continues generally up or down, or whether you are staying more or less at the same elevation. This form of orientation along the route, together with occasional consultation of the map, should help you reconstruct where you are and how you got there, so you don't even begin to get lost.

Day Tripping

Day trips used to be the most common type of adult cycling in the U.S., and are still a very rewarding pastime. Ride the bike around the countryside, have lunch along the way, and return home at night. I purposely left out one common part of the routine: loading the bikes on the car in the morning, driving out somewhere and unloading the bike, to be repeated in reverse order at the end of the tour.

It doesn't have to be done that way, at least not always. It's the way most hikers go about it, and for them it makes sense, since they may not ever reach reasonable hiking terrain on foot or by means of public transportation. On level ground, you move four times as fast as the hiker. Your bike is built to be conveyed on its own two wheels and few people really live so far away from suitable biking terrain that they can't start quite a number of rides from their own home.

Even if you live in the middle of a major city, you'll be surprised how quickly you get out of it on the bike. Besides, it's a real advantage not having to return to a car that's parked somewhere in the middle of nowhere, or to worry about what's happening to it while you're out riding the bike. Feel free to take the car, or some form of public transportation if

you're lucky enough to live close to an operating system that takes bikes, but also consider the alternative of riding your bike all the way.

Overnight Trips and Long Tours

I'd say you start with tours of more than one day only after you have been on several one-day trips. Certainly the first few times, you'll be better off arranging your trip in such a way that you can spend the nights in a hotel or other reliable accommodation. Only after you have become familiar with the various problems encountered on overnight trips, should you consider camping out off the beaten track.

The final stage of touring is the long tour: a ride of a week or more. Certainly if you go camping, or have to camp some nights for lack of other accommodation

Dieter Glogowski photo

Kimberlee Caledonia photo

en route, prepare yourself well. Do that by first taking some overnight camping trips in more familiar terrain. As you accumulate experience, keep track of the various items you might have forgotten to account for. In fact, I consider every trip in some way a learning experience for the next one. As you gain experience and become better at it, you will enjoy touring more each time.

This spot is known as Hole in the Rock. There's no better way to reach it than on your mountain bike.

CHAPTER 12

The Mountain Bike for Transportation

Probably more than any other bicycle design, the mountain bike has found a use amongst utility cyclists. Their specific needs range from messenger services to shopping, commuting and running errands. As it is, perhaps most of this mountain bike use takes place in an urban environment, if only because that's where most bikers live. Even the suburbanite commuting to his place of employment in the city today is as likely to use a mountain bike as he is to ride a conventional drop-handlebar derailleur bicycle.

In the present chapter we shall consider the various aspects of using the mountain bike for basic transportation, primarily in an urban environment. Your equipment should match the particular use. One important aspect is reliability, keeping in mind that— unlike the leisure cyclist—as a utility cyclist, you may have to rely on your bike whatever the

Zipping by on your mountain bike. This commuter has his business suit in his garment carrier.

photograph courtesy Eccosport

weather or time of day. You probably have a time schedule to meet and appointments to keep. The other important criterion is the need to carry luggage.

Bike and Accessories

Just about any kind of mountain bike lends itself to this practical kind of use. Generally, the relatively cheap models with welded frames and somewhat narrower tires are quite adequate, although you may want to use fancier equipment. A hybrid is just fine for most of us, and the new crop of city bikes, which came to us via the European establishments of American companies like Trek and Specialized, fit the bill perfectly. Only if you live someplace where unpaved roads roads are common, should you have to go all the way to a genuine off-road machine with the fattest tires. Just make sure it has the requisite bosses and eyelets for the subsequent installation of accessories.

I feel any utilitarian bike should be equipped with several accessories—or at least it should be easily adaptable to be so equipped. Luggage racks, fenders, and lights should either be permanently installed or available for quick mounting. Although my own utility bike sports all of these all the time, you may prefer to just keep fenders and lights in a bag and have attachments on the bike to install them when needed. The fenders can be held by means of home-made wing bolts, as shown

in Fig. 12.1, to allow quick removal and installation.

Racks and bags for utility use are no different from those designed for touring as described in Chapter 11. What you will need more than anybody else is a lock— and you may have to use it to its full capability every time you leave the bike anywhere. To make sure the removable accessories don't get removed by the wrong people, even while the whole bike is properly locked, use a few simple tricks. As an example, you can wrap some handlebar tape around the pump and the tube against which it is installed—that is usually enough to discourage the person who wants to quickly grab it off the bike.

Don't make the removability of various items too obvious. I'd suggest avoiding quick-release hubs, since wheels with axle nuts are rarely stolen. To keep the saddle on the bike, you can either invest in the Hite-Rite saddle adjusting spring, or you can replace the quick-release by a regular binder

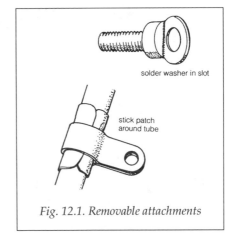

solder washer in slot

stick patch around tube

Fig. 12.1. Removable attachments

bolt—after all, you probably don't have to adjust the height as often as the person who rides his mountain bike mainly up and down steep hillsides.

One home-made accessory that I find extremely handy for carrying odd items, including quite large packages, is the three-sided platform shown in Fig. 12.2. You can put any kind of item in there and restrain it adequately by means of bungee cords or straps. The fact that the weight is off-center seems to have little or no effect on the bike's handling characteristics. I made mine on the basis of a discarded plastic beverage crate, from which I removed two sides. It is attached to the rack by means of clips and bolts with nuts and washers. Mount it far enough to the back to clear your heels and low enough to keep the top platform of the rack free for other items.

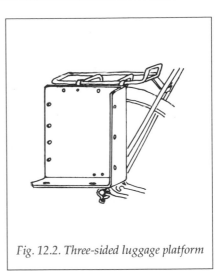

Fig. 12.2. Three-sided luggage platform

Urban Cycling

Most of your utility cycling will probably be done in an urban environment. Even if you live in a smaller community, you will find that the way to the post office and the shopping center requires riding on urban streets with relatively dense traffic. It really is not as hard as some people seem to assume.

Traffic, especially motor traffic, is not as irrational as many of my environmentally zealous friends would have us believe. It operates quite systematically and follows a predictable pattern. Many cyclists seem to have the greatest fear of motor vehicle drivers. Some motorists are indeed either reckless or out to get you. But by and large, you will find that they are a lot more predictable than pedestrians and cyclists, not to mention many of the other typical off-road hazards.

Refer to the various comments about safety, particularly regarding the risk of traffic accidents, outlined in Chapter 6. If you yourself behave sensibly and predictably, reacting logically and considerately to the actions of others, remaining always aware of the potential causes of danger, you will be able to ride in urban traffic with confidence and competence.

Cycling in dense or fast traffic is not an impossible feat, but you have to stay alert. Don't freeze up in panic, expecting the worst to happen any time (if you do, it will). Instead, evaluate the situation consciously, and judge which dangers may be looming where. Along a straight stretch of road there is little risk of someone turning off in front of you, so you can concentrate on the scenery, relaxing a little, providing you keep an eye on the road. Though your inherent fears may tell you differently, the risk of being hit from behind is very remote if you don't suddenly divert from your position in the road. Keep a straight course, and check the road to make sure you can keep it. When you do have to divert, check behind you first.

Increase your level of attention to traffic when you approach a high-risk situation, such as a driveway with a car that may be about to enter the road. When approaching an intersection, become particularly conscious of the traffic situation. Here your choice of the correct path, is of utmost importance, and you have to judge what other drivers are about to do. If you misjudge the situation and have to perform a panic action to avoid a collision, use the knowledge gained in Chapter 8 and 9 about braking and diverting. Judge which way to divert, depending on the course of the 'opponent'.

If you do not at first feel at ease in these situations, start on less densely travelled streets and proceed gradually from streets and areas with relatively slow traffic to more demanding traffic patterns. All the advice given for normal situations also applies to denser or faster trafficked roads only more so. The other side of the coin is that you should not assume you can afford to ride with disregard to others on quieter roads: though the dangers will be fewer and farther between, they must still be considered.

The advice on safe riding techniques in Chapter 6 is really all you need, providing you don't just read it, but practice it. It is easy enough, since it is logical. I taught my children to handle any kind of traffic, including left turns from eight-lane expressways, by the time they were thirteen years old, so figure you can probably learn to do it too.

On the other hand, if you do feel a lack of confidence, don't force things either. If you can't handle that left turn, just get off the bike and cross like a pedestrian, waiting your turn to do each part. It will take you more time if you do it correctly, but it will save your nerves. Just don't try to perform some mix of vehicular and pedestrian behavior within one situation, since that is the most dangerous thing you can do.

One example of incorrect behavior that is only too common amongst novice cyclists wanting to turn, is riding left along the RH edge of the road at an intersection, and then abruptly turning left across the path of those going straight behind you. This self-inflicted danger goes way beyond anything you would risk if you acted like the driver of a vehicle, who would select the correct position in the road or within his lane well ahead of the intersection, after having checked behind to ascertain there is a big enough gap between other vehicles to do so.

With your mountain bike, you have a few advantages over drivers of cars and other cyclists in urban and suburban environments. You can often choose shortcuts that are not available to the drivers of other vehicles, while your equipment is less sensitive than a regular ten-speed. Combine this possibility with that of the considerable speed you can develop, and you may turn out to make progress as fast as motorists in many situations. I know from my own experience that I got to work in San Francisco faster when commuting by bike than I could

either on public transportation or by car.

Commuting by Bike

I would suggest you progress from occasional errands by bike to using it for many of your regular transportation needs within the urban environment, and finally to commuting by bike. The latter is definitely harder, since it generally takes place in rush hour traffic. If you can get flexible working hours, you may be able to avoid the worst traffic, but the problem can't be avoided completely. Confidence comes with practice, so you become an expert urban cyclist.

The mountain bike is perhaps the ultimate urban driving machine. For modest loads the messenger bag is handy, because you can take it with you when you leave the bike.

Dan Gindling photograph

123

Don't let little irritations stop you from using the bike for commuting. Cycling is at its best in nice weather, but you can also ride when it is cold or rainy—yes even in snow and ice, situations that are not entirely pleasant to handle in a car either. It is amusing to notice that in any part of the world cyclists seem to draw the line between suitable and unsuitable weather at a different point. In regions with frequent rains or cold weather, cyclists still ride their bikes —and enjoy it, even when the weather is less than optimal. In areas like Britain, Washington State or British Columbia, where rain is the order of the day any time of the year, a little rain doesn't discourage a commuter from using his bike.

On the other hand, in California experienced cyclists hang their wheels in the willows the minute the forecast includes even the slightest chance of rain. In northern countries with frequent sub- freezing temperatures, a little frost doesn't discourage a cyclist, while in other regions anything below 18°C (60°F) is considered too cold for comfort. Just imagine how much more cycling enjoyment you can get by just raising your tolerance level to what others have to put up with habitually.

It is perfect when you have a place of work with regular safe bike storage facilities, change rooms and showers for your use. However, you can do without if you have to.

If you don't get the use of a shower and change rooms, consider the obvious: don't cycle quite so fast that you perspire. Cycling can be just as enjoyable at 12 mph as it is at 25, and a lot more relaxing. If you want to exert yourself, consider doing the really hard work on the way home, taking it easy on the way to work.

All in all, commuting by bike is easier today than it was in the past. Bicycle commuting is possible, and enjoyable, even under sub-optimal conditions. For most of us, the circumstances are much more favorable than they are in many other parts of the world. If people can commute under poorer conditions, surely there should be nothing to stop you from commuting to work here and now.

CHAPTER 13

Mountain Biking as a Sport

The modern mountain bike is not only a practical means of transportation, but also a fascinating piece of sporting equipment. Its origin can be traced back directly to the casually competitive sport of downhill racing. Even today, with the number of mountain bikes sold each year surpassing the sales of all other adult bicycles combined, sporting competition still plays an important role, both in its technical development and in its actual use.

Traditional road and track racing remains firmly established internationally. But rently, mountain bike racing has found a distinct niche. It is both a popular participation sport and one in which accomplished riders are making money at least semi-professionally.

In recent years, the sport has grown to the point of national recognition. In fact, some of the greatest names in road racing are now also competing in mountain biking events and vise versa. The World Championships, alternately held in Europe and America, an-

Andreas Schlueter photo

nually pit riders from all over the world against each other and are becoming so popular that television coverage is a sought-after commodity.

At the local level, perhaps the most fascinating aspect of mountain bike racing as a sport is the remarkably high rate of participation. Not only is the number of participants relative to spectators very high compared to other sports, there is another significant index that shows mountain bike riding to be a major sport. Compare, if you will, the number of ten-speed riders or joggers to those who participate in the corresponding disciplines competitively: not too many. In mountain bike riding, on the other hand, a strikingly high percentage of riders are also racers.

Mountain Bike Versus Cyclo-Cross

Bicycle racing through rough terrain has been a popular sport for many years, especially in Europe. Cyclo-cross bike racing, although also practiced in the U.S., has little in common with mountain biking. The latter has developed with little regard for this pursuit. They are two distinct sports.

In cyclo-cross, endearingly referred to as 'mud-plugging' in Britain, light and rather fragile drop handlebar racing bicycles are used. These are equipped to make them suitable for the job at hand. Like the mountain bike, they have derailleur gearing and usually can-

tilever brakes. But that's where the similarity ends: they are much lighter and more fragile, running on skinny tires.

The way these featherweights stand up to the abuse of off-road cycling is by means of timely replacement. In fact, this equipment replacement procedure is now driven to the point of absurdity. In many races, competitors not only change bikes after every lap of the short course, to give the mechanics a chance to get them back in working order, they may even show up with different bikes for different sections of the course. As is so often the case, American racers outdo their European mentors in this respect, turning the race into a mechanic's nightmare, scurrying bikes back and forth between fixing and wrecking them.

The modern mountain bike sport is in some way a healthy reaction to this obsession with equipment replacement. It makes it possible to complete a race with just one bike, a true test of both man and machine. The same bike that is used uphill will also go down, ride in sand and on rocks. Instead of being carried over lengthy sections of the course, as is customary in cyclo-cross, it will carry the rider most of the way.

It was probably the well-known California bike racer and mountain bike pioneer Gary Fisher who first served notice that the mountain bike was for real—at a cyclo-cross race of all places. At the 1980 California Cyclo-Cross Championships, he showed up with his fat-tire bike, and ran

away with the senior champion-
ship title.

Though fat-tire bikes had done
well in some cyclo-cross races
before, this was the first big success for the concept of fat tires. It
proved that the mountain bike can
not only do things no other bike
can do, it can also do things for
which more specialized equipment is intended.

While hybrids and other bikes
with narrower tires have their
uses, the terrain is still best handled on bikes with really wide
tires. In Chapter 17 you will find
some additional hints on the selection of tires for particular terrain,
both in racing situations and elsewhere. In general, softer ground

calls for wider and softer tires, and
rougher terrain requires wider and
harder tires. The narrower tires are
only appropriate when racing on
hard and relatively smooth
ground.

Racing Organizations

Initially, the U.S. national bicycle
racing organization, the USCF
(United States Cycling Federation), had not been very quick to
recognize the potential of mountain bike racing. Almost since its
inception, mountain bike racing
has largely been sponsored by
NORBA, the National Off-Road
Bicycle Association. Started in

*Clean looking mountain
bike racers with cool
shades. More often, it's a
dusty or muddy affair.*

Bob Allen photo

127

1983 as a membership-operated organization, the elected directors saw fit to actually sell the organization to one of its founding members—and with it the rights of its membership.

Although the new owner was a benevolent and honorable man, the principle of private ownership, unbeknown to most of the members, set an ugly precedent. The various conflicts with the USCF might have been resolved more elegantly and permanently if there had been at least a pretense of membership control. Glenn Odell, the first owner, put a lot of time and effort into lobbying for access and gaining insurance for the membership, while his industry-backed entourage was more interested in competition and commercial sponsorship.

The combined efforts of organizing races, controlling the membership, dealing with a board of advisers and fighting political battles were more than any man could carry out alone. Three years later the organization was sold to another individual and nasty squabbles soon started.

NORBA has become nothing more (or less) than a race-sanctioning body. Though essential for competition, this left the critical issues of access, safety, and membership participation ignored. Finally, the organization was sold once more, this time to the USCF, where at least mountain bike racing is in competent and powerful hands, and the conflicts between road racing and off-road racing organizers are cleared out of the way.

Off-Road Events

No, I can't teach you here how to race or how to be successful in any of the various off-road events becoming increasingly popular in the U.S. and abroad. You'll learn by doing, and you'll improve by practice and training. To train effectively and to understand the development of the various skills involved, I refer you to the book *Mountain Bike Racing* by Tim Gould and Simon Burney. In this section, we'll compare the various forms of off-road competition.

All competitive off-road events offer the novice the unique opportunity of participating on equal terms with the best. Even though some form of differentiation, similar to the categorization that is established in USCF-sponsored racing, is creeping into the sport, most races are still open to all comers with the appropriate credentials, which may be no more than a liability waiver and a twenty-dollar bill.

Real national celebrities in the world of off-road racing may be within touching distance, at least at the beginning of a race: they move ahead fast, while the novices are fidgeting to get into the right gear. Since most of these events are not based on the principle of numerous laps around a compact course, typical for cyclo-cross racing, the slow riders don't get in the way of faster ones. Although quite a few organizers are beginning to distinguish between the real gonzos and those of us who are out for the fun of it, this is not an athletic class society. Consequently, it is possible for a talented and determined newcomer to rise to stardom within a much shorter time than is customary or possible in regular bike racing.

Downhill Racing

No doubt the oldest form of the mountain bike race, this is nothing but what the name implies: a scramble down a steep open hillside or trail. The terrain may be marked to show where you are supposed to ride and where you're not. Generally, all competitors start together on an open section of road some distance from the actual hill, in order to weed them out a little before the real work starts. Then you show how fast you can get down.

The larger the group, the more you have to rely, not only on pure riding skills, but also on conflict avoidance technique and luck. Sometimes this kind of race is not a mass start event but rather a time trial, where riders start at intervals, and each rider is timed individually. After the race, which tends to be short and snappy—generally only a few minutes—you've got all the time in the world to get back up some other way, to watch how the others are doing and listen to the tall tales told by those who would have

Gary Fisher going full speed at a race at Crested Butte, Colorado.

David Epperson photo courtesy Gary Fisher Bicycles

you believe they could have done better than they did.

Uphill-Downhill

In this kind of event you first have to work up a sweat before you get to break your bones on the way down. Separate times are generally recorded for the two sections and then totalled. Consequently, there may be three winners in any one race: the fastest rider uphill, downhill and overall. Some of these races are hardly longer in distance than the downhill, while others may take you over many miles. Generally, the organizational problems associated with many participants and long distances discourage rides over more than two miles, though they still exist and are perhaps the most exciting to participate in.

Challenges and Enduros

A challenge is not much more than a long uphill-downhill race or one with varied terrain. Though the route will be marked in some critical areas, you may be offered some flexibility of choice, with some daredevil always finding a new and shorter route, which may subsequently be named after him or her. Sometimes, the newly discovered shortcut becomes the established route, which may result in the same race becoming more of a challenge from year to year.

An enduro is more like the typical cyclo-cross race: many laps on a relatively compact course of perhaps one or two miles. The course will include varied terrain. Rather than overall speed, the placings at the end of each lap are recorded, with certain numbers of points awarded to the first six riders after each lap. The point ratings are accumulated and the rider with the highest number of total points is declared the winner.

'Tours'

Some off-road events are still billed as tours, although it can be scary to see the vehement competition that goes on there. The term is not supposed to be taken too seriously by the participants: it is selected to bamboozle the authorities into giving their permission to use public lands for this kind of event. There is nothing wrong with that, since there has never been a report of serious damage done on any of these tours: anybody willing to work this hard at getting somewhere fast has little time to despoil nature.

After a few years, a number of these tours, such as the granddaddy of them all, the Crested Butte-to-Aspen ride in Colorado, had become so popular that the organizers felt obliged to discourage the competitive aspect. They arrived at a formula that seems to have the future of mountain bike participation guaranteed: a non-competitive tour with races before or afterwards. This brings together a highly motivated and know-ledgeable crowd of participant-spectators for a race where the experts can measure their skills with one another.

Observed Trials

This is the kind of event that is highly competitive but has nothing to do with speed—the chess game of off-road biking, so to speak. It was developed mainly in the New England states and seems to trace its heritage back to motorcycling practices in those same parts of the country. The idea is to ride an impossible course without putting a foot on the ground. Bikes with very high bottom brackets, direct steering, soft tires and extremely low gears are used.

Observed trials competition is the ultimate test of skill and requires an entirely different temperament than the speed-and-thrills stuff practiced mainly in the West. Putting on an event like this is a bit of an organizational miracle, because you have to mark off the terrain accurately and you need about as many observers as you have participants. Since not too many spectators and participants can be accommodated, this kind of game will perhaps not get as much attention as it deserves. Even so, it is definitely a fine sport and one that you can practice informally almost anywhere,

In many parts of the world, mountain bike racers are expected to cross streams with their bikes.

Bob Allen photo

Dieter Glogowski photo

alone or in groups. Since it also lends itself better than any other form for television, observed trials racing is becoming more popular as the media pay more attention.

Tandem racing is one of the more unusual, and most difficult, disciplines.

International Competition

In recent years, mountain bike racing has become a truly international sport. Even though some U.S. riders still dominate in a number of events, European, Canadian and Australian racers are quickly catching up with them. World championships, although they nowhere receive the kind of coverage the road racing championships are given (at least in Europe, where the sport is more established), television and press coverage is rapidly increasing. For a good summary of the world of international mountain bike competition, see the book *Mountain Bike Racing* by Tim Gould and Simon Burney.

CHAPTER 14

The Engineered Bicycle

This third part of the book is devoted mainly to the technical aspects of your mountain bike and its individual components. Not all of this may make entertaining reading for everybody. If you are satisfied using your bike the way it is, you may choose to put the book back on the shelf right here.

Just remember to consult these chapters when your bike does develop a problem or if you need advice on the selection of mechanical equipment. I didn't write these chapters just for my own satisfaction: you will find lots of useful information here that can help you select and maintain your equipment more expertly.

When designers get their hands on the mountain bike, as here, only engineering analysis will tell whether it's good or not.

IFMA photo

This particular chapter will explain, in some detail and in simple terms, the technical considerations that went into the design of your bike and its components. In the remaining chapters, you will get more intimately acquainted with the various 'building blocks' that make up your bike: frame, steering system, saddle, drivetrain, gearing mechanisms, wheels, and brakes. Many of these components may either all come from the same manufacturer and be related insofar that they are all from the same 'gruppo,' or group-set (a component package), or they may be selected from the products of several makes and models.

If you are not familiar with the various terms, refer to the illustration in Chapter 2, which shows the complete mountain bike with its individual components labelled, to refresh your memory. The most obvious differences between the mountain bike and other derailleur machines are those that make the mountain bike more suitable for harder use on rougher terrain. These differences are not arbitrary: some real engineering thinking has gone into the design of your bike.

Relax, I shall not try to convert all readers to engineers. But I will acquaint you with the technical background that can help you determine whether your bike and its components are suitable for their use. First we shall take a look at the kind of forces to which a bicycle and its components are subjected. Following that, I shall outline some of the design criteria

that allow the materials to withstand the resulting stresses.

Static Forces and Weight

The simplest case of engineering analysis is referred to as static loading. In this form of analysis, the bike is considered standing still with the weight of the rider on it. Under these conditions the force applied to each part of the bike can be easily calculated. Dividing this force by the strength of the material used, considering an empirically determined safety factor, gives the cross section required to make the part strong enough to withstand the force. Selecting a stronger material allows the part to be made with a smaller cross section, resulting in a design that is equally strong but lighter, assuming the two materials have the same density, or specific weight.

Light weight, after all, is one of the most desirable qualities in a bicycle, provided it is not at the expense of strength. The lighter bike is more efficient, comfortable and responsive to handle. This is especially significant when it comes to accelerating and climbing, and on rough surfaces, where the lighter bike absorbs the road shock much better than the heavier one, leading to more controlled handling and less fatigue.

Another approach to achieving a lighter design is to select a material with a lower density, such as aluminum instead of steel. Designing for the same strength, this method will only lead to a lighter construction if the chosen material is not proportionally as much weaker as it is lighter. Depending on the particular component's shape, certain aluminum alloys may or may not be used to advantage. For some parts, steel alloys may lead to lighter designs of the same strength, despite aluminum's much lower density.

Metals and Their Alloys

Sooner or later in any technical discourse about the bicycle, the word alloy is used—and often misunderstood. Contrary to popular belief,

alloy has nothing inherently to do with aluminum or light weight. It means nothing more than a mixture of several different metals—any metals, mixed in any ratio. Depending on the most prevalent metal in any particular mixture, you will encounter steel alloys as well as aluminum alloys. Both are of interest in bicycle design. In both cases, other elements are added in order to improve upon certain qualities of the base metal. This may be done to achieve greater strength, improved corrosion resistance, increased ductility, or superior hardness.

Two things alloying does not significantly affect are density and rigidity. The rigidity issue will be

Most major mountain bike manufacturers now have their own testing equipment to make sure their designs live up to their expectations.

photo courtesy Enik

135

covered later, but the various steel alloys are no lighter than pure steel, nor are any aluminum alloys markedly lighter than pure aluminum. If the alloy components are lighter than their equivalents made of a pure metal, it is not on account of reduced density, but because the stronger material allows the use of reduced cross sections.

In fact, alloying is only one of several ways to achieve stronger metals. Other methods used to this end include the addition of nonmetallic components (strictly speaking, that would still be an alloy), heat treatment, and certain procedures in the manufacturing process.

Steel is no more than iron with a little carbon added. Steel gets stronger (and more easily corroded) as a higher percentage of carbon is added. Relatively strong high-carbon steels are suitable for bicycle parts, and are widely used for the frames of many reasonably priced mountain bikes.

The next step in the chain of improving the properties of the material is the alloying process. Steel is often alloyed with manganese, chromium, molybdenum and vanadium, while aluminum may be alloyed with magnesium, copper and zinc.

The material properties can also be affected by the manufacturing process. This is most dramatically demonstrated by the very lightest alloy frame tubing materials. They are of interest to the builders of lightweight mountain bikes, since the rolling, draw-

ing, and sometimes heat treating, that has gone into making these tubes actually increases their strength to such a level that they can be made with extremely thin walls, resulting in phenomenally light frames.

These processes have their drawbacks. The strongest tubes with their very thin walls must be handled carefully, since they may easily become so brittle as to break if they are treated at too high a temperature for some time during the frame-building process. There is also a limit to decreasing the wall thickness of tubing, since it can easily dent, or even collapse like an aluminum beverage can, when the ratio between diameter and wall thickness exceeds 50 to 1.

Titanium

Titanium is becoming more popular for frames and certain parts. This material is lighter and more flexible than steel, but heavier and stronger than aluminum. It is also very expensive and hard to work, which does more to explain its popularity as a high-tech material than any real advantage.

Titanium's combination of strength and flexibility can be used to advantage in items such as handlebar stems, giving the bike a softer feel by absorbing some of the vibrations; for many other parts, where rigidity is actually a desired quality, it may be less satisfactory than the price suggests. Titanium frames are invariably welded.

Joining Methods

In the construction of a bicycle frame and other tubing structures, such as forks and handlebar stems, the joints are made either by brazing or welding. In the welding process the base metal of the two parts to be joined is heated so that they fuse together, while a filler metal that is similar to the base metal may be added.

Only materials of rather generous wall thickness can be welded. This process is suitable for mass-production techniques, since it can be automated and is suitable for both steel and aluminum tubing. When applied to high-strength aluminum tubing, a subsequent heat treatment is generally required to return the material to its original strength, but a few special aluminum alloys have been developed that, although less strong, get by without heat treatment.

Most frame welding processes are carried out in an inert gas atmosphere, which protects against corrosion. This is generally referred to as TIG, (for tungsten inert gas) welding, whereby tungsten is the material of which the welding electrode is made.

Brazing, on the other hand, is done at much lower temperatures and is not suitable for frame joints using tubes of aluminum and its alloys. In the brazing process, the base metal is heated to a dark red first. Only then is a brazing rod of a different material with a much lower melting point added. The brazing material melts and runs into the space between the two parts, and when cooled fuses with them in a strong bond. It can be done with much thinner tubes than welding, but is more energy- and labor-intensive, and consequently more expensive. The nature of the metal determines how high the brazing temperature is allowed to be, and the brazing rod used must be selected to match this temperature, melting at some point well below.

Brazing rods are melted between lugs and frame tubes to join them. They comprise mainly copper, alloyed with zinc or silver and cadmium. The term *silver brazing* refers to the use of rods that are actually neither pure silver nor even predominantly silver: they merely contain *some* silver and melt at lower temperatures. These rods must be used to join the most sensitive tubes of very thin, high-strength materials, which might be damaged if heated too far.

Even the brazing process, despite its relatively low temperatures, can negatively affect the strength of the tubing material. As we've seen above, this applies mainly to fancy thin-walled tubes. The point affected is often not so much the area of the joint itself, but the so-called heat affected zone, some distance further along the tube. Thus, after one or two years of use, the tube may break at some point about 12 to 25 mm (½ in to 1 in) back from the joint along the tube, which just happened to be exposed to a particularly unfavorable temperature sequence during the brazing process, particularly if the frame builder heated the joint too long.

Another material that should be mentioned here is resin embedded fiber, usually referred to as carbon. Different varieties of this material may be used for various parts of widely different quality. Thus, the cheapest pedals are of one variety of this material, while some of the most expensive frames are of another. When used for frames, tightly woven or matted carbon or boron fiber material, embedded in a minimum of resin, is generally selected, which is very strong and mortally expensive. Cheap parts are made with very short fibers embedded in lots of resin. One way of making cheap mass-produced frames is by moulding them together forming ugly black lugs around the joints. Be prepared to see new applications of this type of material in the near future.

Tubing Materials

Many components of the bike, not just the frame, are constructed of tubular materials. On the outside they all look more or less the same. There are welded, plain gauge seamless, and butted seamless tubes, as illustrated in Fig. 14.1. The differences between these various materials will be discussed in this section.

The cheapest tubes are welded. A flat plate of the thickness required for the finished tube is rolled into a tubular shape and welded up. You can tell that it's welded by feeling the welding seam or ridge inside the tube from inside the bottom bracket shell. There is nothing wrong with welded tubing, just rather heavy for any given strength, or weak if it is light.

More sophisticated frames are made of seamless welded tubes, such as those frequently used for mid-range bikes these days. The basis is a welded tube of a relatively strong steel or steel alloy that is then pulled over a die to remove the weld seam and to increase its strength. Wall thicknesses tend to be less, typically around 1.0 mm, resulting in lighter structures.

On even higher quality bikes, cold-drawn tubes are used. These are made by pushing a mandrel through a solid bar, and rolling it into the desired tubular shape and size. These tubes may either be plain gauge or butted. Plain gauge tubes have the same wall thickness over their entire length, while butted tubes are drawn in such a way that the ends have a greater wall thickness than the rest of the tube. This serves both to compensate for the reduced strength at the joint as a result of brazing or welding and to prevent damaging the tubing material where it is heated close to the lug, as well as to accept the raised stresses at the ends of the tubes where they meet.

The new crop of seamless welded tubes can also be made with butted ends. In fact these are very nice materials for reasonably priced welded structures, since the butts can be made thick enough to allow welding. The term *butted* does not necessarily tell you the whole story, nor is a frame that is claimed to be made of double, triple, or even quadruple butted tubes necessarily better than one that is merely referred to as butted. Most of these terms are of course strictly incorrect, since a tube can never have more than two butts (ends), but what is meant is the number of different wall thicknesses used somewhere along the length of the tube.

Recently tubing designed to take the load where it is needed most have been offered under the name Ritchey Logic. Here the butts are in the right places and of the right sizes. Like all other components of that name, they are well designed from an engineering standpoint.

Although most of the discussion up to this point has been based on the frame, similar considerations are applicable to the design and construction of other components, whether tubular or not. Spokes can either be plain or butted, to add strength at the point where they are stressed the most. Cranks, handlebars and rims are also shaped or reinforced to concentrate the material where it is most needed, and the welding or brazing operations explained here apply similarly to many other parts of the bike.

Variable Forces

So far, we've only talked about the static forces: those that are applied to the bike and its components even when bike and rider are standing still or merely rolling along a smooth surface. More important, and more complicated to predict or determine, are the variable stresses applied by a whole array of different influences. These range from the rolling of the wheels, the turning of the cranks, the torqueing effect of braking, to the jolts and blows caused by the abuse encountered when cycling off-road, not to mention what happens upon the impact of a collision.

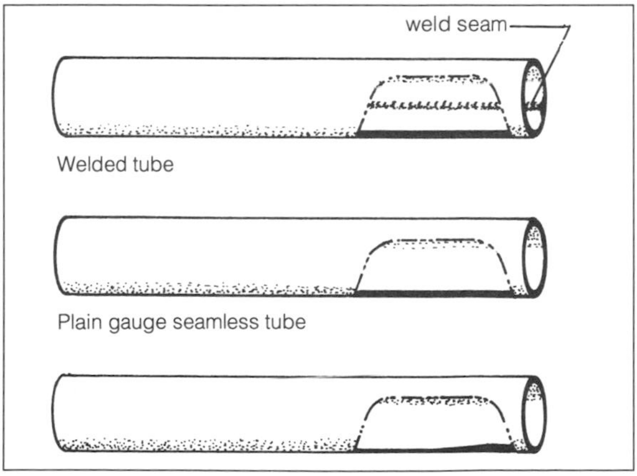

weld seam

Welded tube

Plain gauge seamless tube

Fig. 14.1
Three different types of tubing used for mountain bike frames of different quality. From top to bottom: welded, plain gauge seamless, and butted tubing.

139

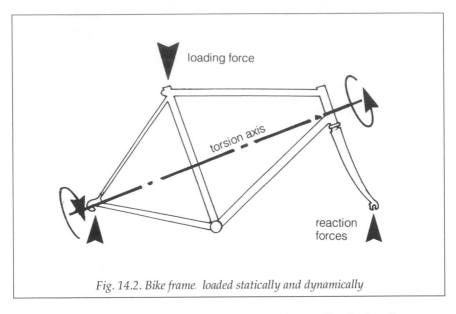

Fig. 14.2. Bike frame loaded statically and dynamically

Two aspects are of particular interest in this respect: bending stresses and fatigue. Bending stresses come into play when determining the rigidity of a structure. Fatigue is important for parts that are loaded intermittently. Engineering analysis and the technology based on it make it possible to design bikes and parts strong enough to also withstand these effects.

To design a structure to withstand bending stresses, not only the strength of the materials, but also another property, referred to as the modulus of elasticity, must be taken into consideration. Whatever the strength of an alloy, the modulus of elasticity remains essentially the same as that of the base metal. Consequently, all types of steel and its alloys, from the cheapest to the most exotic, deform equally far in response to a given bending stress, which is the quotient of force divided by cross sectional area. Similarly, all aluminum alloys deform equally— about three times as much as steel and its alloys. There is of course a difference in reaction between a very strong metal and a weaker alloy of the same base metal. Given a certain stress, both bend equally far but the former is more likely to spring back again when the force is released. Thus, permanent deformation is more likely with the weaker material. But we have seen that weaker materials should be made of greater wall thickness so that they don't bend as much, eliminating the risk of permanent deformation if properly designed.

Temporary, or elastic, deformation, which makes a bike or a part less rigid, is therefore greater for a sophisticated component made of a strong alloy, due to the smaller cross section used. Since rigidity is actually a desirable quality, which affects how well a bike tracks and how precisely it handles, there is a certain incongruity here. Essentially, the cheaper bike is more rigid than the fancy light bike made of the strongest materials. Fig. 14.3 shows what effect various factors have on rigidity.

As you can see from these illustrations, there are three ways to make a part of a given material more rigid, resulting in less deformation: either a slightly larger tube diameter, a considerably greater wall thickness, or a shorter member will do the trick. The two latter methods have been put into practice in mountain bike design for high-quality machines, which need as much rigidity as can be achieved without sacrificing lightness.

The advantage of the shorter member accounts for the tendency to design components, ranging from whole frames to minor items such as cantilever brake parts, with minimal clearances, so that they can be kept short and light. Larger diameters, consistent with a moderate wall thickness, are applied in the design of all mountain bikes. This will be evident when comparing their tube diameters with those used on other types of bikes: they are greater than those used for ten-speeds.

Due to their much lower modulus of elasticity, aluminum frames and components are potentially less rigid, making them particularly sensitive to these restraints. Fig. 14.4 compares typical dimensions of alloy steel and aluminum tubes resulting in similar strength and rigidity. The increased tube diameter is very much in evidence on high-quality aluminum frames, such as those built by aluminum bike frame pioneers Gary Klein and Charlie Cunningham, as well as many mass-produced bikes,

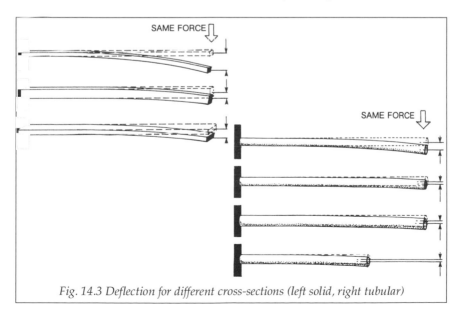

Fig. 14.3 Deflection for different cross-sections (left solid, right tubular)

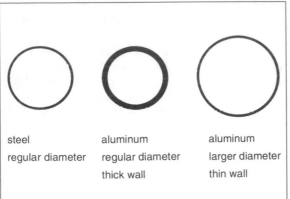

steel
regular diameter

aluminum
regular diameter
thick wall

aluminum
larger diameter
thin wall

Fig. 14.4.
To get the same strength and rigidity with aluminum as with steel, tubes can be made either with a thicker wall or with a greater diameter. The latter method is more effective to reach a suitable weight-to-rigidity ratio.

such as those made by Cannon-dale and an increasing number of other manufacturers.

Fatigue

Many parts of the bicycle are exposed to ever-changing loads, usually in a cyclical pattern. This can lead to fatigue failure if the parts are not designed with this kind of loading in mind. Although the design may be quite adequate to take the highest static force ever encountered, it may fail suddenly after it has gone through many stress cycles. Thus, spokes and even frame tubes may suddenly break after a certain number of miles of use.

The designer must know the fatigue properties of the material selected and apply an appropriate safety factor to compensate for them. In addition, so-called stress raisers must be avoided. Stress raisers are points that are particularly prone to fatigue failure due to their geometry. They occur at every point where a cyclically

loaded part has an abrupt change of cross section or a sharp bend or corner. For minimum fatigue failure risk, look for smooth contours on heavily stressed parts.

Moving Parts

Many parts of the bike move relative to one another. Those that do so cyclically during the course of the ride are generally referred to as moving parts. All have some kind of bearings, either in the form of two sliding surfaces, such as in the various parts of the chain, or in the form of a ball bearing. To minimize friction, the quality and lubrication of the various bearings are critically important.

The bearing surfaces should not only be smooth and perfectly round and aligned, they must also be extremely hard, if wear and the resulting friction are to be minimized. On high-quality bikes and components, the various bearing parts are made of hardened steel that is subsequently ground and polished, resulting in smooth running and low wear.

Most of the critical bearings on the bike are in the form of ball bearings, consisting of an inner race and an outer race that are separated by perfectly matching steel balls, floating in lubricant. The typical bicycle ball bearing is the adjustable cup-and-cone model illustrated in the left hand detail of Fig. 14.5. When properly maintained, this is still the ultimate bearing, offering the best qualities for its weight. It is adjusted by turning the cone or the cup relative to each other, so that the gap between the two, where the bearings balls lie, is closed up a little. As a lubricant, a light grease is used almost universally, being packed in only once or twice a year, whereas oil would have to be replenished frequently.

One problem with this kind of bearing is that it is not perfectly sealed against the elements. A better seal can generally be used on Conrad, or cartridge, bearings, which are the common industrial type, illustrated in the right hand detail. These are not adjustable and generally incorrectly referred to as sealed bearings. They are lubricated for life, which may actually be shorter than it is for a corresponding cup-and-cone model. When this kind of bearing becomes loose or develops increased friction, it must be replaced in its entirety. That generally requires special tools, and so should be left to a properly equipped workshop.

Lubrication of bearings is tricky. Although oil is generally the best lubricant, it tends to run out of the bearings and is messy. That's why grease is used instead, packing it firmly between the races. To keep grease in and dirt out, some kind of seal is required, and the most satisfactory method is the one called Grease Guard, developed by Wilderness Trails Bicycles, the enterprising group of California designers, and licensed to SunTour. In this system, chevron-section flexible seals are installed on either side of each bearing in such a way that the grease is

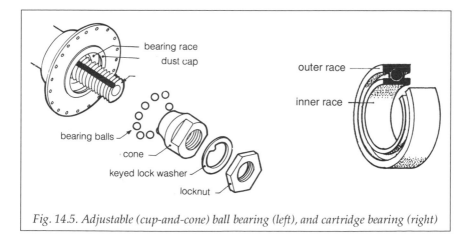

Fig. 14.5. Adjustable (cup-and-cone) ball bearing (left), and cartridge bearing (right)

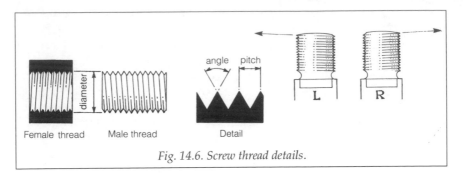

Fig. 14.6. Screw thread details.

trapped in the bearing without filling the entire space in the hub, headset, pedal, or bottom bracket.

Screw Threads

Many of the bicycle's bits and pieces are held together by means of threaded connections, shown in Fig. 14.6. Each of these consists of a part with an exterior, or *male*, thread that fits inside one with an interior, or *female*, thread. Each of the threads is a helical groove, spiralling around the circumference. Obviously, the two threads of matching parts must have the same nominal diameter and thread profile.

The thread profile is defined by the *pitch*—the distance between one groove or ridge and the next, and measured either in mm or as the number of threads per inch (tpi)—and the *thread angle*. Although the thread angle can also vary (either 60° or 55°), this characteristic is rarely quoted on parts. Always make sure you get parts that match perfectly, which in some cases means you have to replace both parts of a connection when only one is worn or

damaged. Ask at the bike shop to make sure you get correctly matching parts.

Some parts are held on with LH thread, while all regular bolts and nuts, as well as most other parts, have regular RH threading. While the latter is turned to the right to tighten, and to the left to loosen, it's the other way round for LH threading: tighten by turning left, loosen to the right. LH threaded parts on your bike are the LH pedal-to-crank connection and (usually) the RH bottom bracket cup, as well as some of the guts inside the freewheel.

The correct treatment of threaded parts includes making sure they are kept clean, slightly lubricated and undamaged. To loosen or tighten a threaded joint, always use tools with adequate leverage that fit exactly. Use wrenches for the bolts, flat screwdrivers for ordinary screws, Allen keys for the type with a hexagonal recess, Phillips head screwdrivers for the type with a cross-pattern head. Wherever possible, place a plain washer under the nut or the bolt head (whichever is the part that will be turned to tighten or loosen), so that contact friction is minimized, to assure the best hold between the threaded parts.

To prevent loosening of bearings on account of vibrations, a thread compound can be used, such as Loctite, which is available in several grades. This is available in different formulations, forming more or less hard to break bonds. For things that need never be undone, it will be safe to select the most durable type, whereas items such as the pedal threads and many other bolts require a less permanent type. Don't use this stuff indiscriminately, but wait until you have established which components on your bike tend to come loose and which do not, and then apply the appropriate type only where necessary.

Mixed media art: Fisher's CR-7 has a welded aluminum main frame and bolted-on steel seat and chain stays.

Finishing Processes

Even the finish applied to the bicycle's various components has a technical significance. Not only is it intended to keep the bike looking pretty, it also protects the underlying material. In some cases the finishing process actually improves the characteristics of the materials. An example of this is the anodizing process used on many aluminum parts, such as the chainrings. If applied to a depth of 0.05 mm, rather than the usual 0.005 mm typical for mere corrosion protection, it actually hardens the material in that area enough to increase the part's wear resistance properties. Parts treated this way may look dull grey, and (in the case of wheel rims) are often incorrectly referred to as heat treated.

Anodizing is an electro-chemical oxidation process that turns

the outer layer of aluminum into a much harder form of aluminum oxide. In recent years it has become popular to mix a colored dye—usually black—in with the anodizing bath to achieve a metallic colored finish. Even to those who think this looks nice in the showroom, it becomes pretty ugly after a while, since the slightest wear or damage shows up as an ugly discoloration— unavoidable in places like the sides of the rims, where the brake blocks wear through the finish in no time.

Bright, shiny parts that are not made of aluminum are probably of chrome-plated steel. The prettiest and most durable chrome plating finishes consist of at least a layer of nickel plating, covered by a layer of chrome plating. Since the nickel is softer, it follows the contours of the material better, even when it gets deformed, whereas chrome may peel off when deformed. For that reason, bolts and spoke nipples are better left just nickel-plated. Protect unpainted finishes like these with a cloth and some wax once a month.

Anodization is frequently used to harden surfaces. In this case it is done to a much greater depth (0.05 mm rather than 0.005 mm as is common for pure corrosion protection). This treatment is quite appropriate on chainrings and other wearing surfaces. However, it is not a good idea on rims: although the process indeed makes them harder, and therefore stronger, it also makes them so brittle that they tend to crack at the spoke holes after one or two years' use.

Paint finishes for mountain bikes have gone through a veritable revolution since the machine was first introduced. Whereas the first models invariably had dull and earthy colors, the brightest, poppiest colors seem barely wild enough these days. Good paint is hard paint, whatever make, color or type is used, and it should cover the bike right up to the tiniest nooks and crannies.

Many components are now frequently coated with a colored resin. Although this makes them easier to keep clean, it is mainly done to save the expense of polishing the blank metal. Since any scratches cut through the finish and show through, I hope this fad will soon blow over. It is certainly not a good idea on any parts subjected to wear.

CHAPTER 15

The Frame

The frame could be called your mountain bike's backbone—the structure that holds it all together. Although the frame used for most mountain bikes at first sight looks like that of any other bicycle, it does differ in a number of points to accommodate the particular kind of use and abuse for which it is intended. In this chapter we shall look at what all bicycle frames have in common, and at what is so special about the frame of your mountain bike.

Fig. 15.1 shows the components that constitute the frame. The main frame comprises four relatively large diameter tubes: top tube, seat tube, downtube and head tube. The rear triangle consists of two seat stays and two chain stays. The smaller members are the bottom bracket, seat lug, upper and lower head lugs (assuming it is a lugged frame), and bridge pieces connecting the pairs of seat stays and chain stays. Finally, there are dropouts and a number of braze-ons. The latter are minor items attached to the tubes, such as brake pivot bosses, cable anchors stops, guides, and bosses.

Not your everyday mountain bike frame. This Kirk Precision frame is made of magnesium. Very strong and light, but a big casting that's not available in many different sizes.

Photo courtesy Kirk/Norsk Hydro

There are at least four different ways to join the tubes of the frame, illustrated in Fig. 15.2. Conventionally, high-quality bike frames have been made by brazing the tubes together with lugs. It is also possible to braze the tubes together directly, referred to as lugless, or fillet, brazing. Alternately, they may be welded, or finally, bonded together with internal lugs.

The welding process commonly used is referred to as TIG welding, which was explained in Chapter 14. The lugless joints of a TIG-welded frame are markedly more abrupt than they are on a fillet brazed frame, except if the contours are hidden by means of a polyester spackling compound. TIG-welding is cheaper than fillet brazing but works very satisfactorily on tubes with slightly thicker ends. All methods can result in equally strong and reliable frames.

Judging Frame Quality

To size up the quality of a mountain bike frame quickly, note the diameters of the various tubes. At least the down tube should be of a larger diameter than the one used on a regular road bicycle of the same material. This is necessary to accommodate the higher stresses resulting from the rougher treatment and the more generous lengths, slopes and clearances of the mountain bike.

Also observe the other details. If the joints are smooth and without gaps, whether lugged or not, the bike is probably of a higher quality than if they are rough and show gaps between the various parts. Finally, note the

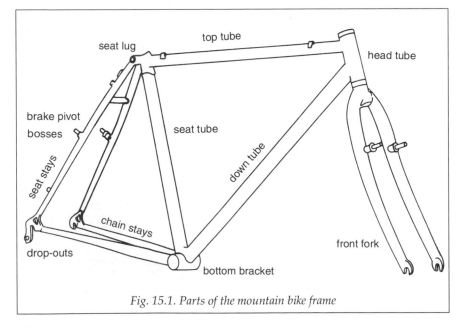

Fig. 15.1. Parts of the mountain bike frame

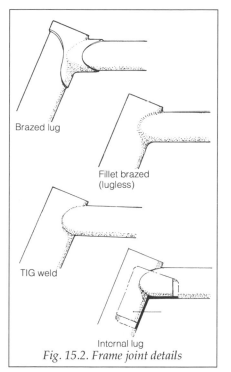

Brazed lug

Fillet brazed
(lugless)

TIG weld

Internal lug

Fig. 15.2. Frame joint details

is not painted at all and where the welds look a little crude at first.

Frame Geometry

Fig. 15.3 compares the geometries of a typical mountain bike and a typical regular derailleur bike for the same size of rider. The differences can be summarized in the following list and will be further explained below:

☐ The mountain bike frame has a higher bottom bracket, despite its slightly smaller wheels.

☐ The mountain bike's top tube is lower. This, in addition to the higher bottom bracket results in a considerably shorter seat tube.

☐ While the seat tube angle should be roughly the same, the mountain bike has a shallower head tube angle.

☐ The top tube tends to be slightly longer on a mountain bike.

paint finish: a good, hard, smooth coat of paint generally indicates a more carefully built machine. Just the same, it is dangerous to judge a book by its cover—or a frame by its finish alone. I know of at least one superb aluminum frame that

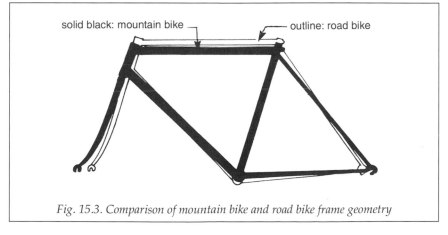

solid black: mountain bike   outline: road bike

Fig. 15.3. Comparison of mountain bike and road bike frame geometry

149

☐ The mountain bike has longer chain stays.

☐ Although not visible here, the clearances for the wheels are more generous on the mountain bike, both radially and laterally.

The last three points add up to a significantly longer total wheelbase, which is the total distance between the front and rear wheel axles.

Fig. 15.4 illustrates the various dimensions and angles, while the following paragraphs offer explanations for the differences and criteria for the selection of an optimum frame geometry. Most manufacturers nowadays include drawings showing the geometries tries of their various models in their catalogs, so you can shop around. Just the same, don't buy a bike without having tried it out, even if the geometry seems perfect on paper: the proof of the pudding is in the eating.

The bottom bracket is typically 30 cm (12 in) or more off the ground, which is at least an inch more than on a road bike. This greater height is required to provide adequate ground clearance in rough terrain, particularly in view of the mountain bike's longer wheelbase, and to prevent damage to the chainring. Even higher bottom brackets make a bike more suitable for extremely rough terrain, such as encountered in observed trials competition.

The top tube is lower to allow a low enough saddle position that makes it possible to reach the ground while seated, and to let you straddle the bike more easily when you are standing still. In general, it should be at least 5 cm (2 in) inches lower than on a ten-speed bike for the same rider. The combined effect of the higher bottom bracket with that of the lower top tube should result in a seat tube length, or nominal frame size, that is about 7.5 cm (3 in) less than it would be for a regular ten-speed. If you can't straddle the frame of a bike with wheels installed, with both feet flat on the ground and at least 5 cm (2 in) of

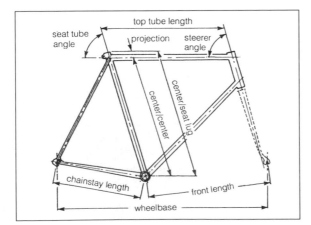

Fig. 15.4 .
Frame geometry terminology: dimensions and angles defined.

crotch clearance, the frame is too big.

Table 1 in the Appendix shows recommended seat tube lengths, measured two different ways, as well as straddle heights. In the English-speaking world, bike frames used to be measured as the length from the center of the bottom bracket to the top of the seat lug. The more logical method of measuring between the center of the bottom bracket and the centerline of the top tube is rapidly becoming universally used for mountain bike frame size designation. Some manufacturers now also refer to the straddling height, or the height of the top of the top tube above the ground.

The seat tube angle merely determines how the seat will be centered relative to the drivetrain. With the common bicycle geometry, 73° is just about right for most sizes—whether mountain bike or not. This angle allows you to get up from the saddle to apply the force of your weight to the pedals quite readily, while keeping your weight reasonably balanced between front and rear wheels when seated. Smaller bikes typically need a steeper frame angle to achieve the proper position for a short-legged rider, though.

The head tube angle influences the steering characteristics, the overall wheelbase and the comfort or springiness of the front end. To this end, any angle between 68° and 72° may be right. It may be as shallow as 68° for a sluggish but comfortable bike that goes downhill without risk and is suitable for the less accomplished rider. It should be more like 72° for a bike that gives a nimbler, though rougher, ride—one that demands more skill on a steep descent.

The longer top tube has two functions. It protects your knees when you are standing up on a steep climb, and it provides an acceptably long wheelbase. My experience suggests that bikes with shorter top tubes for any given frame size tend to be more enjoy-

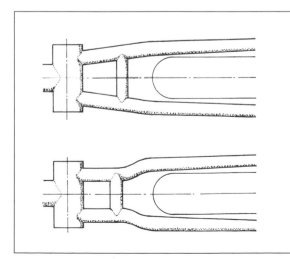

Fig. 15.5. Alternate chainstay configurations. The distinctly curved design may look less sleek, but it does provide the better tire clearance, without weighing more or bringing other disadvantages.

151

able to ride. About 3–4 in more than the seat tube length (measured center-to-center) is about right for most riders. If you still hit your knee caps when grinding uphill, you can get a handlebar stem with more reach.

The longer chain stays provide the greater clearances and contribute to the longer wheelbase. Generally, relatively short chain stays and the resulting shorter wheelbase provide better climbing and sprinting characteristics. I'd say anything less than 17 in (430 mm) chain stays, usually resulting in less than 43 in (106 cm) wheelbase, provides a nimble ride. The frame of a mountain bike intended for the novice should probably be longer than that.

There are various ways to give the mountain bike frame the lateral clearance around the wheels to accommodate the fattest tires, as shown in Fig. 15.5. You need at least 5 mm (3/16 in) lateral clearance on either side. Some frames just don't take the really fat tires. This is not necessarily bad, although I'd prefer one that can be used with any size tire. Measure the distance between the pairs of chain and seat stays at a point 33 cm (13 in) from the drop-out centers; then deduct 10 mm (3/8 in) to determine which is the fattest tire that will fit with adequate clearance.

Different Frame Designs

In recent years, various frame designs have been introduced that

look quite different from that used on the conventional bike. Some of these are mere fads, others may be here to stay.

On smaller frame sizes it has become customary to use a sloping top tube. This allows the use of a reasonably long head tube (a necessity for adequate rigidity) without cramping the rider.

Another popular design is characterized by raised seat stays. This allows using a very short wheelbase and stops the chain from getting caught on the RH chain stay. Even so, it adds unnecessarily to the weight of a frame and is only recommended if it provides a feature you really want for your kind of riding: don't let the presumably cool looks be the determining factor when choosing a particular design.

Then there are the various frames with suspension. Even if the bike only has a front suspension, the frame must be designed with that in mind, since the distance by which the fork gives must be accommodated somewhere in the frame. Frames with a rear suspension are an even more complicated matter, requiring very special frames designed around the particular type of suspension used.

Frame Materials

You may want to refer to Chapter 14 again, where we looked at the various materials and their properties. There are many ways of achieving a frame of adequate quality. The fanciest ones are either made of butted steel alloy tubes that are fillet brazed together (i.e. lugless), of welded and stress-relieved aluminum, or of carbon fiber composits. The first satisfactory mountain bikes were all made without lugs, since at that time none were available to fit the larger diameter tubes needed for a reliable mountain bike. There are now lugs available to fit the large-diameter mountain bike tubes, and many excellent low-price mountain bikes are constructed this way.

I find TIG-welded frames quite adequate, providing high-strength alloy steel tubes are used with a wall thickness of 1.2 mm in the butted sections and no more than 0.8 mm in the center section. Anything thicker and heavier seems to result in a rather harsh and less nimble ride, even though the dif-

ference in weight is only on the order of one or two pounds in all. Mountain bike pioneer Tom Ritchey has designed tubes, referred to as Ritchey Logic tubing and found on many quality frames, matching these requirements as closely as possible.

Any tubing referred to as HiTen is merely carbon steel. These are of necessity either heavier or weaker on account of the material's inferior strength as compared to most steel alloys.

The type of tubing used is generally acknowledged by a sticker, generally attached to the seat tube, especially if it is tubing of recognized quality. Aluminum tubing varies too greatly from one make and design to the other. It should be made of even greater

Framebuilder at work: Jeff Lindsay of Mountain Goat Bicycles in Chico, California.

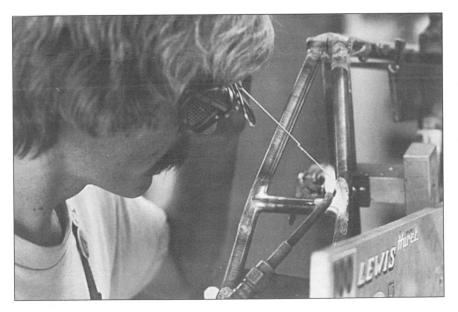

diameters and wall thicknesses than steel tubes to be adequately rigid and strong, respectively.

Frame Details

In addition to the materials and the geometry, several less obvious points affect the quality of your frame. First, the drop-outs are of some importance. These are the flat parts at the points where seat stays and chain stays come together, in which the rear wheel is installed. They should be relatively thick and rounded, indicating that they are made of either forged or investment cast steel. These are superior in strength and, due to the greater thickness, in rigidity to the type made of flat stamped steel plate. Aluminum dropouts had better be really thick, to the point of being ugly.

The slot for the rear wheel in the drop-outs may be either vertical or horizontal. The former method allows closer clearances between the wheel and the chain stay bridge, resulting in a more rigid rear end and a more constant position of a U-brake or a cam-operated brake relative to the rim. Since the wheel can not be adjusted by pushing it forward more on one side than on the other, this kind of drop-out requires a greater degree of precision in building the frame. Check from behind, looking along both wheels, to make sure the wheels track, meaning they are perfectly aligned, when the axle is at the top of the slot on both sides.

There must be a derailleur eye on the RH drop-out. It should be as thick as the rest of the drop-out, to make sure it does not get bent, resulting in derailleur misalignment and consequently in unpredictable gear changing.

The bridges between the chain stays and the seat stays should be attached with perfectly smooth and uninterrupted welds or brazed joints. The same goes for the various other braze-ons, which should include the following:

☐ Pivot bosses for the rear brake. They are generally installed below the chain stays these days, except for cantilever brakes, which have them on the seat stays. Although there is a certain degree of standardization between various makes, check when replacing brakes that they match the bosses on the frame by inquiring about interchangeability at a bike shop.

☐ A rigid anchor for the end of the outer brake cable. To accommodate a cantilever brake, it must be in the form of a tubular bridge between the seat stays with a tunnel or recess in which the cable end is restrained. Roller-cam and U-brakes, which are generally installed below the chain stays, would need a solid lug below the bottom bracket or on the bottom of the down tube just ahead of the bottom bracket.

☐ Guides or tunnels for the brake and gear cables, including stops at those points where outer cable sections are interrupted.

☐ Threaded eyelets and lugs for the installation of a luggage rack and fenders, as well as a hole in the bridge between the seat stays to mount fenders. Even if you don't want to think about such accessories right now, it doesn't hurt to know you can accommodate them if necessary.

☐ Threaded bosses for the installation of water bottles. Generally, three locations are suitable: the front of the seat tube, the top of the down tube, and below the down tube. Your bike will be most versatile if you have all three, so you still have enough bottle-carrying options after you install a lock and a pump.

☐ One or more pegs or anchors for the pump, which can be either clamped between two pegs or between one peg and a corner of the frame. A nice place is along the rear side of the seat tube, if the chain stays are long enough to provide adequate clearance there, leaving the front of the seat tube free for your lock.

Frame Maintenance

Even the mountain bike frame is not indestructible. If it gets seriously damaged, take it to a bike shop to evaluate the possibility of repair. However, some checks and repairs can be carried out by the technically inclined layman. These will be covered in this section.

The first and most important thing to know is how you can judge whether anything is wrong with the frame. This should be done after a serious crash and whenever you get the feeling the bike is not tracking as well as it used to.

The weak point on the frame is the forward section of the downtube, just behind the lower head lug. After a collision, check to make sure there is no bulge or wrinkle at this point, as illustrated in Fig. 15.6. If there is, take the bike to the shop for advice. On a high-quality lugged or fillet-brazed frame, it is quite realistic to get a frame builder to replace the down tube in a case like this.

Other kinds of damage to the frame more typically result in a lateral misalignment. For a simple check, wrap a piece of string

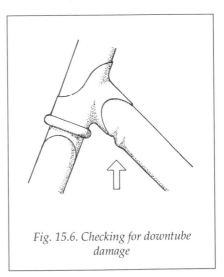

Fig. 15.6. Checking for downtube damage

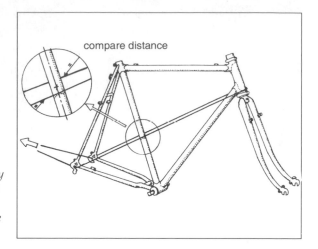

Fig. 15.7.
Checking for frame
alignment. Ideally, the
dimension should be
identical on both sides. Any
discrepancy of more than 3
mm (⅛ in) is definitely
unacceptable and should be
corrected.

around the head tube and the
drop-outs, as shown in Fig. 15.7.
Pull taut and measure the distance
between string and seat tube, comparing it on both sides. If the difference is more than about 2 mm
(3/32 in), the bike will bear some
aligning, which can be done on all
but the most fragile machines.
Once more, this is a job for an experienced bike mechanic.

What you can do yourself, is
touch up the paint when it gets
scratched. Get a bottle of touch-up
paint of the right color at the time
you buy the bike, since the color
choice seems to differ from year to
year, and this year's colors may
not be stocked next year. Sand
only the damaged spot down to
bare metal, then clean with turpentine or paint thinner.

Apply paint with a very small
brush with short bristles, avoiding
overlapping over the undamaged
paint. If you can only get touch-up
paint in a spray bottle, spray a little puddle in a metal bottle cap or
similar small receptacle and apply
it with a brush. Clean the brush
with turpentine or paint thinner
afterwards. Let the paint dry overnight and repeat the application if
necessary.

CHAPTER 16

The Steering System

The mountain bike's steering system is depicted in Fig. 16.1. It comprises front fork, upper and lower headset bearings, stem and handlebars. Each of these items differs somewhat from the corresponding parts installed on other bikes, since your mountain bike's front end is subjected to particularly punishing use and is crucial for the way the machine handles.

Steering Geometry

As explained in Chapter 8, the bicycle is not steered merely by turning the handlebars. In fact, given a reasonably constant road surface, it can be steered successfully without ever touching the handlebars. You can get a good feel for the bike's handling by walking it, holding it only at the saddle. Lean the bike one way or the other and it turns toward that same direction. Bring it back upright, and it will straighten out again.

The position of the steering system changes in response to the lean. At any given speed, a particular lean will point the front wheel under a certain angle. Going faster, a more pronounced lean is required to achieve the same curve radius. Going slower quite a small amount of lean is enough to turn quite abruptly. Standing still, the bike is 'rudderless', unless you hold the handlebars.

While riding, you have to hold the handlebars for only two reasons: to guide the bike when standing still or riding very slowly, and

to dampen the effect of extraneous influences, such as surface unevenness, which would otherwise upset the balance, pushing the front wheel off its course. Such an extraneous force could divert the wheel far enough to lead to a

Front end of a typical modern mountain bike with oversize headset.

diverting type fall, as explained in Chapter 6.

What keeps the bike following its own course at some speed is known as trail, the most significant element of steering geometry. Steering geometry is the entire interrelationship of angles and dimensions of the steering system. Trail is depicted in Fig. 16.2: it is the horizontal distance between the point where the front wheel contacts the ground and the point where a line through the steering axis touches the ground.

All bicycles have positive trail, meaning that the line through the steering axis intersects the road at some point *in front* of the contact point between the tire and the road. The bike's steering and handling would be very volatile if it were the other way round, referred to as negative trail. The amount of trail essentially determines the stability and self-steer-

ing characteristics of the bike. On the other hand, too much trail makes the bike sluggish to handle, so it becomes a matter of fine tuning.

These characteristics also depend on the steerer angle, which is the angle between the steering axis (or the frame's head tube) and the horizontal plane. For any steerer angle, a particular amount of trail results in a certain stability. With a given steerer angle, the trail can be varied by selecting the fork design appropriately. This is achieved by selecting one with more or less fork rake. The rake is the distance by which the fork blades are bent forward. You'll probably never have to worry about that on a new bike: the manufacturer has taken care of that. But when replacing a fork, you have to get one with the right rake to get the same trail.

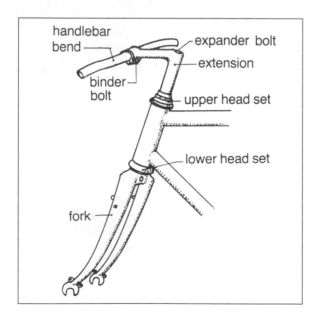

Fig. 16.1.
The parts of the steering system.

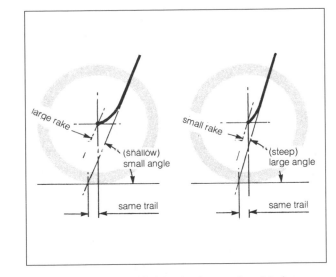

Fig. 16.2.
Definition of steering
geometry and the
factors affecting it.

To obtain the kind of handling that agrees with off-road cycling, the mountain bike should have more trail than a road bike. This increases the bicycle's tendency to go straight, requiring less force to keep it on course when the front wheel is diverted by irregularities in the surface. The granddaddy of today's mountain bike, the Excelsior, had a 68° steerer angle and a 50 mm (2 in) fork rake, resulting in a trail of 60 mm (3¼ in). There probably isn't a better configuration for downhill riding.

However, unlike the California prototypes of the late seventies and eary eighties, most of today's mountain bikes are used for lots of other things, and those that are ridden down steep hillsides are often steered by highly skilled bicycle acrobats. Consequently, different designs are showing up more and more. The range of steerer angles varies from about 67° to 72°, with rakes that differ enough to make one bike a sure descender, another

a nimble climber and a third one a stable low-speed trials machine.

The graph of Fig. 16.3 summarizes the effect of various combinations of steering angle and fork rake, showing two different varieties of trail. The first is what I refer to as simple or *projected* trail, the other one is what I call *effective* trail. The latter measure, derived in the RH graph, is the more accurate one, taking into account the effect of the angle at which trail and rake are measured relative to each other as a function of the steering angle.

Effective trail is what has been referred to by some authors as *stability index*, suggesting some kind of mystical figure, whereas the term effective trail clarifies that it is a measurable dimension. Although the difference between projected and effective trail is minor, it increases as steerer angles diverge more, accounting for the dramatic difference in handling characteristics between two

159

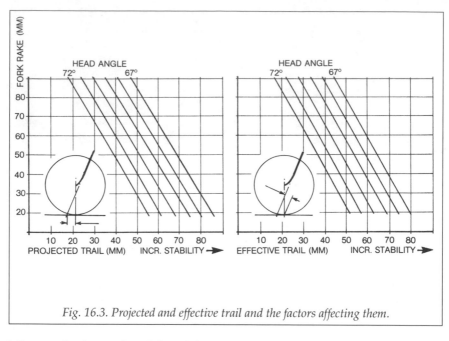

Fig. 16.3. Projected and effective trail and the factors affecting them.

bikes with identical trail, but different steerer angles.

The Front Fork

The front fork not only holds the front wheel, it also serves as a more or less effective suspension system for the mountain bike, elastically absorbing shocks. This shock absorption property is greatest when the head angle is small and the rake correspondingly long. On the other hand, this results in a weaker front end, given the same materials and wall thicknesses, as well as making the bike a little sluggish.

Apart from suspension forks, three basic fork designs are used for mountain bikes, as illustrated in Fig. 16.4. All three types have a steerer tube (steering column in

Britain), two fork blades and fork ends (or front drop-outs). In addition, the traditional front fork, used almost exclusively on non-mountain bikes, has a separate fork crown, into which the blades are brazed. The switchblade design also has a separate fork crown, but here it is clamped around the blades, which are replaceable—whether to achieve a different rake or because of damage.

Most mountain bikes these days use a fork of the unicrown design, on which the fork blades are bent inward near the top and welded to the steerer tube. After bending several conventional forks with a separate crown on my mountain bike, I swear by the unicrown solution. A variation of this type of fork, pioneered by Charlie Cunningham, does away with the forward curve of the blades, which are instead installed under an angle to achieve the same rake.

Although unicrowns are currently the favored design, not all are equal. Some manufacturers take short cuts, and many cheaper bikes come with unicrown forks that are not adequately reinforced. If the fork blades are made of butted tubing with significantly greater wall thickness near the top than elsewhere, the unicrown design works fine. If not, an additional reinforcing piece should have been brazed over the top of the curved section.

Until a few years ago, mountain bike forks had a steerer tube of the same diameter and threading as used on most ten-speeds adhering to the (English) BCI standard dimensions with 1.000 in x 24 tpi screw thread. In recent years more and more manufacturers

have introduced bikes with an oversized model, of which there are now several versions, each requiring a different head tube diameter and handlebar stem diameter—as well as special tools for any maintenance work. All oversize headsets offer more stability and steering accuracy.

Pivot bosses must be installed on the fork blades, to accept the cantilever or roller-cam brakes used on the mountain bike. They should be in the appropriate location and of the right type to match the particular make and model of brake used. Although a brake bolt mounting hole, as is required on a regular road bike with caliper brakes, is not strictly needed, either a normal hole or a threaded one comes in handy to mount fenders or a rack.

The fork ends should be just about as thick as the rear dropouts, and investment cast or

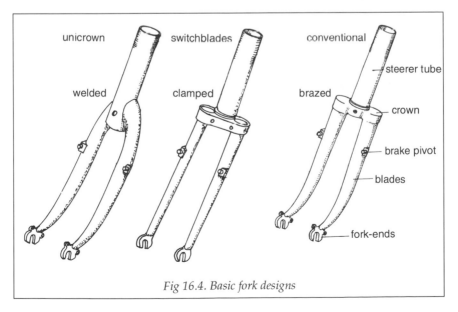

Fig 16.4. Basic fork designs

Lightweight welded steel mountain bike handlebar stems.

forged models are much stronger than those made of stamped steel plate. If the bike is not intended primarily for racing, I'd make sure the fork ends have threaded eyelets for rack and fender mounting. In addition, threaded bosses should be brazed on to the fork blades to install a rack. Bikes sold in Britain should have a threaded boss to mount a lamp bracket for the type of battery light that is used there almost universally. I think that would make sense elsewhere too, but both the British lights and the matching lamp brackets are virtually unknown elsewhere, and other lights do not use standard installation hardware.

Fork Maintenance

The fork is the most likely component to get serious damage when you hit an obstacle head-on.

If there is no evidence of cracks or folds, it may be possible to have it straightened at a bike shop. If the problem is more serious, replace the fork, which you can do yourself. Remove the handlebars and undo the headset as explained below. Take the old fork to the shop to order a replacement of the same size. If they don't have your size, get one with a longer steerer tube and cut it to size with a hacksaw, then remove the burr with a file. Make sure the threaded section is long enough to install the upper headset, being about 3 cm (1 ¼ in). The bike shop can cut the thread further if necessary. To determine the right length, measure the length of the frame's head tube for reference, and take the headset along.

If the steering does not turn freely, and adjusting the headset, as described below, does not do the trick, it may be due to a bent

162

steerer tube. In that case, the fork must be replaced. Whenever you replace, remove or reinstall a front fork, heed the advice contained in the section about headset maintenance below.

The Headset

Depending on the inside diameter of the head tube, your mountain bike may either have a standard headset or an oversized model as mentioned above. Both are built up similarly, as illustrated in Fig. 16.5. Some models have an additional locking device to stop the

Fig. 16.5.
The headset. In addition, many special mountain bike headsets have a clamping device to hold the locknut in place.

locknut from coming loose under the effect of vibrations.

The fixed bearing races are dished and are installed with a compression fit inside the top and bottom of the head tube, respectively. The bearing balls lie in the space between these races, which should be packed with clean bearing grease at least once a season. (If your headset has grease-guard fittings, you don't need to do that, provided you inject clean grease at least once every three months). The bearing balls may be loose but are more usually contained in a retainer. The fork race is held on a shoulder at the bottom of the steerer tube.

Recently, Dia-Compe has introduced its AheadSet, which requires a matching stem and fork, but is easier to maintain without

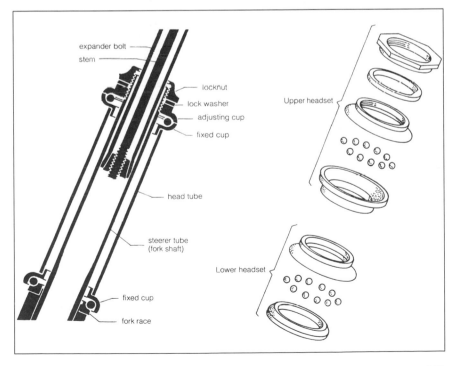

expander bolt
stem
locknut
lock washer
adjusting cup
fixed cup
Upper headset
head tube
steerer tube
(fork shaft)
Lower headset
fixed cup
fork race

special tools (all you need as an Allen key). The design is ingenious, and it may well become a standard item on mountain bikes.

Headset Adjustment

When the steering is either loose or rough, try to solve your problem by adjusting the headset first. The entire headset is adjusted from the top. All you need is a large adjustable wrench and a rag, proceeding as follows:

1. Undo the locknut on top (after loosening the special locking insert screw that is installed on a few models).

2. Raise the lock washer underneath the locknut.

3. Turn the adjusting cup to the right to tighten, the left to loosen.

4. When it feels right—no play in the bearing, yet turning smoothly—tighten the locknut,

while holding the adjusting cup in place.

5. Try again. If necessary, repeat and loosen or tighten a little, perhaps ⅛ turn.

Overhauling or Replacing Conventional Headset

If adjusting does not solve the problem, you'll have to overhaul the entire headset. The same procedure must be followed when you replace either the fork or the headset. Before you start, remove the handlebars, as described in the appropriate section below, and the front wheel, as explained in Chapter 17. You need a large adjustable or special wrench and a rag. If you have to replace the fixed cups and the fork race, rely on your bike shop for this part of the project, since it is best done with special removal and installation tools. If you insist on doing it yourself, refer to my *Mountain Bike Maintenance* for instructions based on the use of improvised tools.

Disassembly procedure:

1. Unscrew and remove the locknut.

2. Remove the lock washer.

3. Unscrew and remove the adjusting race, holding the fork in the frame at the bottom.

4. Catch the bearing balls, which are best replaced together with their retainer each time you overhaul a headset.

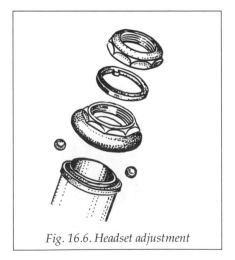

Fig. 16.6. Headset adjustment

5. Remove the fork from the head tube, catching the bearings on the other side similarly.

6. Inspect all parts. Replace any parts that are obviously worn, corroded or damaged. This will be the case whenever grooves, pits or other damage is evident in the bearing surfaces.

7. Buy any replacement parts or an entirely new headset. Make sure you get the right size by taking the old fork and at least one screwed-on headset part to the shop with you to match the new parts for size.

Installation procedure:

1. If applicable, get the fixed bearing cups and the fork race installed at the bike shop.

2. Fill both bearing cups with grease.

3. Turn the frame upside down and place the bearing retainer (or loose bearing balls) inside the lower fixed bearing cup. If held in a retainer, make sure it is installed so that the balls protrude towards you on the inside where they contact the fork race.

4. Place the fork's steerer tube through the head tube until the fork race seats on the bearing balls in the cup. Hold fork and frame together firmly at this point, then turn it back the right way round.

5. Still holding fork and frame together, place the ball retainer or the loose balls in the upper fixed cup.

6. While continuing to hold fork and frame at the lower headset, screw the adjusting cup on the fork.

7. Place the lock washer over the adjustable race, with the flat section of the hole matching the corresponding flat section around the circumference of the head tube.

8. Screw the locknut on by hand.

9. Adjust and tighten the bearing as described above.

Note:

If the adjusting cup cannot be screwed on far enough to adjust the bearing properly, the threaded portion of the steerer tube is too short. If the locknut can not be tightened down fully, the steerer tube is too long. Let a bike shop mechanic shorten the tube or cut the thread further as appropriate.

Handlebars and Stem

Next to the tires, the handlebars most characterize the mountain bike: wide and flat. However not as wide and not as flat as in the early days of mountain biking. Meanwhile, most of us, manufacturers included, have learned that a width of 60 cm (24 in) is generally more than enough. If the bars are too wide, feel free to use a plumber's tube cutter (or in a pinch, a hacksaw) to reduce the width equally on both sides, providing the shape of the bars is such that they can be held and the brakes can be reached comfortably after this kind of surgery. This is important because nowadays the bars are often less straight and flat than they were in the pioneering days.

Welded steel or aluminum stems are all the rage these days, using high-strength materials that give you a light stem. Flexibility of the stem is a desirable feature to absorb some of the vibrations. Titanium stems are most effective in that respect, as are titanium handlebars. There are also several stems with a built-in shock absorber on the market to increase rider comfort even more—at a reasonable price (compared to suspension forks, anyway).

The handlebars should be adjustable, except perhaps if they are tailor-made for a particular rider.

Adjustability is achieved by means of a separate stem clamped around the bars with a binder bolt. On fixed designs, the bars are welded to the stem. Both the handlebars and the stem may be of aluminum, steel or titanium alloy. Steel is often actually lighter than aluminum, if a strong enough alloy with a small enough wall thickness is selected. Titanium is more forgiving on the hands, absorbing some of the shock on account of its low rigidity. All types of bars require a reinforcing sleeve that projects at least one inch on either side of the stem's binder clamp.

Although the old V-shaped stem with double binder bolts holds the handlebars very firmly, the problem is that, with today's shorter frame designs, it gets in the way of your knees when standing on the pedals to climb.

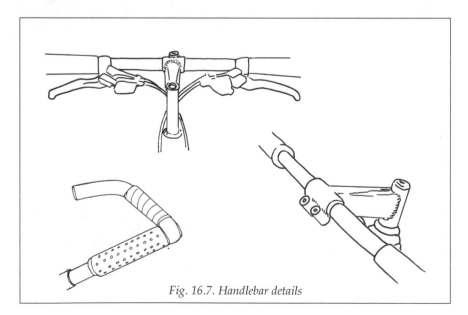

Fig. 16.7. Handlebar details

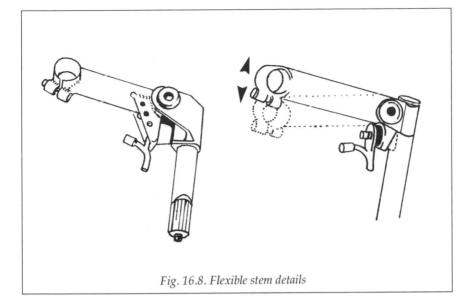

Fig. 16.8. Flexible stem details

Many stems have an integral guide and anchor for the front brake cable; on some models the guide takes the form of a roller, which assures minimum cable friction. Whether with or without roller, it's still a stupid solution, since the brake cable has to be readjusted, and the cable clamped at a different point, whenever the handlebars have been adjusted, even if only slightly.

The stem itself is held in the fork's steerer tube by means of a wedge-shaped item that is pulled into or against the end of the stem by means of an expander bolt. The latter is accessible from the top of the stem. In Chapter 4, you have been shown how to adjust the bars with the aid of this device. Here you will be shown how to replace the stem or the handlebars, which will also be necessary when you want to overhaul the headset or replace the fork.

Bar Ends

In recent years, many mountain bike riders have found that the straight bars do not provide adequate positioning flexibility. Consequently, they have started to mount extensions in the form of handlebar ends, also known as bull-horns, that point forward from the ends of the bars.

Several types are available, as well as bars that have them integrated. The clamp-on conversions may either be clamped around the ends of the straight bars, or they may be installed inside the ends of the bars with an expander bolt, in the same way the stem is held in the steerer tube. You may have to experiment a little before you have found the optimum angle for the bull horns, but once you have, you probably will not want to do without anymore.

167

Replacing Handlebars with Stem

For this job you need an Allan key to match the expander bolt (usually 6 mm), and sometimes a mallet or a hammer. Before you start, release the front brake tension, as explained in Chapter 20.

Removal procedure:

1. Holding the front wheel firmly clamped between your legs, loosen the expander bolt about 4 turns.

2. If the stem comes loose immediately, just pull the combination of stem and bars out.

3. If it does not come loose immediately, raise the wheel off the ground by pulling up from the handlebars; firmly tap on the expander bolt to loosen the wedge, after which the stem should be loose in the steerer tube. If not, put some oil in at the point where the stem disappears inside the upper headset locknut, and try again after waiting a few minutes. Pull the combination of handlebars and stem out of the top.

Installation procedure:

1. Put some vaseline or similar lubricant on the part of the stem that goes in the steerer tube.

2. Make sure the expander bolt is loose enough to fit in line with the stem, yet not so loose that the wedge can be turned more than part of a turn. If a conical expander is used instead of a wedge, the ribs on the outside of the cone should lie inside the slots in the stem.

3. Straddle the front wheel, clamping the front wheel between your legs. Insert the stem in the steerer tube at the upper headset. Lower it as far as seems comfortable, making sure at least 6.5 cm (2.5 in) of the stem is seated inside the steerer tube, which is the minimum safe insertion depth.

4. Holding the handlebars straight and at the desired height, tighten the expander bolt firmly.

Replacing Handlebars or Stem Separately

To sever the connection between stem and handlebars, or to install the one on the other keep the stem on the bike, so you can use the latter for leverage. You need an Allan key to fit the binder bolt and usually a big screwdriver. Before you proceed to the actual work, release the brakes, as described in Chapter 20; then remove the hand grip, the brake handle and the thumb shifter on at least one side of the bars.

Removal Procedure:

1. Holding the bike from the front, clamping the front wheel between your legs, undo the binder bolt or bolts on the stem that hold the hand handlebars by four or five turns.

2. See whether you can twist the bar out from the stem. Usually the stem fits around the bar too tightly. In that case, use the big screwdriver to wedge open the stem's binder clamp, perhaps after removing the binder bolt or bolts altogether. Twist the bar while pushing it out of the stem until it can be re moved.

Installation procedure:

1. Apply a thin layer of vaseline to the part of the stem that goes in the steerer tube.

2. Remove any accessories that may be installed, at least from one end of the handlebars. Hold the bike from the front, clamping the front wheel between your legs. If you are installing a new item, ascertain that bar and stem match with respect to bar diameter.

3. Open up the stem's binder clamp, while guiding the bar through. When it is centered, tighten the binder bolt somewhat.

4. Move to the rider's position and put the bar in the desired orientation, then tighten the binder bolt fully.

5. Install the various accessories on the handlebars.

Different Handlebar Designs

Although most mountain bike riders love the flat bars that make it so easy to reach the brake levers, some more experienced cyclists prefer drop 'racing' bars, even on their off-road machine. Some manufacturers supply their top hybrid bike equipped with a spread out version of drop bars.

Comparison of regular and oversize headsets for mountain bike use.

photo courtesy Gary Fisher Bicycles

169

To get at least more leverage, which is considered desirable off-road, you may spread the ends of regular drop bars to about 50 cm (20 in). Again, bars and stem must match with respect to diameter.

Handgrips

Rigid or foam plastic handgrips are typically used on mountain bikes. The most comfortable are models made of a relatively firm type of foam.

To remove or replace them, you may have to add a drop of dishwashing liquid between grip and bar lifting the grip locally with a screwdriver. To avoid loosening the grips unintentionally, remove all traces of the liquid before installing the handgrips. If you use drop bars, you should probably install foam sleeves, such as Grab-On, rather than conventional handlebar tape, to minimize the numbing effect on the hands caused by vibrations when riding over rough surfaces.

Front Suspension

Several systems of front suspension have been introduced in recent years. The first step was the introduction of titanium stems, which are considerably more flexible than aluminum and steel models, since the high strength of the material allows the use of a relatively modest wall thickness and diameter.

The next step up the evolutionary ladder was the FlexStem, a stem with a built-in spring. Finally came the various telescoping devices that have become popular lately. Some of these use air and oil shock-damper elements that can be regulated by increasing or decreasing the air pressure via a sort of valve nipple on top. These are quite bulky.

Front fork suspension solutions are legion and their number increases from season to season—until the process of natural selection sorts out the useful ones from the gimmicks. In Chapter 22 you will find a comprehensive treatment of the suspension issue.

CHAPTER 17

The Wheels

Nothing characterizes the mountain bike more than its fat-tired wheels. And those fat tires usually carry as pronounced a tread pattern as a pair of vibram-soled hiking boots. But apart from the size and a few other details, the mountain bike's wheels are like those of any other bicycle.

A typical bicycle wheel is shown in Fig. 17.1. It is a tension-spoked wheel with wired-on (also known as clincher) tires. The latter consist of a separate inner tube and a tire that is held on in a deep-bedded metal rim by means of beads that are wire-reinforced. The other components of the wheel are the hub and the spokes that connect the hub with the rim.

The Hub

The hub, shown in Fig. 17.2, forms the heart of the wheel. It may be either attached to fork or frame by means of a quick-release mechanism or by means of axle nuts. These days, the former solution is often chosen for almost all mountain bikes, to allow easy wheel removal for transporting the bike. Although theoretically the solid axle used for wheels that are held with axle nuts is slightly stronger, modern quick-release hubs have

Several different mountain bike wheel hubs:
Top right: SunTour XC hubs with quick-release.
Bottom left: Campagnolo hubs without quick-release—the solid axle is somewhat stronger.
Bottom right: Wilderness Trail Bicycles hub with Grease-Guard lubrication fittings.

photo courtesy SunTour

photo courtesy Shimano

photo courtesy WTB

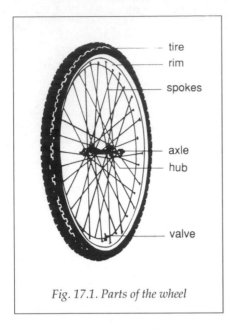

Fig. 17.1. Parts of the wheel

with flanges, to which the spokes are attached. The wheel axle is suspended on a set of bearings inside the hub shell. Bearings may be either of the adjustable type shown or non-adjustable cartridge bearings. Either way, they should be equipped with good dust seals for mountain bike use. The hub must have the same number of spoke holes as the rim, usually 36, but sometimes only 32.

Wheel Removal and Installation

Taking the wheel out and putting it in is a matter of undoing the axle nuts or the quick-release. Although this is a very basic operation, it bears some instructions to do it effectively. In the case of a wheel with axle nuts, you need a matching wrench. For the rear wheel, you may need a rag to keep your hands clean while holding back the chain. Proceed as follows:

proven quite adequate for mountain bike use. If the hub does not have a quick-release, the preferable type of axle nuts are those with integral washers.

As shown in the illustration, the hub consists of a hollow shell

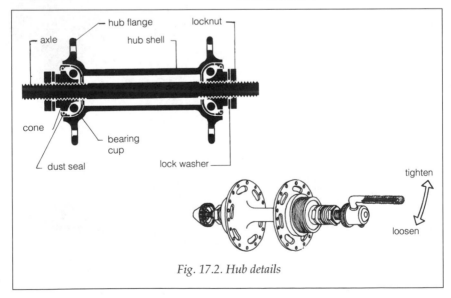

Fig. 17.2. Hub details

Removal procedure:

1. Either support the bike upright with the wheel off the ground, or turned upside-down, supported so that nothing on the handlebars gets damaged. When removing the rear wheel, select a gear with the smallest sprocket in the back and either the intermediate or the small chainring in the front, to minimize tension on the derailleur and the chain.

2. Loosen the axle nuts on both sides or undo the quick-release. The latter is loosened by twisting the lever into the 'open' position (see note below).

3. Release or open the brake. On a cantilever or U-brake, do that by removing one end of the straddle cable; by twisting the cam out from between the rollers on a cam-operated brake. With either type, push the brake arms against the rim to release the cable tension while releasing the cable nipple or the cam plate.

4. Pull the wheel out. For the rear wheel, hold back the chain by means of the derailleur as shown in Fig. 17.3.

Installation procedure:

1. Take the preparatory action described under points 1, 2, and 3 under *Removal procedure.*

2. Keep any brake parts out of the way while inserting the wheel, and hold back the derailleur on the rear wheel.

3. Align the wheel carefully, so that it has the same clearance on both sides, and the brake blocks match the sides of the rims when the brake arms are pushed together. Tighten the axle nuts or the quick-release lever (see note), while holding the wheel in the right position.

Note:
The quick-release is not opened or closed by unscrewing or tightening the thumb nut, but by twisting the lever in the appropriate direction to tighten or loosen the internal cam mechanism. Only if the wheel does not come out with the lever set in the *open* position, should you loosen the thumb nut one or two turns. Do not forget to tighten it again when installing the wheel *before* twisting the lever.

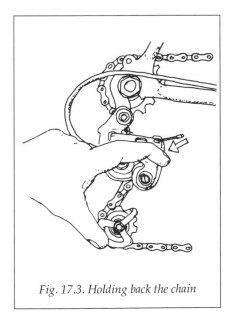

Fig. 17.3. Holding back the chain

173

Hub Maintenance

Virtually all hub bearings are packed with grease for lubrication. By and by, dirt and moisture enter the hub and mix with the grease, causing wear. The best solution is to install hubs with Grease-Guard fittings, which have chevron-sealed bearings and a grease nipple. Use the matching grease gun to inject the grease. On other hubs, disassemble the bearings and replace the grease at least once a year following the instructions below.

When the hub bearings are too loose or too tight, it is time to lubricate and adjust the hub bearings. You will need an open-ended wrench and a set of cone wrenches in sizes to match the make and model of the hubs, purchased from a bike shop. Refer to Fig. 17.2, and proceed as follows (after the wheel has been removed from the bike):

1. Loosen the locknut on one side, while holding the underlying cone with one of the cone wrenches. When adjusting, back it off only two turns. Unscrew the locknut all the way to repack or overhaul the bearing.

2. To adjust, merely lift the lock washer a little, then adjust the cone relative to the opposite cone (to loosen) or the opposite locknut (to tighten).

3. To repack the bearings, remove lock washer and cone, after which the axle can be removed; catch the bearing balls. Clean and inspect everything, repack the cups with grease and insert the bearing balls. Reassemble it in reverse order.

4. When the cone is adjusted so that the bearings turn freely without play, and the lock washer is in place, tighten the locknut, while holding the cone with the cone wrench.

5. Inspect the bearing once more. Tightness is most easily detected with the wheel removed, looseness with the wheel installed on the bike.

The Spokes

The spokes, shown in Fig. 17.4, should be of stainless steel. Each spoke is held to the hub flange by its head, and to the rim by means of a screwed-on nipple. The latter should be kept tightened to maintain the spoke under tension. This actually prevents a lot of spoke breakage.

The spokes run from the hub to the rim in one of several distinct patterns, two of which are shown in the illustration: 2-, 3-cross and 4-cross. The latter pattern appears to be most suitable for the rear wheel, as it has been demonstrated to hold up best.

The rim, with the tire, must be centered over the ends of the bearing locknuts. On the rear wheel, this normally creates a significant off-set relative to the hub flanges, due to the presence of the freewheel on the RH side. The illustration also shows several ways the wheel may be centered. The usual off-set at the rear wheel results in much higher forces on the spokes leading to the RH flange than in those on the LH side of the wheel. This frequently leads to broken spokes on the RH side and makes it hard to keep the wheel trued. A noticeable improvement ensues when a special balanced hub is used in the rear, such as the Shimano Cassette Freehub, which has the freewheel built in, resulting in a more nearly equal spoke tension and fewer wheel problems.

The length of the spoke is measured as shown in the illustration. It depends on the actual rim size, the type of hub and the spok-

ing pattern. Before replacing a broken spoke, or when buying spares to take on a longer tour, check which sizes are needed for your wheels. They may be different for front and rear, and in the rear even from one side to the other.

The strength is a function of the thickness. At least 2.0 mm (14 gauge or less) is the minimum required for off-road use. Butted spokes have a thinner section in the middle. They are as strong as regular spokes that are as thick as their thickest section (the lower gauge number in their size designation). If a spoke should break, carry out a repair according to the following description:

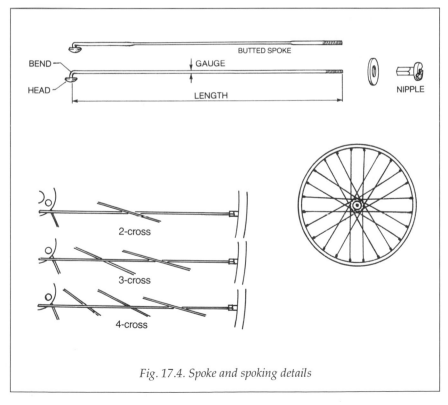

Fig. 17.4. Spoke and spoking details

Replacing Broken Spoke

1. Remove the freewheel, if the hole in the hub that corresponds to the broken spoke lies inaccessibly under the freewheel.

2. Remove the old spoke. If possible, unscrew the remaining section from the nipple, holding the latter with a wrench. If this is not possible, the tire must be deflated and locally lifted first, after which the nipple may be replaced by a new one.

3. Locate a spoke that runs the same way as the broken one: every fourth spoke along the circumference of the rim runs similarly. Check how it crosses the various other spokes that run the other way, using it as an example.

4. Thread the nipple on the spoke until it has the same tension as the other spokes of the wheel, or on the same side of the rear wheel.

5. If the spokes do not seem to be under enough tension, tighten all of them half a turn at a time, until they all seem equally taut and the wheel is reasonably true. If necessary, follow the instructions for *Wheel Truing* below to correct the situation.

Note:

For an emergency repair of the spokes on the (inaccessible) RH side of the rear wheel, you may carry some special bent spokes, made from oversize spokes, bent according to Fig. 17.5, and hooked in the hub flange without removing the freewheel. Take the bike to a bike shop to get these provisional spokes replaced as soon as possible. You can also do it yourself, after removing the freewheel, or the stack of sprockets from a cassette unit, following the instruction in Chapter 18.

The Rim

Fig. 17.6 shows typical rim cross sections. For a mountain bike of any quality, the rims must be made of aluminum. In addition to being light, aluminum ensures much better braking when wet than the chrome plating used on steel rims.

The rim should match the tire, which will be discussed below. The trend in recent years has been towards narrower rims. Right now, the universally preferred

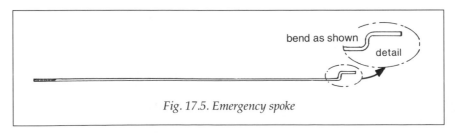

bend as shown

detail

Fig. 17.5. Emergency spoke

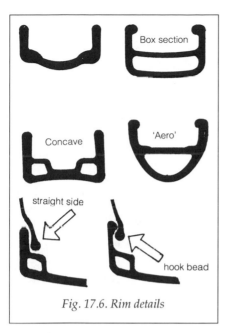

Fig. 17.6. Rim details

The spoke holes in the rim should be reinforced by means of ferrules. To protect the tube, a strip of rim tape should cover the part of the rim bed where the spoke nipples would otherwise touch the inner tube.

Wheel Truing

If the rim is bent, it may or may not be the result of a broken spoke. Either way, you will have to straighten it by retensioning certain spokes. After checking to make sure all spokes are intact, and replacing one that is broken, proceed as follows, as shown in Fig. 17.7:

mountain bike rim seems to be 20 mm wide (measured inside). Stronger models tend to be those that are a little heavier but well worth the extra weight.

1. Establish where it is offset to the left, where to the right, by

Fig. 17.7. Wheel truing details: Left: Correcting radial misalignment; right: lateral misalignment

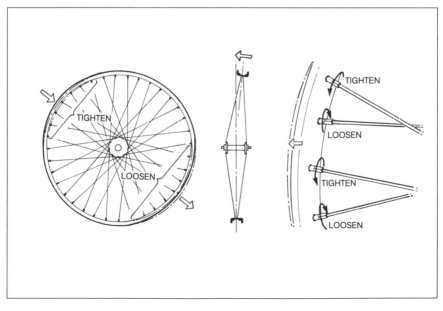

turning it slowly while watching at a fixed reference point, such as the brake shoes. Mark the relevant sections.

2. Tighten LH spokes in the area where the rim is off-set to the RH side, while loosening the ones on the LH side and vice versa.

3. Repeat steps 1 and 2 several times, until the wheel is true enough not to rub on the brake. This will get you by but, unless you are quite good at it, I suggest you get the job done properly by a bike mechanic as soon as possible.

The Tires

The size of the tire defines the nominal size of the wheel, although the nominal size does not necessarily coincide exactly with the wheel's actual outside diameter. To give an example, fat 26-in tires normally measure as big in circumference as some tires referred to as 700 mm, although 700 mm would be more like 28 in.

The rim for a mountain bike tire has a rim bed diameter of 559 mm. Add to that twice the actual tire cross section, and you have the tire's outside diameter, illustrated in Fig. 17.8. Even though this system has been adapted as a (worldwide) ISO standard, it continues to be ignored by U.S. and some Asian manufacturers, who seem to prefer bewildering their customers with designations that bear little reference to the actual dimensions.

See Chapters 2 and 3 for advice on selecting the appropriate tire width and pressure for the terrain you will encounter.

Most people have the mistaken notion that a tire's rolling resis-

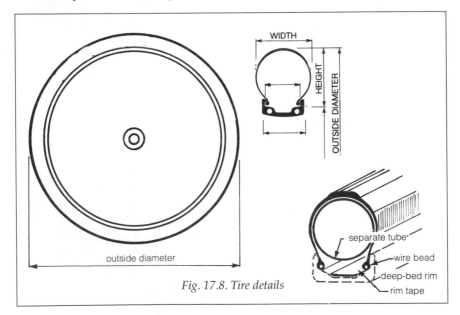

Fig. 17.8. Tire details

tance necessarily increases with its width. Actually, the rolling resistance of a tire is a function of the extent to which the tire or the road deform at their contact area. The LH detail of Fig. 17.9 illustrates this. Clearly, on a smooth hard road, the only way to fly is with a tire that is inflated really hard. On soft or rocky ground, on the other hand, that tire had better be a little softer.

Soft ground calls for pressures of no more than 1.7 bar (25 psi) at low speeds, a little higher at higher speeds. On smooth asphalt or other smooth hard surfaces, you may go all the way to 6 bar (75 psi) for high-speed cycling. All other combinations lie somewhere in between. Experiment with tire pressures for different kinds of riding, frequently checking with a tire pressure gauge, until you have developed a feel for the pressure that is best for certain conditions.

To judge a new tire before buying, note that a light and flexible model stretches as shown in the illustration, and it should have easily deformable sidewalls. All these factors are associated with better running characteristics. Select a diameter, a weight and a tread pattern that matches your needs.

There are numerous different tread patterns. What will be best for you depends on where and how you ride. The very knobby tires that are characteristic of early mountain bikes are still ideal for off-road cycling, especially on soft ground or snow. Knobs that are offset relative to one another, so that distinct interruptions are formed between rows of knobs along the circumference, provide best-soft ground traction. Patterns on which the knobs are offset in a continuous pattern provide less rolling resistance. Very durable are

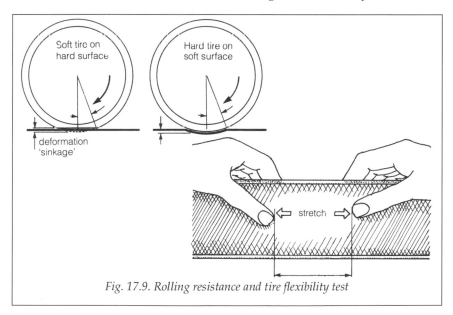

Fig. 17.9. Rolling resistance and tire flexibility test

tires with a so-called negative tread pattern, with large projections and small recesses, such as the very fine Continental tires. Patterns with a raised center ridge provide neither good traction nor particularly low rolling resistance, and they handle unpredictably in curves.

The perfectly smooth tires, called *slicks*, that have become available for mountain bikes as well as for ten-speeds, work only under certain circumstances. They are fine on regular roads and hard rocky surfaces, even when it is wet. On rough rocky surfaces they should be inflated to a low pressure; otherwise, especially when it is wet, they work best when inflated to their maximum pressure.

For icy conditions, there are studded tires. The Finnish Nokia company has made them as long as I can remember, but hard to get in the U.S. These studded tires are presently available only in versions to match the European 650 and 700 mm wheels with the larger diameter 584 and 622 mm rims, respectively. The latter size fits on any hybrid bike, while the former size would require the brake pivots to be mounted in a different location, a little farther from the wheel axle. More recently, IRC has introduced its studded Blizzard tire in the U.S., which is available in a size to match the standard 559 mm mountain bike rim.

Tube and Valve

The inner tube is inflated by means of a valve, several types of which are illustrated in Fig. 17.10. By far the most suitable is the Presta valve, since it requires much less force to inflate properly. Unscrew the round nut at the tip

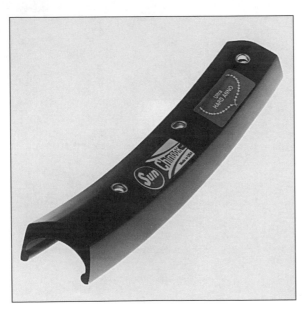

Sun Shinook mountain bike rim in cross section. By and large, the more metal there is in cross section, the stronger the rim. However details such as the presence of ferrules around the spoke holes are equally important.

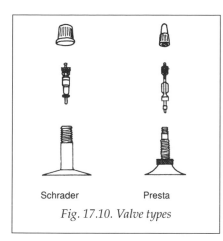

Schrader   Presta

Fig. 17.10. Valve types

before inflating, and tighten it again afterwards. Unfortunately, Presta valves can't be inflated with a gas station air hose, unless you have an adapter nipple. And even if you do, chances are the thing leaks air. This is the reason most manufacturers still install tubes with the cruder Schrader valves used on car tires.

The tube should preferably match the size of the tire, although most tubes stretch enough to go anywhere from 1.5 to 1.9 in (for the narrower ones), or from 1.75 to 2.2 in cross section (for the wider ones), respectively. The lowest rolling resistance is offered by the lightest and most flexible tubes.

Thin latex tubes are the lightest and provide the lowest rolling resistance. Use them only for tires that have about the same nominal cross section, since they don't hold the air properly if stretched too much. At the other extreme, very thick butyl tubes lend themselves to terrain with thorns and other tiny, sharp objects. They offer little advantage in other conditions,

since the typical flat is not caused by a penetrating pointed item, but in the sidewall area when the tube gets pinched between the rim and a hard object.

Finally, there are tubular tires. These are also referred to as sew-ups in the U.S. or tubs in Britain. Formerly only used on track and road racing bikes (where they are slowly being edged out by high-pressure regular tires), they actually hold more promise in off-road cycling. Since they are not as likely to be pinched between the rim and a rock due to the absence of a narrow rim edge, they are very satisfactory in mountain bike sizes, providing the lowest weight and the lowest rolling resistance.

Fixing a Flat

Sooner or later every cyclist gets a flat, and you should be able to handle this repair yourself. Carry a puncture kit, three tire levers, a pump and perhaps a spare tube. The adhesive quality of the patches in your kit deteriorates over time, so I suggest replacing them once a year. Proceed as follows:

1. Remove the wheel from the bike. On a rear wheel, first select the gear with the small chainring and sprocket, then hold the chain with the derailleur back, as shown in Fig. 17.3 at the beginning of this chapter.

2. Check whether the cause is visible from the outside. If so,

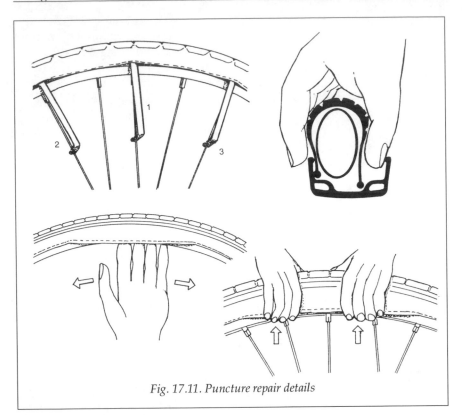

Fig. 17.11. Puncture repair details

remove it and mark its location so that you will know where to work.

3. Remove the valve cap and unscrew the round nut (if you have a Presta valve); then remove the locknut at the base of the valve stem, if installed.

4. Push the valve body in and work one side of the tire into the deeper center of the rim.

5. Put a tire iron under the bead on that side, at some distance from the valve, then use it to lift the bead over the rim edge and hook it on a spoke.

6. Do the same with the second tire iron two spokes to the left and with the third one two spokes to the right. Now the first one will come loose, so you may use it in a fourth location, if necessary.

7. When enough of the tire sidewall is lifted over the rim, you can lift the rest over by hand.

8. Remove the tube, saving the valve until last, when it must be pushed back through the valve hole in the rim.

9. Try inflating the tire, and check where air escapes. If the hole is too small to see, pass the tube

slowly past your eye, which is quite sensitive. If still no luck, dip the tube under water a section at a time: the hole is wherever bubbles escape. Mark its location and dry the tire if appropriate. Check the whole tube, since there may be more than one hole.

10. Make sure the area around the patch is dry and clean, then roughen it with sand paper or the scraper from the puncture kit, and remove the resulting dust. Treat an area slightly larger than the patch you want to use.

11. Spread a thin, even film of rubber solution on the treated area. Let dry about 3 minutes.

12. Remove the foil backing from the patch, without touching the adhesive side. Place it with the adhesive side down on the treated area, centered over the

hole. Apply pressure over the entire patch to improve adhesion.

13. Sprinkle talcum powder from the patch kit over the treated area.

14. Inflate the tube to a moderate pressure and wait long enough to make sure the repair is carried out properly.

15. Meanwhile, check the inside of the tire and remove any sharp objects that may have caused the puncture. Also make sure no spoke ends are projecting from the rim bed—file flush if necessary and cover with rim tape.

16. Let enough air out of the tube to make it limp but not completely empty. Reinsert it under the tire, starting at the valve.

17. Pull the tire back over the edge of the rim without using a tool.

The mountain bike's relatively wide tire and rim make it easy to push the tire over the rim by hand. In fact, some people even manage to remove the tire without tire levers.

photo H. C. Smolik

Start opposite the valve, which must be done last. If it seems too tight, force the part already installed deeper into the center of the rim bed, working around toward the valve from both sides.

18. Make sure the tube is not pinched between the rim and the tire bead anywhere, working and kneading the tire sidewall until the tube is free from the tire and the rim.

19. Inflate the tire to about a third of its final pressure.

17. Center the tire relative to the rim, making sure it lies evenly all around on both sides, then install the locknut.

21. Inflate it to the final pressure, then install the wheel. If the tire is significantly wider than the rim, you may have to release the brake and tighten it again afterwards. For the rear wheel, hold back the chain with the derailleurs set for a small chainring and a small sprocket.

Note:

If the valve leaks, or if the tube is seriously damaged, the entire tube must be replaced. Follow the relevant steps of these same instructions. Replacement of the tire cover is done similarly. Always make sure the rim tape covering the spoke ends is intact.

CHAPTER 18

The Drivetrain

The mountain bike's transmission comprises the various components that transmit the rider's effort to the rear wheel: bottom bracket, cranks, chainrings, pedals, chain, and freewheel. The derailleur system, which allows this transmission to operate at the desired gear ratio, will be treated separately in the next chapter.

Although each one of the components described here is also installed on other bikes, most of them are designed differently for mountain bike use. This is necessary to stand up to the particular kind of treatment they receive off-road. Even so, since the early days of mountin biking, most of these components have gone through some changes, making them lighter easier-running.

The Crankset

The crankset can be considered the heart of the drivetrain. It comprises several different components, which will each be described in the following sections. These are the bottom bracket with its bearings, the cranks, and the chainrings. Generally, all these components are supplied as a group of matching parts by the

The heart of a modern mountain bike's drivetrain. This one has a cartridge bottom bracket held in place with two Allen bolts.

photo courtesy Gary Fisher Bicycles

185

same manufacturer. However, it is entirely possible to select parts from various manufacturers or different models to make up the system.

The Bottom Bracket

Sometimes referred to as crank hanger in Britain, the bottom bracket is the set of bearings that lie in the frame's bottom bracket shell, together with the spindle or axle to which the cranks are attached. For mountain bikes, two types are in common use: the conventional adjustable BSA bearing and the system with cartridge bearings, both shown in Fig. 18.1. On both types, the spindle usually has tapered square ends for the installation of cotterless cranks.

On high-quality bottom brackets, the spindle is hollow and the cranks are held with bolts, where-

as some cheaper models use solid axles with threaded protrusions to which the cranks are held with nuts—once these have been disassembled, they'll hardly ever get back together firmly enough, always making creaking noises.

Although the cartridge bearing is often thought to be superior, the size of the bearings relative to the total unit is actually bigger on the adjustable model, which makes that one stronger, all else being equal.

As long as parts of adequate quality are used and they are adjusted and lubricated regularly, a regular BSA bottom bracket can give excellent service. They are certainly not inherently inferior to the cartridge bearing variety, as is sometimes implied.

If you've never heard of cartridge bearing units, it's because of the almost universal use of the incorrect term *sealed bearing*,

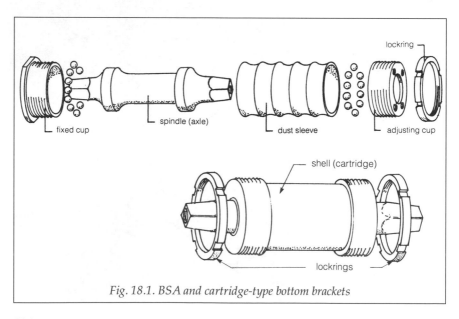

Fig. 18.1. BSA and cartridge-type bottom brackets

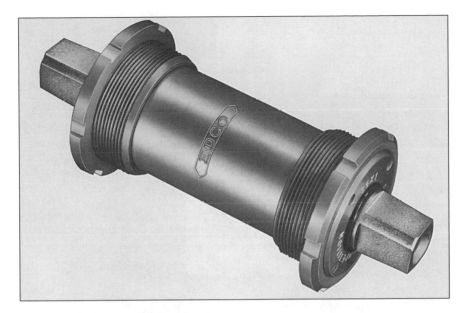

photo courtesy Ed. Dubied S.A.

Edco cartridge bottom bracket unit held in place by means of lockrings.

when, in fact, cartridge bearing is meant. Either type of bottom bracket can be provided with seals to keep dirt out and lubricant in. Neither type can be perfectly sealed, so some cleaning and lubrication will be required from time to time. This is easier on the adjustable model than it is on the cartridge type, which may have to be replaced in its entirety.

Bottom Bracket Maintenance

To take a look at the cartridge bearing units first, little maintenance work is possible, or required for that matter. You may succeed in cleaning and lubricating the bearings: A little careful manipulation of the seal with a very thin small screwdriver generally allows you to remove it. Rinsing with a thick oil will both clean and lubricate the unit. The disadvantage is that

you have to keep repeating this process frequently once you start it, since the oil will run out again. Alternately, you can install Wilderness Trails' grease fittings to lubricate this and other bearings with a grease gun. Some high-end Sun-Tour components have these fittings as a standard feature.

The only other maintenance operations you can easily carry out yourself on some cartridge bearing bottom brackets are side-to-side adjustment and replacement. The former may be necessary to adjust the chain line: to align the plane of the middle chainring with that of the middle sprocket (or, on a freewheel with six sprockets, with the middle of the freewheel block). On many designs these units are held in the bottom bracket shell by means of

187

an internal spring clip, in which case the side-by-side adjustment is generally not possible. Other units are equipped with an adjustable lockring on the LH side, allowing this adjustment by loosening the lockring. Subsequently, the whole unit can be moved either to the left or the right, using the special matching bottom bracket tools, and then tightened in the new position.

The conventional way to lubricate any kind of bicycle bearing is with grease, which is packed inside the bearing races where the bearing balls are embedded. This is done in the factory and must be repeated at least once a season for all adjustable units. To do this, first lift the chain off the chainring and remove the cranks, as described in the appropriate sections below. Next proceed as follows, using either improvised tools or preferably, the special wrenches for the particular make and model installed on your bike. These are available from most bike shops.

1. Remove the lockring on the LH side by unscrewing it to the left.

2. Remove the bearing cup on the LH side by unscrewing it to the left, while catching the bearing balls which may lie loose or may be held in a retainer, when it comes off.

3. Pull the spindle out, catching the bearing balls on the other side.

4. Clean all parts and inspect them. Replace anything that is pitted, grooved, damaged or corroded.

5. Generally, the fixed bearing cup can be left in place on the RH side. If it must be replaced, remember that it has LH thread (at least on most bikes sold in the U.S. and Britain). Consequently, it must be removed by turning to the right, and installed by turning to the left.

6. Pack the cups with bearing grease, then reassemble in reverse order and adjust, following the procedure below.

Note:
Although the use of matching special tools is preferable, improvised tools may be used for this and many other jobs—very carefully. To loosen or tighten the lockring, use a blunt screwdriver and a hammer, tapping the lockring from the notches in the circumference. To loosen or tighten the adjustable

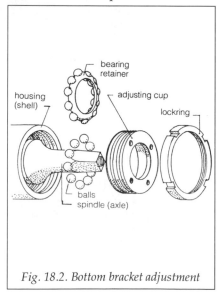

Fig. 18.2. Bottom bracket adjustment

bearing race, use a hammer and a drift or similar roughly pointed object with a blunt end. To remove or tighten the fixed or RH cup, use either a really big adjustable wrench (crescent wrench), or clamp the cup in a metalworking vice with the frame horizontal, and turn the frame. To assure correct alignment, always finish the removal and start the installation process by hand, rather than using tools, whether provisional or not.

Adjusting Bottom Bracket

After overhauling the bottom bracket, or anytime the adjustable bearing is loose, it must be adjusted. Cartridge bearings are not adjustable and must be replaced. This job should be left to a bike shop, unless you have the special tools to do it yourself. To adjust a

BSA bottom bracket, you need the same tools as for overhauling.

1. Loosen the lockring by one turn, unscrewing to the left.

2. Loosen or tighten the adjustable bearing cup as appropriate.

3. Retighten the lockring, making sure the adjustable cup does not turn with it, restraining it with the matching tool.

4. If necessary, repeat the procedure until the bearing runs smoothly without play. Smoothness of operation is checked by hand, preferably with the cranks removed; looseness of the bearings is best established using the leverage of the installed crank.

Today's mountain bike pedals have lost a lot of the weight that was supposed to be necessary in the early days. These are SunTour XC pedals

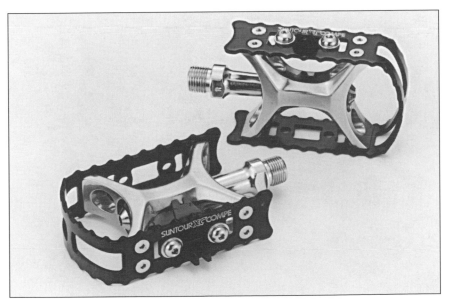

photo courtesy SunTour

189

The Cranks

Virtually all mountain bikes have aluminum cranks that are attached to the ends of the bottom bracket spindle by means of a cotterless device as illustrated. In this system the crank has a square tapered hole that matches the square tapered end of the spindle. A bolt—or sometimes a nut, if the bottom bracket spindle is not hollow but has threaded projections—clamps the crank over the spindle and a dustcap covers the recess from the outside.

The RH crank is equipped with an attachment spider for the chainwheels. The pattern of the holes in the latter varies greatly from make to make and even from model to model. It must correspond to the particular chainrings installed. On a new bike the manufacturer installs cranks and chainrings from the same manufacturer. In fact, a complete standard crankset, including cranks, as well as bottom bracket and chainrings from the same component manufacturer, is generally installed. When replacing either cranks or chainrings, consider the interchangeability restrictions.

The square taper is not standardized. Thus, you may find when replacing either the cranks or the bottom bracket, that a crank either hits the chainstay, or conversely does not seat fully on the spindle. Consult a bike shop to find out what fits and what doesn't. A comprehensive source of interchangeability information in general is *Sutherland's Handbook for Bicycle Mechanics*, which any good bike shop should have available for reference.

SPD (Shimano Pedaling Dynamics) pedals with matching shoes have revolutionized high end mountain bikes.

photo courtesy Shimano

Cranks are made in several different lengths. Some mountain bike riders swear by longer cranks, rather than the standard length of 170 or 175 mm. This dimension is measured from the center of the bottom bracket spindle hole to the center of the pedal hole. If you have longer legs than average, a longer crank of 180 mm or even 185 mm may be justified.

Crank Maintenance

Here, I'll cover two maintenance jobs: tightening and replacement. The crank attachment must be tightened when the square tapered hole is not fully seated on the spindle's square end. The crank has to be replaced when the crank cracks or gets bent and no amount of straightening will do the trick. You can tell when a crank is bent, since the pedal develops a strange wobbling behavior, usually after a fall. Leave the straightening to a bike shop, since it requires a special tool. The simple crank extractor, used for removing and tightening the crank, is something you should buy yourself. Make sure it fits the particular crankset installed on your bike.

Crank Tightening

To do this, you need a crank extractor tool matching the particular make and model of crankset installed on your bike. Actually, you only need the

wrench part of this two-part tool, but you have to buy the whole thing, which should be done when you buy the bike, so that you have it on hand when needed. You will most need it within the first few weeks, when the material of the crank is deforming slightly.

1. Remove the dustcap, using a fitting tool or a coin, depending on its shape.

2. Tighten the bolt or the nut that lies under the dustcap, using the wrench part of the crank tool.

3. Reinstall the dustcap.

Replacing Cranks

This operation may be necessary in order to do bottom bracket maintenance or to replace a defective crank or bottom bracket part. For this work, you need both parts of the crank extractor tool to match the particular make and model of your crankset.

Removal procedure:

1. Remove the dustcap, using a fitting tool or coin.

2. Restraining the crank, unscrew the bolt or the nut that lies under the dustcap. Remove both the bolt or the nut and the underlying washer.

3. Withdraw the inner part of the extractor part of the crank tool and thread the tool into the threaded recess in the crank.

191

4. Restraining the outer part of the tool that is installed in the crank, screw in the inner part, which pulls the crank off the spindle.

5. Restraining the crank, unscrew the tool from the crank.

Installation procedure:

1. Inspect all contact surfaces and all parts, to make sure they are clean and free from serious corrosion or damage. Sparingly apply lubricant to the threaded parts, as well as to the matching surfaces of spindle and crank hole.

2. Place the cranks on the spindle, 180° offset from each other, making sure the one with the chainring attachment spider is on the RH side.

3. Install the washer, followed by the bolt or the nut; then tighten

the latter with the wrench part of the crank tool, restraining the crank.

4. Install the dustcap.

5. At about 50-mile intervals during the first 200 miles, retighten the bolt until it is fully seated.

The Chainrings

These items, also referred to as chainwheels, are available in a wide range of sizes for the mountain bike. Generally, three are installed, as described in the chapters devoted to the gearing system. In this chapter we shall ignore gearing theory and size selection, looking only at the mechanical aspects of the chainrings.

They are attached to the RH crank by one of the methods shown. In my experience, the

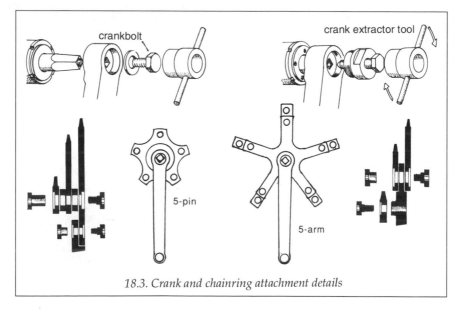

18.3. Crank and chainring attachment details

method shown in the RH detail is generally the more satisfactory. It results in greater strength and rigidity, leading to fewer cases of bent and buckled chainrings. Of course, it also depends on the hardness of the materials used, which accounts for a lot of the price difference between superficially similar cranksets.

For a number of years, most mountain bikes, particularly those intended for less-experienced riders, were equipped with chainrings that are not truly round. The Shimano Biopace design was the most popular of these. Meanwhile they have fallen out of favor. Yet if you want to experiment with them, they are quite interesting in providing a different distribution along the pedaling cycle, by mounting them one way or the other—feel free to rotate them to get a different feel.

Chainring Maintenance

The maintenance operations that may be required comprise straightening a chainring when either the teeth or the entire unit is bent, as well as disassembly or removal to replace one that is worn or damaged. Fig. 18.4 will help you identify a worn chainring.

If only individual teeth are bent, you can grab each of these separately with a crescent wrench that is adjusted to just fit just around the bent tooth. Then bend it back carefully. Inspect the result, replacing any chainring on which

teeth are either seriously damaged, cracked or broken.

If the entire chainring is warped, resulting in intermittent scraping of the chain against the cage of the front derailleur or the RH chainstay, you can use a wedge-shaped piece of wood to carefully straighten it out. A crude roadside alternative may be to use a wide screwdriver instead. If you have particularly soft chainrings, such as some of the cheapest models, you may use a mallet to straighten the entire chainring. If in doubt, I suggest you take it to a bike shop or replace the entire chainring.

To replace the chainrings, simply loosen the bolts that hold them to the spider or to each other, countering at the other side. Take care not to lose any of the bolts, nuts and washers, also noting where each of these parts was installed. In the case of the Shimano

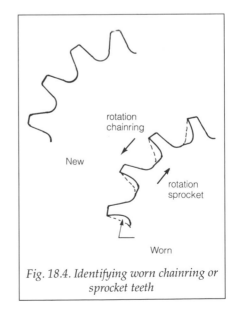

Fig. 18.4. *Identifying worn chainring or sprocket teeth*

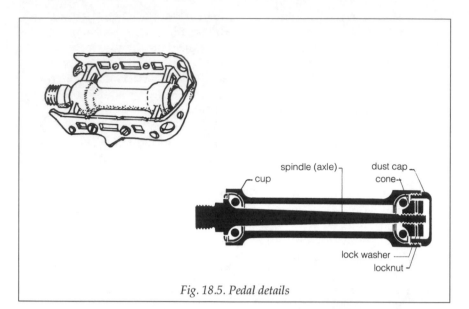

Fig. 18.5. Pedal details

Biopace and other non-round chainrings, observe where the label sits relative to the RH crank and, reinstall it with the label in the same place.

The Pedals

Early mountain bike pedals were designed for more grip on regular shoes than those installed on ten-speed bikes. More recently, riders and manufacturers have found out there is no real advantage to such vicious ragged-looking implements as the 'bear paw' pedals, so now quite elegant pedals are *en vogue*. Some cheap bikes have pedals made of moulded resin-embedded graphite fiber. My preference is for light metal pedals that have angled sides front and rear, because these are the easiest to get on and off, whether with or without toeclips.

At least as important as the pedal's exterior shape are its guts, shown in Fig. 18.5 for a typical mountain bike pedal. The most important difference relative to any old pedal is that there should be a dust seal on the crank side bearing. Some models have cartridge bearings, which are not necessarily superior. Although they are better sealed and probably run perfectly smoothly when new, the cartridge bearings must be replaced in their entirety when they develop play or run rough.

Recently, clipless pedals, which hold the (special) shoes by means of a device reminiscent of a ski binding, have become popular for mountain bikes too. These require the use of a matching shoe. The most common type, Shimano's SPD (for Shimano Pedaling Dynamics), works remarkably well, is reversible, is reasonably light, and can be used with regular shoes. Do avoid non-reversible models that have to be a certain way round to work, because it will be hard to coerce them into the right direction when trying to get your feet in and they will be impossible to ride in regular shoes.

Pedal Removal and Installation

This job has to be carried out whenever either the cranks or the pedals are replaced, or in order to store or transport the bike. All you need is a wrench that fits the stub with which the pedal is screwed into the crank. It is best done with the crank installed on the bike, proceeding as follows:

Removal procedure:

1. Restrain the crank, if necessary with a rod stuck through the frame. To remove the RH pedal, stop the crank from turning counterclockwise, clockwise to remove the LH pedal.

2. Using a thin, flat wrench, grab the flattened section of the stub that is screwed into the crank. If the stub has a hexagonal recess, use an Allen key from the back of the crank to remove the pedal. Unscrew the RH pedal to the left; the LH pedal, which has LH screw thread, to the right.

Installation procedure:

1. Inspect all threaded parts to make sure they are clean and undamaged, then put a little

lubricant on them. To protect the crank face, you may install a thin steel washer that fits around the threaded stub on the pedal axle, also applying a little grease there.

2. Establish which is the RH pedal and which the LH one, consulting the illustration if they are not marked.

3. Carefully aligning the threads, screw the pedal in as far as you can by hand. Holding the crank in place with one hand, screw the RH pedal in clockwise, the LH pedal counter-clockwise.

4. Restraining the crank as appropriate, tighten the pedal with the wrench.

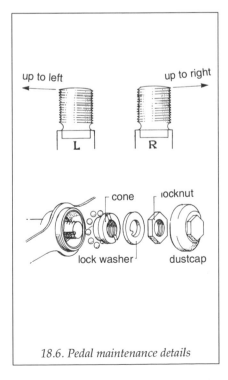

18.6. Pedal maintenance details

Pedal Maintenance

The bearings may have to be lubricated or adjusted when the pedal bearings are loose or do not run smoothly. If the problem cannot be eliminated this way, replace the entire pedal or—if the problem is due to a bent axle—adjust the latter, following the instructions below for assembly and disassembly. You will need a wrench or prizing tool to remove the dustcap, a wrench to fit the locknut underneath, either a wrench or a thin screwdriver to adjust the bearing cone, and sometimes a small screwdriver or Allan key to remove the cage of the pedal if it hinders access to the bearing.

1. Remove the dustcap.

2. Remove the locknut, or merely loosen it 2–3 turns if you do not want to lubricate it or replace any parts.

3. Lift up the keyed lock washer and tighten or loosen the underlying bearing cone as appropriate to adjust the bearing. Remove these parts to overhaul or lubricate the pedal.

4. To overhaul or lubricate, pull the pedal housing off, catching the bearing balls on both ends. Replace or clean and lubricate all the parts, packing the bearing cups with grease, after which the bearing balls are embedded in the grease.

5. Reinstall in reverse order, then adjust as explained under point 3 above.

6. Tighten the locknut, restraining the adjustable bearing cone, e.g. with the thin screwdriver. If the cone can't be stopped from turning, replace the lock washer, making sure the key that fits in the groove of the pedal axle is not worn off so far that the washer can turn on the axle.

7. When the pedal operates smoothly, reinstall the dustcap and, if appropriate, the pedal cage.

The Chain

Mountain bikes are equipped with the same $1/2$ x $3/32$ in chains that are used on other derailleur bikes. These dimensions refer to the length between two consecutive pins, and the internal width between the inner link plates, respectively. The chain should be long enough to wrap around the largest chainring, the largest sprocket and the derailleur pulleys, while still leaving a little spring travel in the derailleur mechanism.

Two typical chain constructions are shown in Fig. 18.7. If the bike has a freewheel block with 7 or 8 sprockets, you should use a narrow chain. These have the same nominal dimensions and the same internal size, but the pins protrude less far. Personally, I don't like the kind of chain with 'bulging' link plates, because they wear and literally stretch. Just the same, the latter are extremely popular on account of their greater lateral flexibility which eases shifting. Shimano's Hyperglide chain is designed to match the Hyperglide tooth pattern on the sprockets, although in a pinch you can use another chain.

Chain Line

The chain line is the orientation of the chain relative to the centerline through the frame. It should preferably be such that the intermediate chainring lines up perfectly with the middle sprocket on a freewheel block with 7 sprockets, the point between the third and the fourth if it has 6, between fourth and fifth if it has 8 sprockets. Unfortunately, this situation is very hard to achieve with a mountain bike, due to the constraints of the bike's geometry. Since the correct chain line results in less lateral twisting of the chain and guaran-

tees the most efficient transmission of power, as well as the smoothest gear shifting possible, you should at least try to optimize it. Corrections to the chain line are made by adjusting the bottom bracket, by inserting spacers, or by straightening the frame if it is bent. These jobs are best left to an experienced bike shop mechanic.

Chain Maintenance

The chain is removed, installed, lengthened or shortened by means of the chain tool illustrated in Fig. 18.8. Frequent cleaning and lubrication of the chain contributes to drivetrain efficiency. Although it is possible to lubricate the chain on the bike, the most thorough way is to remove it. Rinse out in a 10:1 mixture of a solvent, such as kerosene (paraffin in Britain) with mineral oil. The

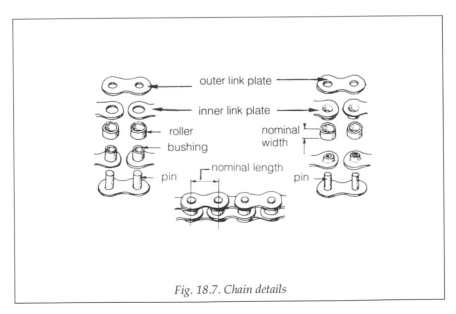

Fig. 18.7. Chain details

mineral oil prevents rust and provides lubrication in hidden nooks and crannies once the solvent has evaporated.

Let it drip dry and then immediately lubricate it with a waxy lubricant, such as special motorcycle chain lube. Wipe the exterior off with a rag. This lubrication will last about six weeks in rainy weather on the road, twice as long in dry weather, but still only one day under dusty off-road conditions.

If you never take the bike out in wet weather, especially if dust is your primary problem, you may consider lubricating the chain in paraffin (American paraffin this time, which is known as candle wax in Britain). Don't heat it directly on the hot plate, but in a

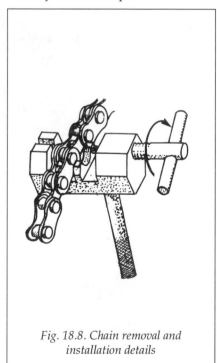

Fig. 18.8. Chain removal and installation details

can that's standing in a saucepan of boiling water. When the paraffin is liquid, take the can out of the boiling water and dip the chain in. Let it soak about one minute, then remove it before the paraffin begins to solidify. Wipe the exterior of the chain with a rag while it's still hot.

Chain Removal and Installation

The chain has to be removed to allow thorough lubrication or to be replaced. It wears with use and must be replaced by a new one from time to time—I'd say once a year. Follow these same instructions to shorten or lengthen the chain.

If the chain seems to jump off the largest sprocket after it has been replaced, it may be due either to a stiff link or a worn sprocket. First check for a stiff link, which can be loosened as explained under point 6 of the *Installation procedure* below. If that does not do the trick, replace the sprocket or the entire freewheel assembly, since this means the sprocket has been worn down by the old chain. To remove or install the chain, all you need is a chain rivet tool and a rag, proceeding as follows:

Removal procedure:

1. Place the tool on one of the pins somewhere midway between chain wheel and sprockets, as shown in the illustration. Turn the handle until the

pin of the tool pushes against the pin of the chain.

2. Turn the handle clockwise by six full turns, which pushes the pin out of the chain far enough without allowing it to come unseated.

3. Screw the handle back, so that you can retract the tool.

4. Wriggle the chain apart. If it can't be done yet, reinstall the tool and give it another half turn or so and try again.

Note:
If you should push the pin out all the way, install some new links, which you can pick up at a bike shop, making sure they are of the same chain make and model. Remove a section of your old chain and insert this part instead.

Installation procedure:

1. To establish the correct length, wrap the chain around the largest chain wheel, the largest sprocket and both derailleur pulleys, passing through the front derailleur cage. Determine its correct length so there is a little spring movement left in the derailleur mechanism, removing or adding links if needed.

2. Place the chain on a combination of the smallest chainring and an intermediate or small sprocket, to release the spring tension in the derailleur, still keeping it routed as before.

3. Place the inside of the protruding pin in the hole of the corresponding link at the other end of the chain, and hold the two ends together.

4. Place the chain rivet tool over the pin and screw the handle in, making sure the pin is pushed through the bushing and comes out the other end. If not, wriggle the various parts relative to each other until they line up.

5. Retract the tool when the pin protrudes equally far as the other pins on both sides.

6. Check whether the links are flexible with respect to each other at this point. If not, twist the chain sideways until they are freed. Alternatively, place the chain in the other slot of the chain tool (the one marked spreader position in the illustration) and gently turn the handle clockwise by about a quarter of a turn to loosen the links. If necessary, repeat from the other side until the chain runs smoothly.

Note:
The Shimano Hyperglide chain can only be disassembled using the matching special tool. This chain has a specially marked link with a black pin, which is the only location to take the chain apart. When reassembling, put in a new one of those special pins and pinch its protruding end off with sharp pliers.

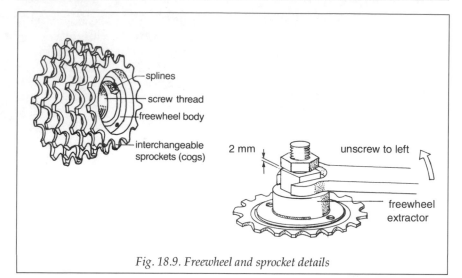

Fig. 18.9. Freewheel and sprocket details

The Freewheel

The freewheel mechanism used to be contained in a separate freewheel block, shown in Fig. 18.9. It comprises both the mechanism and the 6, 7 or 8 sprockets, or cogs. Generally, it is a separate unit screwed onto the threaded portion on the RH side of the rear hub.

Some different solutions more frequently used on mountain bikes include the cassette type hubs, such as Shimano's Freehub (but now similar designs are available from many other manufacturers as well). These include the freewheel mechanism in the rear hub, and the various quick-replacement type freewheels recently introduced by various French manufacturers. The first widely used variant of the latter type was the Maillard Helico-Matic, which most riders find unsatisfactory for mountain bike use due to its tendency to break down when grit gets inside the mechanism.

On cassette hubs, the sprockets are held on splines and are easily replaceable once you unscrew the smallest sprocket with the appropriate tool.

Freewheel Removal and Installation

The freewheel may have to be removed and reinstalled in order to replace a broken spoke on the RH side of the rear wheel. In addition, it may have to be replaced if it is worn or damaged and does not run smoothly, or when the sprocket teeth are worn, so that the chain jumps or skips teeth. You will need a large crescent wrench and a special freewheel tool to match the make and model of the freewheel used on your bike. Special freewheel mechanisms, such as the cassette system are covered separately below. On a regular freewheel, proceed as follows:

1. Remove the rear wheel from the bike (see Chapter 17) and place it in front of you with the freewheel side facing up, after removing the axle nuts or the quick-release.

2. Place the freewheel tool over the splines or notches of your freewheel, then reinstall the axle nut or quick-release with about 2 mm (3⁄32 in) space, as shown in the illustration.

3. Restraining the wheel, e.g. by stemming it with your body against two perpendicular walls in the corner of a room, use the crescent wrench to turn the freewheel tool to the left.

4. After one or two turns, when the freewheel tool hits the axle nut or the quick-release, loosen the nut by another two turns.

5. Repeat steps 3 and 4 until the freewheel comes off easily by hand.

Installation procedure:

1. Inspect all screw-threaded surfaces for damage, wear and cor-rosion. Clean or replace parts as appropriate and lubricate the threaded surfaces using grease or vaseline sparingly.

2. Place the wheel horizontally in front of you with the threaded side of the hub facing up.

3. Carefully align the thread on the freewheel with that of the hub, then screw it on by hand as far as it will go.

4. Final tightening of the free-wheel takes place 'automat-ically' when you have installed the wheel on the bike and you apply force to the pedals.

Cassette Freewheels

More and more mountain bikes are being equipped with these in-tegrated units of rear hub and freewheel mechanism. Their major advantages are easy sprocket re-placement and a less pronounced difference between the LH and RH side of the rear wheel, which leads to less likelihood of spoke breakage, as was explained in Chapter 17.

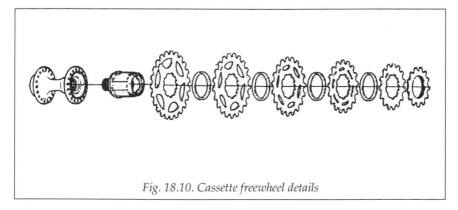

Fig. 18.10. Cassette freewheel details

To replace the sprockets on a cassette hub, use the manufacturer's special wrench to first unscrew the smallest sprocket, then pull off the other sprockets (sometimes also spacer rings) in sequence. Reinstall in reverse order.

The entire freewheel mechanism on these is actually much easier to replace than it is on a hub with a separate screwed-on freewheel: Remove the wheel axle, then use a large Allen key to remove the unit, turning to the right (LH thread). Install the freewheel mechanism by turning the internal Allen bolt to the left.

Freewheel Lubrication

I do not suggest carrying out any involved overhauling or adjusting work on the freewheel. However, it makes sense to lubricate it when it shows signs of imperfect running. If symptoms persist, either take it to a bike shop, replace it with a new one, or consult my *Mountain Bike Maintenance* or John Stevenson's *Mountain Bike Maintenance and Repair* to overhaul the guts of your freewheel.

To lubricate the freewheel mechanism, place the bike on its side with the freewheel facing up and with a shallow can under the other side of the hub to catch excess lubricant. Using an oil can with a thin spout, pour SAE 40 or thicker oil into the gap between the moving and stationary part of the mechanism, turning the freewheel in the freewheeling

mode. If it has a special oil nipple, such as is standard on the SunTour Winner freewheel, enter the oil through it. Either way, keep pouring in oil until what comes out the other side is about as clean as what you pour in. Let it drip, catching the excess, and wipe everything clean when finished. Take the recovered oil to a gas station for disposal.

Micro Drive and Other Novelties

The most recent developments in drivetrain technology include entries from SunTour, Campagnolo, and Shimano to reduce the weight, especially for top-of-the-line mountain bikes. All three now offer systems based on smaller chainrings and sprockets. This way, you can still achieve the same gearing, but with fewer teeth both on the chainring and the sprockets. Not only does the smaller parts save some weight, they also increase the clearance between the ground and the chainrings. Finally, this also makes it possible to keep the cranks a little closer together, a feature some manufacturers refer to as a 'small *Q-factor.*'

Shimano's other entry in this department reduces the weight in the rear by using a freewheel on which the sprockets are not mounted directly to a heavy freewheel block but to an intermediate attachment spider, which also spaces the sprockets more accurately.

CHAPTER 19

The Gearing System

The theoretical aspects of the mountain bike's derailleur gearing system were discussed fully in Chapter 7, while the mechanical details of sprockets and chainrings were covered in Chapter 18. Here we shall concentrate on the derailleur mechanisms and their control devices: shifters and cables.

On the mountain bike, special versions of derailleurs and shifters are used. The derailleurs accommodate the wide-range gearing typically used on these bikes, while the shifters are designed to be installed on the handlebars. Indexed rear derailleurs have taken over on mountain bikes completely in the last few years, replacing conventional derailleur systems, on which there were no definite positions of the shift lever for the individual gears selected.

The Rear Derailleur

Fig. 19.1 illustrates a typical indexed mountain bike rear derailleur. It comprises a spring-tensioned hinged parallelogram mechanism that is free to pivot over a certain arc around the mounting bolt, and to which a spring-tensioned cage with two little wheels, or pulleys, is attached at the other end.

When the cable is pulled or released, the mechanism moves over to the next position to the left

Typical modern gearing system for most mountain bikes, with indexed 21-speed derailleurs—also many bikes now have 24-speed gearing.

203

or the right, corresponding to a different gear. As your pedaling motion pulls the chain forward, it is guided by the two pulleys in the cage to the next sprocket position, engaging the appropriate higher or lower gear. The amount of cable travel is determined by means of the shift lever which in turn also has a ratchet mechanism, stepped to correspond to these same rear derailleur positions.

Even today not all derailleurs are of the indexed type. There are lots of people who bought their equipment years ago, before the advent of the indexed gearing craze, and feel no desire to replace their derailleur system just yet. In fact, some of us more experienced riders still prefer the old-fashioned derailleurs. We only had to develop a little more sensitivity to master the art of shifting. This equipment is quite similar, except that there are no ratchet mechanisms in the shifters.

The wide gearing range of mountain bike derailleurs is achieved with a relatively long cage, with the two pulleys lying quite far apart. Virtually all wide-range derailleurs available in the U.S. are those made by either Shimano or SunTour. European manufacturers offering similar products include Sachs-Huret, Mavic, and Campagnolo. After initial problems, most of these now are just as good as the Japanese competition within the same price category.

Rear Derailleur Maintenance

The most frequent maintenance job on the rear derailleur is the adjustment of the lateral travel for

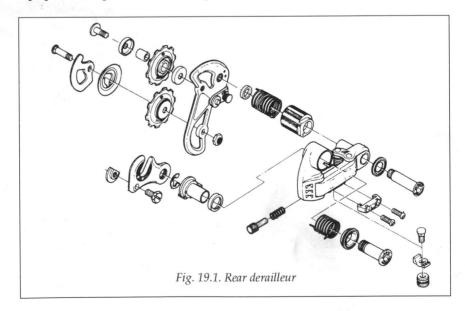

Fig. 19.1. Rear derailleur

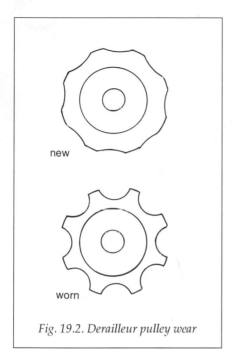

Fig. 19.2. Derailleur pulley wear

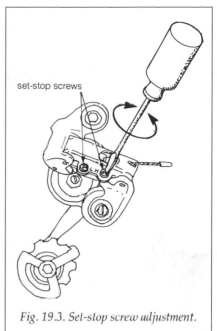

Fig. 19.3. Set-stop screw adjustment.

the cage, if it does not shift the chain over properly.

The derailleur has to be adjusted whenever the chain gets shifted past the biggest or smallest sprocket, or does not get shifted far enough to reach these extreme gears. The other work consists of cleaning, inspection and lubrication.

Clean the entire system after every demanding ride in dirty terrain or wet weather. Work a rag in between the cage and the pulleys as well as in the various other nooks and crannies, wrapping the rag around a narrow screwdriver to reach these tight spots. Replace any damaged or badly worn parts. Especially check the pulleys, of which Fig. 19.2 shows new and worn versions for comparison. To adjust the derailleur, proceed as described in the following section, using a small screwdriver.

Adjusting Rear Derailleur

1. Establish which form of adjustment is necessary. Note whether the chain is pushed too far or not far enough, on the inside for the low gear or on the outside for the high gear.

2. Set the rear derailleur in an intermediate gear by means of the shift lever, pedaling forward with the rear wheel raised off the ground.

3. The derailleur is equipped with two set-stop screws, usually marked with an L for low gear and an H for high gear adjustment. Tightening these screws

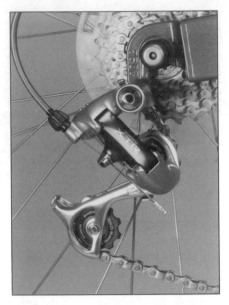

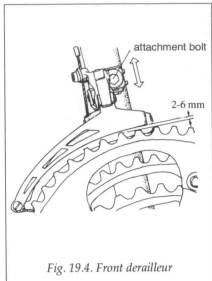

Fig. 19.4. Front derailleur

Shimano XTR rear derailleur set-up with matching freewheel and cogs mounted on a lightweight spider. All this is done to save some ounces off the top-of-the-line bikes.

Next, clean the cable and the mechanisms and lubricate the derailleur, using thin oil. If still no luck, I suggest you take the bike to a bike shop for professional advice.

restricts the derailleur's travel in the corresponding direction, loosening them expands it.

4. Using a small screwdriver as shown, screw in the necessary direction—about half a turn at a time. Repeat the operation, checking the result until you can change properly, without either overshifting or missing the extreme gear.

Note:
If it turns out to be impossible to achieve a satisfactory result, first check the movement of the shift lever and the cable, including its adjustment as explained below.

The Front Derailleur

Shown in Fig. 19.4, the mountain bike's front derailleur, often called changer in Britain, is a much simpler mechanism. It is attached to the seat tube just above the chainrings and consists of a cage through which the chain is guided, attached to a simple hinge or parallelogram mechanism to move it sideways, carrying the chain over to the next chainring. Today, these are not indexed, and there seems little point in it. Move the shifter, pedaling with reduced force, until you notice that it shifts onto the next chainring, then back off a little if necessary to get it to run smoothly without scraping.

As far as maintenance is concerned, there is little to do here. Keep the mechanism clean and the pivots slightly lubricated. Make sure it is attached at the right height and with the cage parallel to the plane of the chainrings. When you can't reach the extreme gear or conversely overshift, dumping the chain, you should adjust the travel of the cage. That's done with the set-stop screws, following essentially the same procedure explained above for the rear derailleur.

New Developments

Many new developments in bicycle componentry are introduced from time to time, though few seem to prove as useful as the manufacturers would have us believe. The most interesting and perfectly operating innovation that I have tried to date was the front gear system introduced by the Browning company, now licensed by SunTour. It is an electronically controlled unit on which the chain is not pushed sideways by a derailleur; instead, sections of the chainrings are hinged to pick up and deliver the chain to the next one.

It worked like a charm, even though I dislike the idea of battery-powered toys on my hitherto perfectly mechanical bicycle. In the meantime, however, the shifting ease afforded by conventional derailleurs with special shaped tooth patterns has made this kind of high-tech approach superfluous.

Another interesting item is SunTour's new derailleur that is mounted directly to the RH chainstay, rather than to the dropout. Although it is technically un-

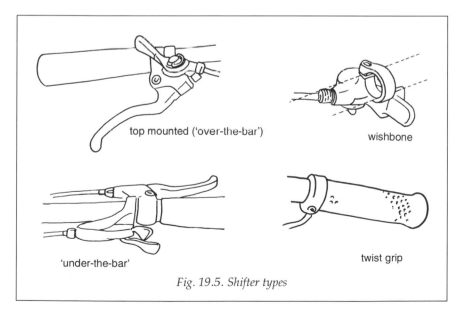

top mounted ('over-the-bar')

wishbone

'under-the-bar'

twist grip

Fig. 19.5. Shifter types

questionable, this is another one of those cases that removes the bike farther from the assembly of standard parts that has made its maintenance so simple. I'd prefer to have standard components.

Shifter Mechanisms

Lately there has been a lot of change in this arena. Up to early 1990 all mountain bikes were shifted with single-lever shifters that were mounted on top of the handlebars. Since then, first double-lever shifters, mounted under the handlebars, were introduced, soon followed by wishbone designs and more recently by the twistring and twistgrip, which work similar to those on a moped.

All of these are fully indexed, both for the front and the rear, meaning that they change gear in definite steps. Only the conven-

tional top-mounted shifters often have an auxiliary lever with which the indexing mode can be overridden in case there are alignment problems, leaving you at least the opportunity to shift in the socalled friction mode, just like older derailleur systems.

To assure the most reliable and predictable shifting possible, make sure shifters and derailleurs are designed for each other. That does not necessarily mean they must be of the same make and model (for instance, Grip-Shift's version of the twistring is specifically designed to work with other manufacturers' derailleurs and really should be a big success in hybrids and beginners' mountain bikes.

Several manufacturers offer a combination brake lever and shifter unit. Only if the two levers are mounted separately, can you get both in the ergonomically op-

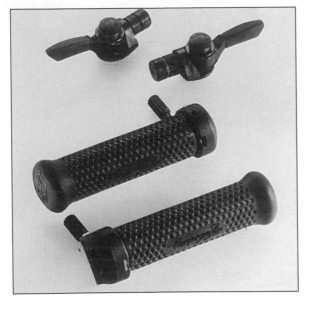

Shifting options from Campagnolo: regular top-mounted indexed shifters and Bullet twist grip shifters.

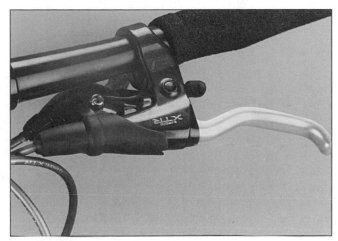

Shimano XTR integrated shift lever and brake lever. Total integration is the word from Shimano, and some of us don't like the idea, although we all agree it works fine—until a small problem forces you to replace several hundred dollars worth of equipment.

photo courtesy Gary Shimano

timum position to match your hand. Twist and turn the attachment until it is convenient to operate, whether changing to a higher or a lower gear both front and rear.

I shall not bore you with the technical details hidden inside the shifters, which pull the derailleur cable in and out to shift the derailleur to the desired position. For the rear, it is always a ratchet mechanism with a spring-tensioned pawl to arrest the lever in positions corresponding to the individual gears. The shifter for the front derailleur may be either a simple friction or a ratchet mechanism. The lever controlling the rear derailleur is mounted on the right, and the one for the front on the left.

One option not mentioned above is the bar-end shifter, which can be used to advantage if your bike has drop handlebars, which are sometimes used on high-quality hybrids. To install bar-end shifters yourself, refer to Fig. 19.4.

Route the cables along the handlebars, and hold them with pieces of tape in some position where they don't get in your way. Then cover the bars with handlebar tape.

Derailleur Cables

The shifters are connected to the derailleurs by means of flexible Bowden cables. The cable for the indexed derailleurs should be relatively stiff and thick, also requiring a larger diameter outer cable,

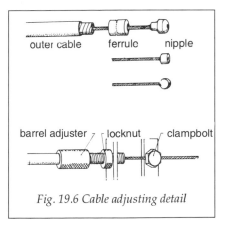

outer cable   ferrule   nipple

barrel adjuster   locknut   clampbolt

Fig. 19.6 Cable adjusting detail

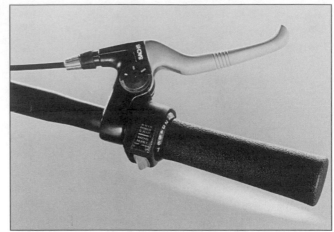

A minor player, but promising products: Sachs offers this Power Grip twist ring and matching derailleurs. Prepare to hear more from this and other Europeans in the near future.

and are usually sold in complete sets of fixed length. Fig. 19.6 shows a cable with its nipple, which is inserted at the shifter end, while the other end of the inner cable is clamped at the derailleur in an eye bolt or under a notched plate with a pinch bolt. Between the shifter and the derailleur, the cable is routed over and through guides mounted on the frame.

Cable Care

The indexed gearing used today require special cables that are rather stiff and run in low-friction sleeves. Other than cleaning and making sure they don't get damaged (and replacing them if they do) these require no maintenance or lubrication.

Remove the inner cables to clean them at least once a season. Lubricate the cable of a non-indexed derailleur with a rag soaked in vaseline or grease. The cable of

an indexed system should be cleaned but not lubricated. At the same time, check to make sure there are no broken strands or frayed ends and that they run freely in the outer cables, which should not be pinched anywhere. Cables are cheap enough to replace if you're in doubt about their condition. Pull the cable taut, with the derailleur and the lever both set for the smallest sprocket in the rear or the smallest chainring in the front, before tightening the pinch screw at the derailleur.

The tension of the derailleur cable may be adjusted when the shifting range cannot be fully covered despite adjustment of the derailleur's set-stop screws. To do this, use the barrel adjuster shown in Fig. 19.6. Hold the barrel while loosening the locknut, then turn the adjuster in the appropriate direction to tighten or loosen, and finally hold the barrel while tightening the locknut again. Check the operation of all the gears, and readjust if necessary.

CHAPTER 20

The Brakes

For anyone who has watched the introduction of new products since its inception, it is remarkable to note that today's mountain bikes are virtually all equipped with the same type of brakes as the first ones: cantilevers. On the other hand, it is equally remarkable how much weight they, and particularly their control levers, have shed in the meantime and how much easier they are to control than the early ones. In this chapter we'll look at theory and practice of mountain bike braking.

Your mountain bike's brakes are important, but not just for coming to a sudden halt. Consider what happens when you come thundering down a steep slope, heading straight for a giant sequoia or whatever clutters the backwoods in your part of the world. You have four choices: run into the obstacle, ride around it, stop before you get there or some combination of the latter two. Usually,

you will use the last option, slowing down to a lower speed, at which you can safely divert to avoid the obstacle. But whatever you do, you need brakes.

From a technical standpoint, whether slowing down or coming

Campagnolo Centaur gruppo, or component group. In addition to the fanciful brakes shown here, it is also available with regular low-profile cantilever brakes.

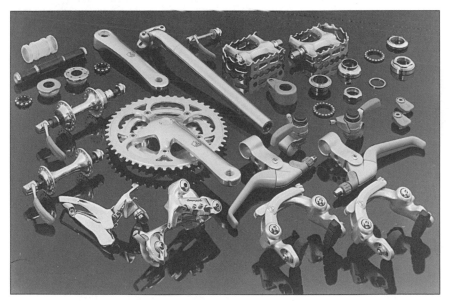

photo courtesy Campagnolo

to a complete halt, you have to decelerate the bike. There's a lot of kinetic energy stored in the moving mass of bike and rider. The brakes are used to dissipate some of that energy. If you did not dissipate the energy by braking, you'd eventually do it by hitting the obstacle—with disastrous results.

In practice, two forms of braking can be distinguished: to regulate speed gently or to come to a sudden stop. Speed regulation is not only the more common, but also the more demanding, since it requires more feeling. Whatever form of braking is practiced, the kinetic energy of the moving mass is transformed into heat.

The amount of heat generated while slowing down gradually or stopping suddenly on a long steep downhill is quite substantial. The predecessor of the modern mountain bike used to be equipped with a coaster brake, also known as a back-pedaling brake, built into the hub of the rear wheel. If you take a look at one of those and consult a high school physics text, you'll be able to figure out why that was not such a good way of braking on a long downhill. You need lots of bare metal surfaces for friction and cooling, and the coaster brake is tiny inside and out, compared to the area of the rim, which represents the friction and cooling surface on a bike with rim brakes.

Types of Rim Brakes

There are several different types of rim brakes suitable for mountain bikes: the cantilever brake, the pivot-mounted roller-cam brake, and the U-brake. Newer versions of the cantilever, referred to as low-profile (more correctly narrow-profile) brakes are similar to the conventional cantilever but are designed in such a way that they don't project sideways as much. These types are all depicted in Fig. 20.1. In countries with more rain and mud than steep hills, you will find mountain bikes equipped with hub brakes. In the U.S., these are rare enough to be ignored here—you will find instructions for handling such brakes in my *Bicycle Repair Book* or *Bicycle Technology*, in case you are interested.

On all rim brakes, a pair of brake blocks is pushed against the sides of the rim when the brake is applied. On the cantilever and U-brake, this is done by means of a cantilever system pulled together with a connecting cable. On the roller-cam brake, the cantilever arms are spread apart at the opposite end by means of a wedge-shaped plate guided between rollers on the brake arms. On all of these, the brake arms are installed on pivot bosses that are attached directly to the fork for the front brake, to the seat or chain stays for the rear brake.

Mountain bike riders are fortunate compared to racing cyclists, because the best brakes for their application are reasonably priced. The paramount criterion for a

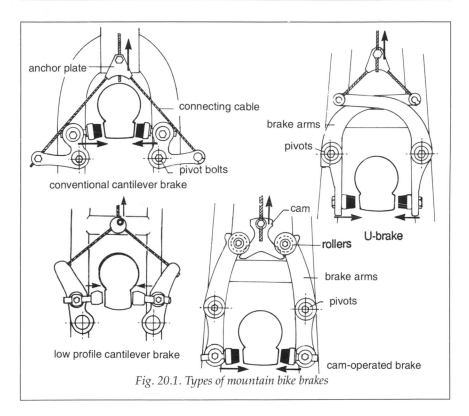

Fig. 20.1. Types of mountain bike brakes

good brake is that it must be rigid, while still opening up far enough to clear the fat tires. All of these designs allow this, although you must ascertain whether the pivot bosses are installed in a position that allows the use of the particular brake you select.

When comparing different versions of the same basic system, look for a type that provides maximum rigidity and smooth operation. One particularly effective brake is the SunTour self-energizing Scott Pederson brake, a cantilever model with a mechanism that increases the pressure between brake block and rim by means of the energy from the rotating wheel. U-brakes and cam-operated models have the advantage that they do not project as far as the original cantilever brake, but the modern low-profile cantilever versions are just as narrow.

Brake Controls

The brake lever, a typical one of which is shown in Fig. 20.2, has lost a lot of weight since the introduction of the first mountain bikes, and tiny two-finger brake levers are *en vogue*—and they do the trick quite well. Since it is easier to design a lever strong enough when it is shorter, this is a rather logical development. The major advantage to the rider is

213

that these levers allow you to hold the handgrip with the free part of the hand while braking with two fingers.

The levers should also be designed very rigidly. It must work smoothly and be easy to reach, while allowing full application of the brake, leaving about 2 cm (¾ in) clearance between the handlebars and the lever. The type of levers designed for mountain bikes are quite suitable for any bike with flat handlebars, providing the attachment clamp matches the bar diameter. If you like to use drop handlebars, you will need normal racing brake levers.

With any rim brake, the force applied by pulling the lever is transmitted to the brake unit by means of flexible Bowden cables, shown in Fig. 20.3. These cables are partly contained in flexible outer cables and restrained at anchor points on the frame. The force is transmitted to the part of the brake unit to which the cable is attached.

All rim brake controls have an adjustment mechanism that allows you to take up any slack in the cable. Although all mountain bike levers have such an adjuster integrated, there may be an additional one at one of the cable anchor points. If you use a drop bar with racing levers, this will be your only adjuster. The adjustment is described below.

Some brakes themselves have a quick-release mechanism to allow easy wheel removal and installation, without affecting adjustment of the brake. If not, they can be loosened by pushing the brake blocks against the rim and at the same time removing the connecting cable on the cantilever or U-brake, or the cam plate on the roller-cam brake, respectively.

Brake cables should not be elastic or 'spungy,' to allow applying adequate force. Relatively thick, preferably stainless steel, inner cables and non-compressing outer cables with a PTFE or other low-friction liner are best for use with any make or model of brake. Brake cables should be routed as short as possible, providing they are not forced into excessively tight bends in any position of the handlebars.

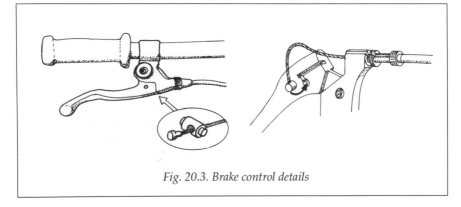

Fig. 20.3. Brake control details

The straddle cable, connecting the two parts of the cantilever brake—especially on low-profile models—must make a rather wide angle of at least 120° to be effective. The most frequent cause of inadequate braking is too narrow an angle, which can be increased by moving in the second clamping point to shorten it, and making the necessary length adjustment of the main cable.

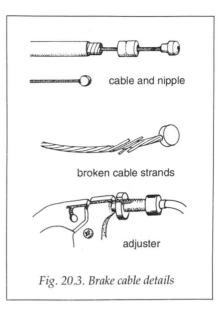

Fig. 20.3. Brake cable details

Brake Blocks

The brake blocks should be of a composition material that provides adequate friction even in the rain, which is not the case with plain rubber brake blocks. Contrary to popular belief, longer brake blocks are not necessarily better. Although they may last longer, they actually provide poorer braking than shorter ones, especially in wet weather. This is due to the fact that the pressure, and thus the ability to remove water between the brake block and the rim, is greater for a smaller brake block, since the pressure is the quotient of the force—which is the same in both cases—divided by the area. Typically, mountain bike brake blocks can be adjusted in all three dimensions.

Brake Check

To make sure the brakes work reliably, check whether they are attached properly and then test them at low speed. Try them out separately at walking speed, which is perfectly safe and still gives a representative test of the deceleration reached with each brake when travelling at speed. Used alone while riding the bike, the rear brake must be strong enough to skid the wheel when applied firmly. The front brake should decelerate the bike so that the rider feels the rear wheel lifting off when it is fully applied. If their performance is inadequate, carry out the adjustment described below.

Be particularly careful to adjust the brake blocks close enough to the rim to assure that the brake block contacts the rim fully when applied. On a cantilever brake, brake block wear left unchecked will eventually cause the brake block to slip off the rim and hit the spokes, whereas on U-brakes and roller-cam brakes the brake blocks will eventually rub on the tire

215

sidewall, which—though not as dangerous—may cause tire wear instead of good braking performance.

Brake Adjustment

Usually the brake must be adjusted because its performance is insufficient. In this case, the cable tension must be increased by decreasing its length. Should the brake touch the rim even when not engaged, the cable tension must be reduced, to lengthen the cable slightly. The adjuster mechanism is also shown in Fig. 20.3.

Before starting, check to make sure the brake blocks lie on the rim properly over their entire width and length when the brake is applied. Ideally, the front of the brake block should touch the rim just a little earlier than the back. If necessary, adjust by loosening the brake block bolt, moving the block as appropriate. Retighten it while holding the brake block in the right position. If necessary, the brake block may be replaced. Proceed as follows:

1. Release brake quick-release if installed.

2. Loosen the locknut on the adjusting mechanism for the brake cable, which on mountain bikes is usually installed on the brake lever.

3. While holding the locknut, screw the barrel adjuster out by several turns; then tighten the

quick-release again, if your brake has one.

4. Check the brake tension: the brake must grab the rim firmly when a minimum of 2 cm (¾ in) clearance remains between the brake lever and the handlebars.

5. If necessary, repeat steps 1 through 4 until the brake works properly.

6. Tighten the locknut again, while holding the adjusting barrel to stop it from turning.

Brake Centering

If the brake drags on the rim on one side, while the other side is still some distance away, the unit must be centered. On cantilever brakes, this is done by bending the springs on the pivots in or out a little. This job can only be done by disassembling the unit, after establishing which pivot spring has to be tightened or opened a little. Use two thin pliers to bend the spring into the required shape. Reassemble and check again—repeat if necessary.

To center a roller-cam brake, each arm has its own separate spring that can be adjusted individually. To do this, first check to make sure the fixing nuts on the brake arm pivot bolts are tight. Then use a 15 mm cone wrench (or any flat open-ended wrench of this size) to turn the pivot bushings immediately under the brake arms by only a very slight angular amount, until the two brake arms are centered relative to the rim.

The U-brake is centered by means of a tiny Allen screw installed vertically down just below one of the brake pivots. Tighten or loosen this screw by one or two turns to bring the brake arm on the same side closer to, or farther from, the side of the rim.

Brake Cable Replacement

To avoid the unsettling experience of a brake cable snapping just when you need it most, I suggest you replace it as soon as individual strands show signs of damage at the end nipple, as shown in the illustration. Since a cable may have to be replaced while you are away from home, you should to carry a spare. Make

sure the spare cable has a nipple that matches the particular brake lever used on your bike. Proceed as follows:

1. Loosen the brake quick-release, if installed, or squeeze the brake arms together, removing the cam plate on the roller-cam brake or the straddle cable on other types of mountain bike brakes.

2. Loosen the eye bolt that holds the cable at the brake anchor plate, until you can pull the old cable out.

3. Push the old cable out, working toward the lever where you can dislodge the nipple as shown in the illustration, after turning the locknut until its slot lines up with the one in the barrel adjuster.

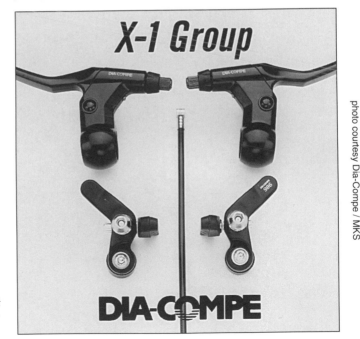

This Dia-Compe cantilever brake set the trend to lighter low-profile brakes.

photo courtesy Dia-Compe / MKS

217

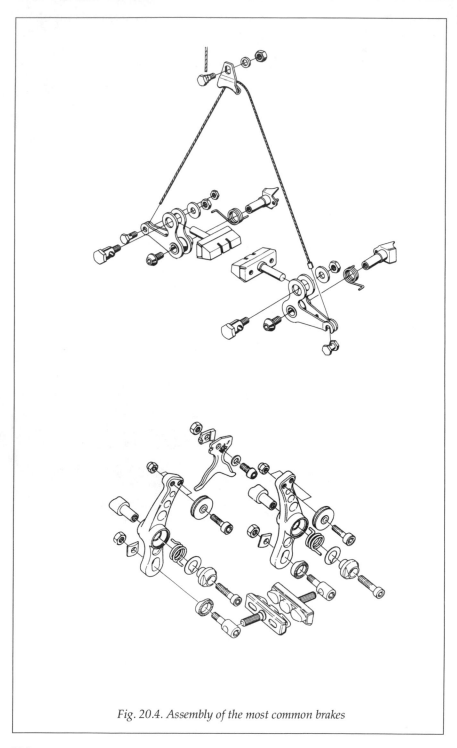

Fig. 20.4. Assembly of the most common brakes

4   Then pull the entire inner cable out, catching the outer cable section or sections, as well as any other parts, memorizing their installation locations.

5. Lubricate the new cable with grease or vaseline. Back off on the locknut, then screw the adjusting barrel in all the way.

6. Starting at the lever, push the new cable through, securing the nipple by pulling it taut. Thread the inner cable through the various anchor points, outer cable sections and other parts. Finally push it through the eye bolt or the pinch plate at the brake.

6. Locate the nipple in the lever's recess, then pull the cable taut from the brake end and tighten the eye bolt or pinch bolt, using tools with enough leverage on both parts of the screwed connection.

7. Adjust the cable tension, following the preceding instruction.

8. Test the brake in operation, followed by a final adjustment if necessary.

9. Finally, cut off the free end of cable until about 3 cm (1¼ in) projects, using sharp cutters.

Overhauling Brakes

Sometimes you may find that no amount of adjusting solves your brake problems. In that case, it is time to overhaul the mechanism. Refer to the exploded views in the accompanying illustrations for cantilever, cam-operated and U-brake, respectively.

Proceed systematically, taking the lever, the brake mechanism, and the cable one at a time. Disassemble, inspect, clean, lubricate and rebuild the items the way they were originally. Replace any parts that are beyond repair. I have included exploded view drawings of some typical assemblies for your guidance. Use your imagination to establish

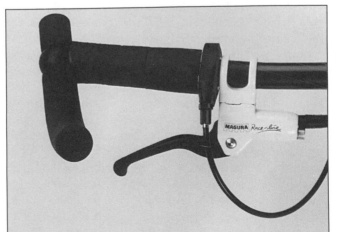

Hydraulic brakes for your mountain bike are here. This Magura brake lever for that same company's hydraulic brake unit has finally caught up with today's trends.

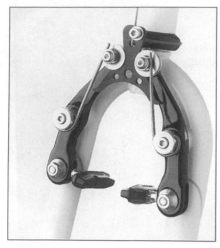

Sole survivor: Wilderness Trail's roller cam brake has outlasted the mass produced models based on the same patent

what may be the problem. Take the bike to a bike shop if you can't solve it.

Other Brakes

Ever since the introduction of the mountain bike, various manufacturers, inventors and tinkerers have tried to improve upon the brakes. Although none have been able to edge out the cantilever in the long run, some are quite interesting. These include the hydraulically operated versions by Mathauser and Magura, as well as a symmetrical U-brake by Campagnolo and the Scott-Pederson self-energizing brake now licensed by SunTour. The advantage of hydraulic operation has long been established in motor vehicles: virtually no resistance in transmission of brake force between the lever and the point of application.

Interestingly, without being aware of the new market, Magura was a factor in early mountain bike development. Magura's moped brake levers were the choice of mountain bike pioneers, long before the major component manufacturers copied their design for mountain bike use.

The other interesting brake is one of Campagnolo's entries. Campagnolo, long the road and track racing component specialist, was a late entrant in the race for the mountain bike rider's favors. On their beautiful U-brake—though rather heavy and outright expensive—the one brake arm has a slot, through which the other brake arm moves. Consequently, the brake arms are not twisted relative to each other as they are on other U-brakes.

The force that can be applied with the rear brake is limited by the flexibility of the seat stays. There are stiffening brackets available that go over the top of a U-brake to reduce the twisting that results without such reinforcement. On front suspension forks, such a bracket is integrated.

Finally, there are even more unusual brakes. Several of the rear suspensions, and one of the suspension forks for the front preclude the use of rim brakes. This is on account of the varying distance between the axis and the rim. In these cases, either drum brakes or disk brakes must be used (in fact, some are sold as a package complete with the fork). Some city bikes also rely on drum brakes.

CHAPTER 21

Saddle and Seatpost

Although the saddle, or seat, and the seatpost that connects it to the frame are not amongst the bicycle's most technically intricate items, they are important for the rider's comfort and justify a chapter of their own. They are shown in Fig 21.1, together with the customary quick-release used on almost all mountain bikes.

The Saddle

On the mountain bike, you will probaby spend more of your time actually sitting on the saddle than in the case of a 10-speed bike with drop handlebars. And since generally a larger proportion of the rider's weight rests on the saddle, due to the different geometry, comfort is something to look out for.

This comfort is enhanced by means of some kind of padding between the nylon base and the thin leather or fabric cover and, at least as important, by the shape.

To be comfortable when a lot of weight rests on a saddle, while still allowing the legs to move freely while pedaling, the saddle should be relatively wide in the back and long and narrow in the front. These criteria are satisfied by most special mountain bike seats these days. Yet women, who tend to have a wider pelvis, should probably look for a model that is even wider in the rear.

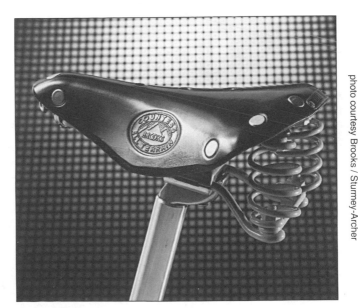

Brooks Countess All Terrain leather saddle.

photo courtesy Brooks / Sturmey-Archer

Choosing the rear portion about 4–5 inches wider than the distance between the two protrusions that make contact with a hard surface when you sit on it gives you about the right saddle under most circumstances.

Personally, I like to use a firm leather saddle, such as the Brooks models with coil springs in the back. These require a special adaptor to mount them to most modern seatposts.

The Seatpost

Today, virtually all mountain bikes come with a forged or cast aluminum micro-adjusting seatpost. The illustration shows various types, all of which will do the job. More important than the adjusting detail is the length: a mountain bike seatpost should be at least 30 cm (12 in) long to allow enough up and down adjustment while still clamped in properly.

There should be a marking on the seatpost indicating how far it may extend outside the seat lug. If there is not, the minimum clamping length should be 65 mm (2½ in). If necessary, measure that point and mark it yourself using an indelible marking pen to make sure it is always clamped in safely.

Recently, in conjunction with the trend towards suspension, a few sprung seatposts have made it to the market. To date, none of them have been very convincing, but such a device could well be made satisfactory if it included a damper to prevent uncontrolled oscillations. Another approach is that of the Allsop, in which the seat is mounted without a seatpost to a fiber composite girder that serves as a leaf spring—quite good for downhill riding but still questionable for other uses.

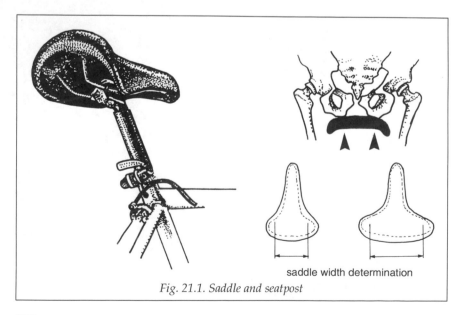

saddle width determination

Fig. 21.1. Saddle and seatpost

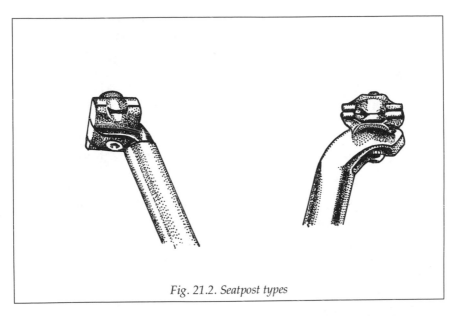

Fig. 21.2. Seatpost types

Quick-Release Binder Bolt

You will occasionally want to lower or raise the saddle to optimize the bike's behavior in difficult terrain. Specifically, you will want to lower the saddle when going down a steep descent. This is achieved easily by means of a quick-release binder bolt shown in the illustration. It is loosened and fastened quickly and conveniently by flipping the lever. If it is too tight or too loose to fully release or hold the seat, first put the lever in the open position and then adjust the thumbnut on the other side. Some frame builders don't use quick releases, and that's OK.

Hite-Rite

The up-and-down adjustment of the saddle is greatly eased by the installation of a Hite-Rite seat ad-

justing spring. Developed by mountain bike pioneer Joe Breeze, it is clamped between the eye of the seat lug and the appropriate point on the seatpost. First install it loosely, then adjust the saddle height, and finally tighten the clamp on the Hite-Rite.

The main advantage is that the seat remains perfectly aligned when you quickly adjust the height. Even if you are not too impressed by the effect it has on

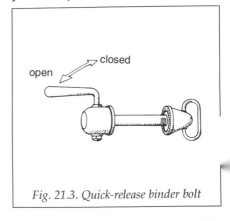

Fig. 21.3. Quick-release binder bolt

223

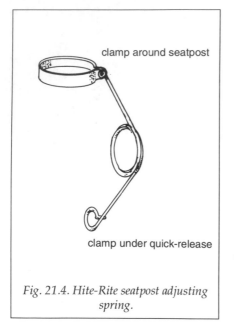

clamp around seatpost

clamp under quick-release

Fig. 21.4. Hite-Rite seatpost adjusting spring.

adjusting the seat height, it has at least one other benefit: it discourages seat theft.

Saddle and Seatpost Maintenance

The jobs described here will be adjustment of the position of the saddle (also called seat), replacement of saddle and seatpost, and any maintenance needed on a leather saddle.

Adjusting Saddle Height

In this and the following descriptions, we shall merely explain how the actual adjustment operations are carried out, assuming you know how high you want it to be.

1. Flip the lever of the quick-release binder bolt in the open

position in order to loosen the seatpost.

2. The seatpost with the saddle should now be free to move up and down. If it is not, hold the lever and unscrew the thumb nut on the other side by about one turn. If it still isn't, enter some liquid lubricant between the seatpost and the seat lug, wait a minute or two and try again, if necessary twisting the saddle with the seatpost relative to the frame.

3. Place the seat in the desired location (if lubrication was needed, first remove it all the way, then clean the seatpost and the interior of the seat tube and apply some vaseline to the outside of the seatpost).

4. Holding the saddle at the correct height, and aligned perfectly straight forward, flip the quick-release lever in the closed position.

5. Check whether the saddle is now installed firmly. If not, loosen the quick-release lever, tighten the thumb nut perhaps one turn, and try again.

6. Try out and readjust if necessary until the location is satisfactory.

Note:
If your bike has a Hite-Rite spring adjuster, apply just enough downward force on the saddle to achieve the desired location when adjusting. If the range of the Hite-Rite is incorrect for the required

seat position, undo the clamp around the seatpost and attach it higher or lower as required.

Adjusting Saddle Angle and Position

Generally, both of these adjustments are carried out with the same bolts that hold the saddle to the seatpost, which can be reached from under the saddle (except on some special seatposts, such as the Campagnolo Euclid model, which has an adjustment by means of a large knurled button and an additional quick-release—a mild case of overkill). You will need an Allen key or whatever other wrench fits the seatpost adjusting bolts on your particular bike.

Procedure:

1. If the seat must be moved forward or backward, loosen both bolts by about one or two turns each.

2. Holding the clamp on top of the seatpost with one hand and the saddle with the other, move the latter in the correct position.

3. If the seat has to be merely tipped—the front raised or lowered relative to the rear portion—loosen the nuts, and then move the saddle in the correct orientation.

4. Holding the seat in the correct location and orientation, tighten the bolts, making sure the seat does not move while doing so.

5. Check and readjust if necessary.

Replacing Saddle with Seatpost

It is usually easier to remove the combination of saddle and seatpost than to remove the saddle alone. This is also the first step in removing the seatpost. You may need a wrench for the bolt on the Hite-Rite if your bike is so equipped.

The lightest: Flite saddle with titanium rails and, interestingly enough, a leather seat.

photo courtesy Flite

225

Removal procedure:

1. Loosen the quick-release binder bolt until the seatpost can be moved up or down freely, as described under *Adjusting Saddle Height*.

2. Pull the saddle with the seatpost out.

Installation procedure:

1. Clean the outside of the seatpost and the inside of the seat tube, than smear vaseline on the seatpost to prevent cor-

Long's the word in mountain bike seatposts: 330 mm long SunTour seat post.

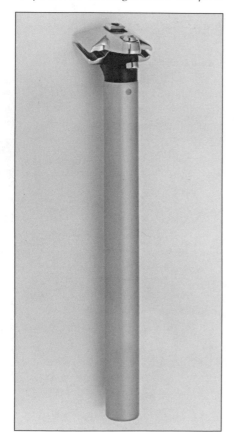

photo courtesy SunTour

rosion and to ease subsequent adjustments.

2. Install the seatpost with the saddle installed and adjust it at the correct height.

3. In case you are installing it with a Hite-Rite, clamp it around the seatpost when it is perfectly aligned and at the maximum comfortable height.

4. Tighten the quick-release binder bolt as described under *Adjusting Saddle Height*.

Note:
If adjustment problems persist, especially if the seatpost won't come loose, it may be necessary to drill out the hole at the bottom of the slot in the rear of the seat lug to about 3 mm (⅛ in)—or drill it yourself, since it prevents the formation of cracks and eases clamping or unclamping the lug around the seatpost.

Replacing Seatpost or Saddle

Not exactly a job that is often necessary, except if a new saddle or seatpost has to be installed—or to get water out of the frame. Just the same, here's how to go about it. You'll need an Allen key or other wrench to fit bolts that hold seat to seatpost, and sometimes a wrench to loosen the nut of the Hite-Rite.

Removal procedure:

1. For the time being, leave the saddle installed on the seatpost

and remove the seatpost complete with the saddle as described under *Replacing Saddle with Seatpost,* loosening the Hite-Rite clamp around the seatpost if installed.

2. Separate the saddle from the seatpost by unscrewing the bolts that hold the saddle's wires to the seatpost clamp.

Installation procedure:

1. Install the saddle on the seatpost.

2. Install the seatpost with the saddle as described under *Replacing Saddle with Seatpost,* entering the seatpost through the Hite-Rite if appropriate.

3. In case you are installing it with a Hite-Rite, clamp it around the seatpost when it is at the maximum height you want the seat to be.

4. Adjust the height, the forward position and the angle of the saddle as described in the relevant sections above.

5. Check and readjust if necessary.

Maintenance of Leather Saddle

If you use a real leather saddle (as opposed to the usual nylon one with a thin leather cover), make sure it does not get wet. Wrap a plastic bag around the saddle when transporting the bike or leaving it outside when there is the slightest chance of rain. If it does get wet, don't sit on it until it is

thoroughly dried out, since otherwise it will deform permanently. To keep it water repellant and slightly flexible, treat it with a leather treatment such as Brooks Proofide at least twice a year.

Adjust the tension of a leather saddle no more than once a year and only when it has noticeably sagged: tighten the bolt shown in the illustration perhaps one turn at the most. Don't overdo this adjustment, since it often causes the saddle to be pulled into an uncomfortable shape.

Still the most comfortable leather saddles, such as the Brooks ATB Conquest, have double wires and coil springs. To install this kind of saddle on a regular seatpost, you will have to install a filler piece between the wires in the saddle. Breeze and Angel, manufacturers of the Hite-Rite, also offer such a filler piece. Place it (or a home-made substitute) between the saddle's two pairs of wires and between the seatpost's

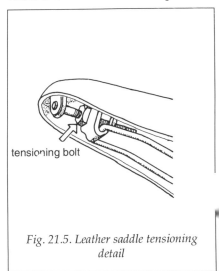

Fig. 21.5. Leather saddle tensioning detail

227

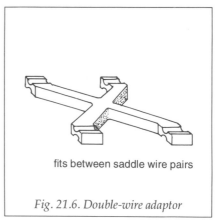

fits between saddle wire pairs

Fig. 21.6. Double-wire adaptor

Typical saddle quick-release.

main part and its clamp, then tighten the bolts and adjust the seat as described above.

There may well be relief on its way in the saddle department.

Modern gel materials and air-cushioned designs are being developed and once their designs have matured, everything you ever heard about seating comfort may be outdated. Not yet, though.

CHAPTER 22

Mountain Bike Suspension

Some form of cushioning is almost essential in off-road riding. Even though the mountain bike's fat tires brought hitherto unknown comfort, the real need for suspension is not just for comfort, but also for traction and control: an effective suspension keeps the wheels on the ground and your hands on the bars.

Although some sprung bikes have long been available, the big boom is quite recent. A distinction can be made between full-suspension bikes and those that are sprung in the front only. In this chapter we will take a look at the various systems that are conceivable, their theoretical basis, and their practical applications as available to date.

The world of bicycle suspension is full of surprises to those used to dealing with motorcycle suspension who try to extrapolate the results from that field to the mountain bike scene. Slingshot was one of the first contenders. Although it seems to break all the rules, it works OK, even uphill. And it weighs less than any other bike in its class..

Bob Allen photo

229

The Basics of Suspension

Actually, the pneumatic tire, perhaps unbeknown to its inventor John Boyd Dunlop, put the suspension in exactly the right place. The theory of suspension, which was largely developed since that time, recognizes that the unsprung mass should be minimized. That's another way of saying the closer to the road, the more effective the suspension. You can't get any closer to the road than the tires. And the tire's suspension effect can easily be fine-tuned by controlling the inflation pressure: let some air out in terrain that is particularly rough, especially if you go at some speed, inflate them a little harder when the going is smooth.

Until the sudden advances in recent years, most other suspension systems proposed or realized had been mere compromises compared to the pneumatic tire. Not only did all of those other systems leave a significant portion of the bike's mass unsprung (namely whatever is between the spring and the road), most of them also affected dimensions that should remain constant for effective cycling.

However, the tire's problem is the very limited depth by which it can deform without negatively affecting rolling resistance on a smooth road, which is about ½ inch at the most, even on a 2 inch fat tire, and at least 2 inches would be nice in many kinds of terrain. That's why designers did not give up on the idea of separate suspen-

sion systems—and have come up with some real advances in recent years.

Before we go into the pure theory of suspension, here is a brief layman's summary. The quality of the ride is determined by the following factors:

- ☐ Amount of travel, i.e. how big an object the suspension can swallow.

- ☐ Damping, i.e. how it resists unintentional movement up and down.

- ☐ Sticktion, i.e. what minimum force must be overcome to become effective.

- ☐ Geometry effect, i.e. whether the bike will handle differently with the suspension compressed.

Suspension Theory

Virtually all that is known about suspension theory stems from the motorcycle literature, and my own experience indicates that some of it should be taken with a pinch of salt when it comes to bicycle suspension. But to set the scene for an intelligent and informed discussion, here is the established theory on suspension for single-track vehicles as modified for rider-propelled machines.

For the efficient transfer of power to the pedals, the distance between the rider's seat and the crank axle should remain constant. Any suspension system in the seat, the seat post or the seat tube

230

completely ignores this requirement. Oddly enough, such designs
recur on a regular basis. Three
other dimensions that should
preferably remain constant for
maximum control are the wheelbase, the amount of trail, and the
head tube angle. That rules out
several possible suspension systems in the front end.

Finally, the suspension must be
damped, especially on the rebound, to be satisfactory. That
means that after contracting, it
should come to rest in the original
position with a minimum number
of oscillations, as shown graphical-
ly in Fig. 22.1. Two forms of damping are important: initial damping
in response to a sudden load, and
rebound damping on the way
back. Only with hydraulically
damped shock absorbers is the latter form of damping adequately
provided—at a price, because
these things are quite a bit more
expensive than systems based on
compressed or stretched elastomers.

In the rear, the best way is to
design the mechanism to pivot
around the bottom bracket, so
there is no change in wheel base
and chain tension when the
suspension is compressed relatively to what it is under unloaded
conditions. In the rear it also helps
if the design is such that there is
minimal lowering of the bottom
bracket when the suspension is
loaded. In the front a relatively
upright steerer angle keeps the
steering geometry most constant,
providing the right amount of trail
is still provided.

Obviously, all these criteria are
best served if the bike's frame is
designed with the particular
suspension system in mind for the
fork. On the other hand, it is nice
to find a front fork that can easily
be installed in an existing frame.

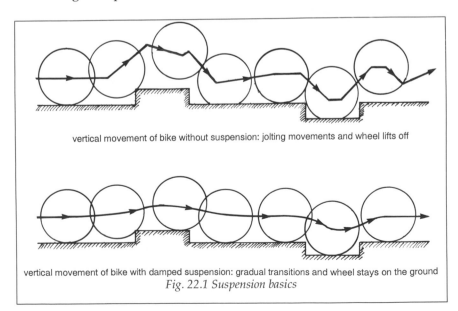

vertical movement of bike without suspension: jolting movements and wheel lifts off

vertical movement of bike with damped suspension: gradual transitions and wheel stays on the ground

Fig. 22.1 Suspension basics

When looking for a suspension system, don't assume that what is best on a bike that is custom designed around a specific suspension should also work best when retrofitting an existing bike: retrofitting is a compromise that is most sensibly handled by something designed for that specific purpose.

Whatever common knowledge on suspension theory is available must be measured by the real experience, and oddly enough much of it does not pass that critical text, as I could establish myself when test-riding several systems. Too much of the available body of knowledge is based on experience with motorcycles, especially the concept that the unsprung mass must be minimized.

As it turns out, one of the most effective forms of mountain bike suspension is by means of a device as simple as the sprung stem: it is more important to insulate the hands from the shocks of the road than to insulate the bike itself. This can largely be explained on the basis of the dramatic difference in weight between motorcycle components and those on the bicycle; as an example, an entire mountain bike often weighs less than does the front wheel and the unsprung portion of telescoping forks on a typical modern motorcycle.

Clearly, the proof of the pudding is in the eating, and I advise you to take nobody's word for it without having tried it yourself under the kind of riding conditions you anticipate for your own use.

Where it Matters

Many suspension bikes are great fun to ride, but only where there is a reason to use a suspension. That applies to downhill riding at speed, not to some other forms of riding, such as technical trails riding. In fact, for trials use, practiced more in the Northwest and Northeast of the U.S., no form of suspension seems to be suitable: you lose the control over the bike that is needed to make it do what you want.

I find it particularly curious to see typical East coast bikes, such as Klein's, whose geometry clearly say 'I'm not built for speed but for technical trails riding' suddenly coming out with suspensions that may be perfectly good, but not for that kind of riding. But for fast downhills it's fantastic what a little shock absorbtion will do. And even at relatively slow speeds going uphill, certainly the front end becomes much more manageable with some springiness.

Forms of Suspension and Damping

I like to divide the various suspension systems into a limited number of main categories, whether used in the front or the rear. As represented in Fig. 22.2, these are:

- ☐ elastomer in compression
- ☐ elastomer in tension
- ☐ torsion rod
- ☐ leaf spring

- coil spring in compression
- coil spring in tension
- pneumatic

The other side of the story is the damping, which is needed to stop the suspension from merely turning jolts into perpetual swinging motion. Damping can take the form of one of the following:

- friction
- hydraulic

Each of these various systems, both for springiness and for damping, has some advantages and disadvantages. All of them can be made to work very well or very poorly, last long or fall apart, depending more on their detail design and the quality of their construction than on their respective principles of operation. In the fol-

lowing section, we'll take a look of their operating principles.

Elastomer in Compression

A cushion of elastomers (a rubbery material) is compressed under the effect of the shock impact. Relatively cheap and simple to make, this method is used both in the front and the rear. In the front, it may be either in the form of two parallel units in the fork blades, that will look just like 'hydraulic' shocks, but will typically have less travel and less rebound damping.

The Alex Moulton small-wheel bikes, hardly known in the U.S. were the first to use this principle satisfactorily both front and rear. The damping is controlled by a knob that is turned to increase or decrease the friction in the

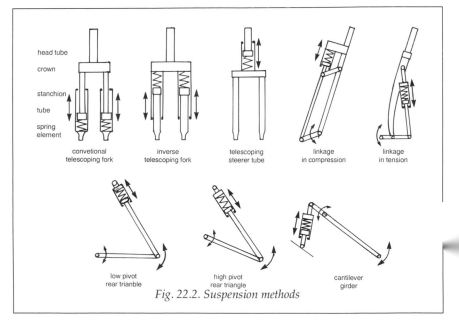

Fig. 22.2. Suspension methods

Suspenders, "upside-down shocks

Pressure control valve on Marzocchi fork

mechanical parts. One of the nicest designs of this type is the one by Browning, used on several makes of bikes since 1992, that is integrated between the headset and the fork crown, with a linkage system that keeps the fork blades rigid relative to each other.

Typically, a combination of elastomer pads of different hardness is installed. Most of these units can be adjusted by selecting the appropriate combination of pads, which are often easily accessible for replacement. The manufacturers should supply a range of color-coded elastomer pads and adequate instructions that tell you how to select and install the right combination for a particular rider's weight

Elastomer in Tension

Rarely used but potentially very simple and quite satisfactory if done right, this is essentially an elastic strap, like a bungee cord, stretched between two points on a linkage mechanism. To work well, the linkage mechanism must be controlled to minimize lateral movement, and there must be an adjustable knob to control the tension for damping control.

The first time I saw this principle applied on a bike was in the late sixties on Captain Dan Henry's bike, which is described in some detail in Fred DeLong's excellent, though somewhat dated book *DeLong's Guide to Bicycles and Bicycling*.

Torsion Rod

The principle used on many independent suspensions on small European cars, it is based on the limited elasticity in twisting or bending a more or less straight piece of an otherwise seemingly rigid material. It was used on the 1992 version of the Merlin titanium bike—easily the lightest suspension bike I've ever seen. An extraneous damping is in this case not as much required because there is very little rebound.

Leaf Spring

Well, in reality it will be a single fiber-reinforced member, rather than a conventional steel leaf spring. The Allsop bike uses this principle to keep the saddle 'afloat', and it is not amongst my favorites for any use except all-out

downhill riding. Laterally, the thing must be rigid enough (yes it is on the Allsop) to resist sideways sway.

Coil Spring in Compression

Often used in the back in combination with a guiding linkage and elastomer pads to limit the impact at final compression, this system is reasonably simple. As long as the linkage is well designed to limit changes in geometry, it can work quite well. These systems are generally dependent on a more or less complex linkage system.

By far the most cleverly designed of these are those by Mert Lawwill, as used in the rear on the Gary Fisher full suspension bike. Lawwill himself markets a front

Works better than you may think: Allsop Softride with carbon fiber 'leaf spring' and flexible stem.

photo courtesy Allsop Softride

fork that uses the same principle and, once in production, it promises to be a real winner.

These particular linkage systems keep the bike's geometry—its wheelbase, steering trail, etc.—identical whether the suspension is compressed or not, resulting in the most surprisingly effective suspension and control over the bike.

Coil Spring in Tension

Rarely used, but this system would work essentially like the elastomer in tension described above. Again the design and construction of the linkage system would be critical.

Pneumatic

Probably still the preferred method for the front, this system uses a chamber with compressed air as the cushion. The chamber can be enclosed in a flexible (e.g. butyl rubber) chamber so it does not leak out. Somewhere there may be a valve to let in more air to increase its tension or let some out to decrease it as appropriate to the rider's weight.

Damping usually is in the form of a hydraulic chamber with a little orifice through which the hydraulic liquid passes slowly enough to form the right resistance. This system is used virtually only in telescoping forks (one in each blade). Rock Shox and Marzochi are perhaps the best known

brands, but there are many more. Adjustment is by increasing or decreasing the air pressure via a special valve and a pump (in most cases a football pump with matching needle).

Other forms of adjustment include the fine-tuning of the damping system by means of selecting a different fluid for the hydraulic system. Generally, ATF 100 (a common automatic transmission fluid) is factory-installed, but more or less damping can be achieved by replacing it with a fluid with higher or lower viscosity, following the manufacturer's service instructions, which can be obtained via your bike shop or directly from the manufacturer.

An interesting variant of the pneumatic suspension principle is the Firestone pneumatic cushion. This is merely an air-filled rubber ball that can be installed between two points and has been successfully used in the rear in combination with some form of friction damping.

Rear Suspensions

Any suspension for the rear requires a heavily modified frame design. This makes it virtually impossible to offer after-market designs that can be retrofitted to an existing bike. There are numerous possibilities to achieve adequate travel in the rear, because here it is possible to use the leverage effect by mounting the spring and damper close to the pivot point (either on the same side or on the opposite side from the wheel).

All of the same methods described above can be used in the spring element. In fact, the spring and damping elements are the easy part of a rear suspension, because they can be bought off-the-shelf, unlike those used in the front. Here the trick lies in the location of the pivot point, its mounting and the linkage mechanism involved. See the section on the effect of suspension on the bike's geometry for more details.

Stiction

Stiction is an acronym made up of the words stickiness and friction. It refers to the directness of response to the impact of a force on the suspension system. Interestingly, it has been described both as a positive and as a negative fea-

ture. Experienced riders, used to a feel of control they get on an unsprung bike consider some degree of stiction positive, because it limits the deflection to cases where the shock is so significant that it is really needed.

Many less experienced riders seem to have what I call the Princess-and-the-Pea-complex ('Did I feel a pea just then?') and want to feel fully cushioned, not aware that their interaction with the bike is largely a function of the extent to which they develop a feel for its movements in the terrain.

As so often, the truth probably lies somewhere in the middle. A little stiction is a good feature, in fact it can be seen as initial damping,

Trek cantilevered rear suspension. The T3C in the name refers to the fact that each inch of deflection of the spring element corresponds to 3 inches of travel at the wheel—which can be achieved with all cantilever designs.

but too much stiction would make the ride too rough, and that's not what you get a bike with suspension for.

Brakes and Suspension

In the rear, there is usually no great problem finding a good place to mount the regular cantilever brakes. However front suspension forks are anathema to conventional braking. The telescoping arms when mounted the conventional way move the crown up and down relative to the wheel axle, so the location of the brake shifts relative to the rim. This is solved by means of a sturdy metal bridge that hold the fork stanchions parallel and to which the brake pivots are installed at a point that stays fixed relative to the rim. Even so, there is some loss of rigidity in most suspension forks, and braking can be less definite, in some cases causing a lock-up of the suspension. Roughly the same applies to most linkage-type of front suspensions.

When the telescoping members are mounted upside down (the thick end at the bottom), you can forget about the whole idea of cantilever brakes, and a disk or drum brake must be used—see Chapter 20.

The Effect of Suspension on the Bike's Geometry

Except for the simple sprung stem, all suspension systems tend to change the bike's geometry. Somewhere, there must be room to accommodate the depth of the range of movement, and since clearances on a modern mountain bike tend to be minimal, the only way to add it is by raising the frame.

In the front, a typical suspension fork requires about 1½ to 2 inches more room, lifting the front end by that much. This in turns shifts the bike's head tube angle to a shallower position—when uncompressed. As you hit an unevenness, and the fork is compressed, this angle changes to a steeper one again, and if the system is not well damped, the angle will change back and forth as the fork oscillates. This can lead to somewhat unpredictable behavior, and it is one reason to keep the unit adjusted on the stiff side to maximize control.

Another measure of interest is the fork trail. As we've seen in Chapter 16, the fork rake and the steerer angle must be matched carefully, yet as the fork is pushed in, and the steerer angle changes, the fork rake remains the same. Some manufacturers pride themselves in their advertisements with a presumably clever design that keeps the rake constant regardless of the angle. But curiously enough this merely indicates that these same manufacturers don't really understand the problem: in fact, the rake should vary to achieve the trail that is right for any particular steerer angle. By and large, systems with variable rake therefore should be preferred to those with constant rake, and even those with constant trail.

In the rear, an important aspect is the response of the suspension to the force applied on the pedals. Preferably, the pivot points should be arranged in such a way that the tension in the chain, resulting from the application of force on the pedals, tends to push the rear wheel down, causing it to maximize traction. This is achieved by placing the pivot point high enough, preferably about in line with the point where the chain runs off the top of the chainring.

Other Suspension Methods

Rather than installing a cheap suspension fork in the front and dreaming of a low cost rear suspension, there are other ways to dampen the ride satisfactorily

without breaking the bank. For the front, I have found sprung stems remarkably effective. They have an enormous amount of travel and give more direct steering than most even the best telescoping front forks. In the rear very much the same could be achieved with a well designed damped sprung seatpost—I'm not holding my breath, but there must be someone out there ready to introduce one that actually works satisfactorily.

Maintenance of Suspension Systems

Keep it clean and check it out. That is about the most important and most generally valid advice with respect to the maintenance of any suspension system. Make sure you keep the manufacturer's descriptive brochure with main-

Left: front fork suspension that increases the wheelbase when compressed.
Right: Lots of travel on flexible stems., and that's perhaps the most important factor.

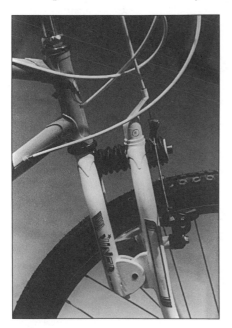

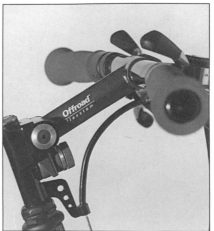

Direct acting rear suspensions have limited travel as compared to cantilevered designs

tenance instructions that apply to your particular type and model.

After every ride, clean the telescoping or otherwise moving parts very carefully. Use a dry cloth and wipe away from the mechanism, making sure you don't push any dirt particles inside. Then use a waxed cloth to go over it again to form a protective layer (don't use vaseline or grease, since that would only attract dirt).

Adjust the tensioning or damping device (either a knob or a valve) to match the rider's weight on the basis of the feel you get in the terrain. Most people tend to adjust them too loose, thinking more cushioning must be better than

less. That is incorrect, since the suspension is only meant to even out real bumps, not to make you seasick swaying up and down.

Check all bolts and nuts and linkage elements to make sure they are neither loose, nor excessively tight, nor bent. If they are loose, tighten them, if they are tight, see whether they can be freed—but leave it to the bike shop mechanic or the manufacturer if things can't be easily corrected. If they are regularly kept cleaned and maintained, most suspension systems will give little trouble.

Of course, like all other mechanical devices, suspensions can actually break. If you notice the thing either gets stuck or moves freely undamped, or works asymmetrically, things are more serious. Even in such cases, a repair may be possible, perhaps merely replacing a seal or a damping valve. In other cases, the whole thing may have to be replaced.

If you carefully read the instruction manual that comes with all the suspensions of any respectable quality, you will have a good feel for when you need to take it to a workshop and what you can fix yourself. Just don't keep riding with an ailing suspension, because that will only aggravate the situation.

Back Matter

Table 1. Recommended frame sizes

leg length		recommended seat tube height				recommended straddle height ground to top tube	
		A center to top of lug		B center-to-center			
cm	in	cm	in	cm	in	cm	in
73	29	35	14	34		65	26
74		36		35		66	
75		37		35	14	67	
76	30	38	15	36		68	27
77		39		37		69	
78		40		38	15	70	
79	31	41	16	39		71	28
80		42		40	16	72	
81	32	43	17	41		73	29
82		44		42		74	
83		45		43	17	75	
84	33	46	18	44		76	30
85		47		45	18	77	
86	34	48	19	46		78	31
87		49		47		79	
88		50		48	19	80	
89	35	51	20	49		81	32
90		52		50	20	82	
91	36	53	21	51		83	33
92		54		52		84	
93		55		53	21	85	
94	37	56	22	54		86	34
95		57		56		87	

Remarks:
The seat tube lengths shown in this table are recommended values. The maximum size is about one inch (2.5 cm) more, the minimum about one inch (2.5 cm) less.

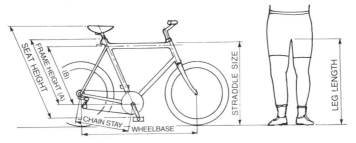

Table 2. Gear table: gear in inches for 26-in wheels

Number of teeth on chainwheel (columns) · Number of teeth on sprocket (rows)

Sprocket \ Chainwheel	24	26	28	30	32	34	36	38	39	40	41	42	43	44	45	46	47	48	49	50	51	52	53
13	48	52	56	60	64	68	72	76	78	80	82	84	86	88	90	92	94	96	98	100	102	104	106
14	45	48	52	56	60	63	67	70	72	74	76	78	80	82	84	85	87	89	91	93	95	97	98
15	42	45	49	52	55	59	62	66	68	69	71	73	75	76	78	80	81	83	85	87	88	90	92
16	39	42	45	49	52	55	58	61	63	65	67	68	70	72	73	75	76	78	80	81	83	85	86
17	37	40	43	46	49	52	55	58	60	61	63	64	66	67	69	70	72	73	75	76	78	80	81
18	35	38	40	43	46	49	52	55	56	58	59	61	62	64	65	66	68	69	71	72	74	75	77
19	33	36	38	41	44	47	49	52	53	55	56	57	59	60	62	63	64	66	67	68	70	71	73
20	31	34	36	39	42	44	47	49	51	52	53	55	56	57	59	60	61	62	64	65	66	68	69
21	30	32	35	37	40	42	45	47	48	50	51	52	53	54	56	57	58	59	61	62	63	64	66
22	28	31	33	35	38	40	43	45	46	47	48	50	51	52	53	54	56	57	58	59	60	61	63
23	27	29	32	34	36	38	41	43	44	45	46	47	49	50	51	52	53	54	55	57	58	59	60
24	26	28	30	32	35	37	39	41	42	43	44	45	47	48	49	50	51	52	53	54	55	56	57
25	25	27	29	31	33	35	37	39	41	40	43	44	45	46	47	48	49	50	51	52	53	54	55
26	24	26	28	30	32	34	36	38	39	40	41	42	43	44	45	46	47	48	49	50	51	52	53
27	23	25	27	29	31	33	35	37	38	39	39	40	41	42	43	44	45	46	47	48	49	50	51
28	22	24	26	28	30	32	33	35	36	37	38	39	40	41	42	43	44	45	46	46	47	48	49
30	21	23	24	26	28	29	31	33	34	35	36	36	37	38	39	40	41	42	42	43	44	45	46
32	20	21	23	24	26	28	29	31	32	33	33	34	35	36	37	37	38	39	40	41	41	42	43
34	18	20	21	23	24	26	28	29	30	31	31	32	33	34	34	35	36	37	37	38	39	40	41
38	16	18	19	21	22	23	25	26	27	27	28	29	29	30	31	31	32	33	34	34	35	36	36

Number of teeth on sprocket

Table 3. Gear table: development in meters for 26-in wheels

Number of teeth on chainwheel

Teeth on sprocket	24	26	28	30	32	34	36	38	39	40	41	42	43	44	45	46	47	48	49	50	51	52	53
13	3.80	4.10	4.50	4.80	5.10	5.40	5.70	6.10	6.20	6.40	6.50	6.70	6.90	7.00	7.20	7.30	7.50	7.70	7.80	8.00	8.10	8.30	8.50
14	3.60	3.90	4.10	4.40	4.70	5.00	5.30	5.60	5.80	5.90	6.10	6.20	6.40	6.50	6.70	6.80	7.00	7.10	7.30	7.40	7.60	7.70	7.90
15	3.30	3.60	3.90	4.10	4.40	4.70	5.00	5.30	5.40	5.50	5.70	5.80	5.90	6.10	6.20	6.40	6.50	6.60	6.80	6.90	7.10	7.20	7.30
16	3.10	3.40	3.60	3.90	4.10	4.40	4.70	4.90	5.10	5.20	5.30	5.40	5.60	5.70	5.80	6.00	6.10	6.20	6.40	6.50	6.60	6.70	6.90
17	2.90	3.20	3.40	3.70	3.90	4.10	4.40	4.60	4.80	4.90	5.00	5.10	5.20	5.40	5.50	5.60	5.70	5.90	6.00	6.10	6.20	6.30	6.50
18	2.80	3.00	3.20	3.50	3.70	3.90	4.10	4.40	4.50	4.60	4.70	4.80	5.00	5.10	5.20	5.30	5.40	5.50	5.60	5.80	5.90	6.00	6.10
19	2.60	2.80	3.10	3.30	3.50	3.70	3.90	4.10	4.30	4.40	4.50	4.60	4.70	4.80	4.90	5.00	5.10	5.20	5.40	5.50	5.60	5.70	5.80
20	2.50	2.70	2.90	3.10	3.30	3.50	3.70	3.90	4.00	4.10	4.30	4.40	4.50	4.70	4.80	4.90	4.90	5.00	5.10	5.20	5.30	5.40	5.50
21	2.40	2.60	2.80	3.00	3.20	3.40	3.60	3.80	3.90	4.00	4.10	4.20	4.20	4.30	4.40	4.50	4.60	4.70	4.80	4.90	5.00	5.10	5.15
22	2.30	2.50	2.60	2.80	3.00	3.20	3.40	3.60	3.70	3.80	3.90	4.00	4.10	4.15	4.20	4.30	4.40	4.50	4.60	4.70	4.80	4.90	4.95
23	2.20	2.30	2.50	2.70	2.90	3.10	3.20	3.40	3.50	3.60	3.70	3.80	3.90	4.00	4.10	4.15	4.20	4.30	4.40	4.50	4.60	4.70	4.80
24	2.10	2.20	2.40	2.60	2.80	2.90	3.10	3.30	3.40	3.50	3.50	3.60	3.70	3.80	3.90	4.00	4.10	4.15	4.20	4.30	4.40	4.50	4.60
25	2.00	2.20	2.30	2.50	2.70	2.80	3.00	3.20	3.25	3.30	3.40	3.50	3.60	3.70	3.70	3.80	3.90	4.00	4.10	4.15	4.20	4.30	4.40
26	1.90	2.10	2.20	2.40	2.60	2.70	2.90	3.00	3.10	3.20	3.30	3.40	3.40	3.50	3.60	3.70	3.80	3.85	3.90	4.00	4.10	4.15	4.20
27	1.85	2.00	2.20	2.30	2.50	2.60	2.80	2.90	3.00	3.10	3.20	3.25	3.30	3.40	3.50	3.55	3.60	3.70	3.80	3.80	3.90	4.00	4.10
28	1.80	1.90	2.10	2.20	2.40	2.50	2.70	2.80	2.90	3.00	3.05	3.10	3.20	3.30	3.35	3.40	3.50	3.60	3.65	3.70	3.80	3.90	3.90
30	1.70	1.80	1.90	2.10	2.20	2.40	2.50	2.60	2.70	2.80	2.90	2.95	3.00	3.05	3.10	3.20	3.30	3.35	3.40	3.50	3.55	3.60	3.70
32	1.60	1.70	1.80	1.90	2.10	2.20	2.30	2.50	2.55	2.60	2.70	2.75	2.80	2.90	2.95	3.00	3.05	3.10	3.20	3.25	3.30	3.40	3.45
34	1.50	1.60	1.70	1.80	2.00	2.10	2.20	2.30	2.40	2.45	2.50	2.60	2.60	2.70	2.75	2.80	2.90	2.95	3.00	3.10	3.15	3.20	3.25
38	1.40	1.50	1.60	1.70	1.80	2.00	2.10	2.20	2.25	2.30	2.40	2.45	2.50	2.55	2.60	2.70	2.75	2.80	2.85	2.90	2.95	3.00	3.10

Number of teeth on sprocket

Table 4. Troubleshooting Guide

Problem/symptom	Possible cause	Required correction	For description see
bike hard to ride (high resistance when coasting and pedalling)	1. insufficient tire pressure	inflate and/or mend tire (use high-pressure pump)	chapter 17 (tires) chapter 5 (pump)
	2. wheel rubs on brake, fork or frame	adjust brake; adjust or straighten wheel; install narrower tire if insufficient clearance	chapter 17 (wheels) chapter 20 (brakes)
	3. dirt build-up on wheel or bike	clean bike	chapter 2
	4. resistance in wheel bearings	lubricate, adjust or overhaul wheel bearings	chapter 17
bike hard to pedal (but coasts alright)	1. accumulated dirt on chain	clean chain, chainwheels, sprockets and derailleurs	chapters 2, 18, 19
	2. insufficient lubrication on chain	lubricate	chapter 18
	3. resistance in bottom bracket or pedal bearings	lubricate, adjust or overhaul bearings	chapter 18
chain drops off chain-wheel or sprocket	1. derailleur out of adjustment	adjust derailleurs	chapter 19
gears do not engage properly	1. shift lever dirty, loose or defective	clean, adjust, lubricate or replace	chapters 2 and 19
	2. derailleur cable anchor or guides loose, or cable corroded	tighten attachments or replace cable	chapter 19
	3. derailleur out of adjustment	adjust derailleur	chapter 19
	4. chain too short or too long	correct or replace	chapter 18

Problem	Cause	Remedy	Reference
inadequate braking	1. rim or brake wet, greasy or dirty	clean rim and brake	chapters 2, 17, 20
	2. brakes out of adjustment	adjust brakes	chapter 20
	3. friction in brake cables	replace or lubricate	chapter 20
	4. brake shoe worn	replace brake shoe	chapter 20
brakes squeak	1. brake attachment loose	adjust and tighten	chapter 20
	2. brake pad worn	replace	chapter 20
	3. rim or brake pad dirty	clean or replace pad	chapters 2 and 20
	(if none of these causes: don't worry, some brakes just squeak)		
chain slips	1. chain and sprockets dirty	clean and lubricate	chapters 2 and 18
	2. rear derailleur out of adjustment	adjust	chapter 19
	3. chain worn (especially when used with new freewheel)	replace chain	chapter 18
	4. freewheel sprocket worn	replace sprocket or freewheel	chapter 18
irregular pedalling movement	1. crank or pedal loose	tighten cranks and pedals	chapter 18
	2. pedal or bottom bracket bearing out of adjustment	adjust or overhaul	chapter 18
	3. crank, chainwheel or pedal axle bent	replace or get straightened	see bike shop
steering vibrates or is inprecise	1. wheels out of true or not in line	center and true both wheels and, if necessary, get frame and fork aligned	chapter 17 / see bike shop
	2. head-set bearings loose or worn	adjust, overhaul or replace	chapter 16
	3. wheel bearings loose	adjust or overhaul	chapter 17

Organizations and Offices

Australian Cycling Council
153 The Kingsway
Cronulla
Sydney 2230, Australia

Bicycle Federation of America
1818 R St. N.W.
Washington, D.C. 20009, USA

Bicycle Federation of Australia
399 Pitt Street
Sydney 2000, Australia

Bikecentennial
Box 8308
Missoula, MT 59807, USA

British Cycling Federation
70 Brompton Road
London SW3 1EN, Great Britain

British Cycling Federation
Touring Bureau
3 Moor Lane
Lancaster, Great Britain

British Cyclo Cross Association
208 Ecclesall Road
Sheffield 511 8JD, Great Britain

Bureau of Land Management
U.S. Department of the Interior
18th and C Streets, NW
Washington, D.C. 20240, USA

Canadian Cycling Association
Touring Department
333 River Road
Vanier Ontario KlL 8B9, Canada

Cross Country Cycling Club
5 Old Station Cottages
Ford, Arundel, West Sussex
BNl8 OBJ, Great Britain

Countryside Commission
John Dower House
Crescent Place
Cheltenham GL50 3RA
Great Britain

Cyclists' Touring Club
69 Meadrow Godalming, Surrey
GU7 3HS, Great Britain

Effective Cycling League
726Madrone
Sunnyvale, CA 94086, USA

League of American Wheelmen
6707 Whitestone Road Suite 209
Baltimore, MD 21207, USA

Mountain Bike Club
3 The Shrubbery
Albert Street Telford TF2 9AS,
Great Britain

National Park Foundation
PO Box 57473
Washington, D.C. 20037, USA

National Park Service
U.S. Department of the Interior
18th and C Streets NW
Washington, D.C. 20240, USA

NORBA (National Off-Road
Bicycle Association)
PO. Box 1901
Chandler AZ 85244, USA

Rough Stuff Fellowship
9 Liverpool Avenue
Southport, Merseyside PR8 3NE,
Great Britain

Sierra Club
730 Polk Street
San Francisco, CA 94109, USA

United States Forest Service
U.S. Department of Agriculture
PO Box 2417
Washington DC, USA

U.S. Geological Survey
1200 South Eads Street Arlington,
VA 22202 , USA
(map distribution for states east of
Mississippi River)

US Geological Survey
PO Box 25286
Denver, CO 80225, USA
(map distribution for states west
of Mississippi River)

Periodicals

Adventure Bike
1127 Hamilton Street
Allentown, PA 18102, USA

Bicycle Action
136/138 New Cavendish Street
LondonW1M 7FG, Great Britain

Bicycle Magazine
PO Box 381
Mill Harbour
London E14 9TW, Great Britain

Bicycle USA
10 E. Read St.
Emmaus, PA 18098, USA
(LAW members' magazine)

Bicycling
33 E. Minor St.
Emmaus, PA 18098, USA

Cycletouring
69 Meadrow
Godalming, Surrey GU7 3HS,
Great Britain
(CTC members' magazine)

Cyclist
PO. Box 907
Farmingdale, NY 11737-0001, USA

Bicycle Guide
711 Boylston St.
Boston, MA 02116, USA

Mountain Bike
33 E. Minor St.
Emmaus PA 18098, USA

Mountain Bike Action
PO Box 9502
Mission Hills, CA 91345, USA

Mountain Biking
7950 Deering Ave.
Canoga Park, CA 91304, USA

Mountain Biking UK
Woodstock House, Luton Road
Faversham, Kent ME13 8HQ,
Great Britain

New Cyclist
14 St. Clement's Grove
York YO2 1JZ, Great Britain

Rough Stuff Journal
A. J. Matthews
9 Liverpool Avenue
Southport, Merseyside PR8 3NE,
Great Britain

Bibliography

Advanced First Aid. New York: Doubleday; The American National Red Cross, 1973.

American Youth Hostels Handbook. Delaplane, VT: American Youth Hostel Association (annual).

Ballantine, R, and R. Grant. *Richard's Ultimate Bicycle Book*. New York: London, Dorling Kindersley, 1992.

Bicycle Touring Atlas. New York: American Youth Hostel Association, 1969.

Biestman, M. *Travel for Two*. Sausalito, CA: Pergot Press, 1986.

Bridge, R. *Freewheeling: The Bicycle Camping Book*. Harrisonburg, PA: Stackpole Books, 1974.

———. *Bike Touring*. San Francisco: Sierra Club Books, 1979.

Bunelle, H. and S. Sarvis. *Cooking for Camp and Trail*. San Francisco: Sierra Club Books, 1984.

Burney,S , and T. Gould. *Mountain Bike Racing*. Hudersfield (GB): Springield; San Francisco: Bicycle Books. 1992.

Campground and Trailer Park Guide. Chicago: Rand McNally, (annual).

Carlson, R. (ed). *National Directory of Budget Motels*. New York: Pilot Books, (annual).

Climates of the States. Port Washington, NY: United States National Oceanic and Atmospheric Administration, 1974.

Coello, D. *The Mountain Bike Manual*. Salt Lake City: Dream Garden Press, 1985.

Coles, C.W., H.T. Glenn, and J. Allen. *Glenns Complete Bicycle Manual*. New York: Crown Publishers (2nd Ed.), 1988.

The Complete Guide to America's National Parks. Washington, D.C.: The National Park Foundation, 1984.

The CTC Handbook. Godalming, Surrey (GB): Cyclist's Touring Club, (annual).

Cuthberson, T. *Anybody's Bike Book*. Berkeley, CA: Ten-Speed Press, 1991.

———. *Bike Tripping*. Berkeley, CA: Ten-Speed Press, 1984.

DeLong, F. *DeLong's Guide to Bicycles and Bicycling*. Radnor, PA: Chilton Books, 1978.

Eastman, P. F. *Advanced First Aid for All Outdoors*. Centerville, MD: Cornell Maritime Press, 1976.

Editors of Bicycling Magazine. *Best Bicycle Tours*. Emmaus, PA: Rodale Press, 1981.

Faria, I. E. *Cycling Physiology for the Serious Cyclist*. Springfield, MS: Thomas, 1978.

Fletcher, C. *The New Complete Walker*. New York: Knopf, 1974.

Food and Nutrition Board. *Recommended Dietary Allowances*. Washington, D.C.: National Academy of Sciences, 1974.

Forester J. *Effective Cycling.* Cambridge, MA: MIT-Press, 1984.

Gatty, H. *Finding Your Way on Land and Sea.* Brattleboro, VT: Stephen Green Press, 1983.

Gausden, C. and Crane, N. *The CTC Route Guide to Cycling in Britain and Ireland.* Oxford: Oxford Illustrated Press; Harmondsworth: Penguin Books, 1980.

Gordis, K. and G. LeMond. *Greg LeMond's Complete Book of Bicycling.* New York: Putnam, 1989.

———. *Greg LeMond's Pocket Guide to Bicycle Maintenance and Repair.* New York: Putnam, 1989.

Greenhood, D. *Mapping.* Chicago: University of Chicago Press, 1964.

Hefferson, L. *Cycle Food.* Berkeley, CA: Ten Speed Press, 1976.

Howard, J. *The Cyclist's Companion.* Brattleboro, VT: Stephen Green Press, 1984.

Inside the Cyclist. Brattleboro, VT: Velo-News, 1984.

International Bicycle Touring. Mountain View, CA: World Publications, 1976.

Kals, W. S. *Land Navigation Handbook.* San Francisco: Sierra Club Books, 1971.

Keefe, M. *The Ten Speed Commandments.* Garden City, NY: Doubleday, 1987.

Keller, K. *Mountain Bikes on Public Lands.* Bicycle Federation of America, 1992.

Kellstrom, G. *Map and Compass.* New York: Charles Scribner's Sons, 1973.

Kelly, C. and N. Crane. *Richard's Mountain Bike Book.* New York: Ballantine Books; Oxford: Oxford Illustrated Press, 1988.

Lynn, L. et al. *The Off-Road Bicycle Book.* Butterset (GB): The Leading Edge, 1987.

Nasr, K. *Bicycle Touring International.* San Francisco: Bicycle Books, 1992.

National Atlas of the United States. Washington, D.C.: U.S. Department of the Interior, Geological Survey, 1970.

Nye, P. *The Cyclist's Source Book.* New York: Putnam Publishing, 1991.

Olson, J. *Mountain Biking.* London: Salamander Books; Harrisburg, PA: Stackpole Books, 1989.

Rafoth, R. *Bicycling Fuel.* San Francisco: Bicycle Books, 1988.

Rostaing, B. and B. Walton. *Bill Walton's Total Book of Bicycling.* New York, Toronto: Bantam Books, 1985.

Sloane, E. *Eugene A. Sloane's New Complete Book of All-Terrain Bicycles.* New York: Simon & Schuster, 1990.

———. *The New Complete Book of Bicycling.* New York: Simon & Schuster, 1981.

Stevenson, J. *Mountain Bike Maintenance and Repair.* Huddersfield (GB): Springfield; San Francisco: Bicycle Books, 1992.

Thomas, D. *Roughing it Easy.* Provo, UT: Brigham Young University Press, 1974.

Van der Plas, R. *The Bicycle Commuting Book.* San Francisco: Bicycle Books, 1989.

——. *The Bicycle Racing Guide.* San Francisco: Bicycle Books, 1986.

——. *The Bicycle Repair Book.* San Francisco: Bicycle Books, 1985.

——. *Bicycle Technology.* San Francisco: Bicycle Books, 1991.

——. *The Bicycle Touring Manual.* San Francisco: Bicycle Books, 1987.

——. *Cycle Repair Step by Step.* Huddersfield (GB): Springfield Books, 1988.

——. *Mountain Bike Maintenance.* San Francisco: Bicycle Books, (2nd Ed.) 1992.

——. *Mountain Bike Magic.* San Francisco: Bicycle Books, 1991.

——. *The Penguin Bicycle Handbook.* Harmondsworth (GB): Penguin Books, 1983.

——. *Roadside Bicycle Repairs.* San Francisco: Bicycle Books, (2nd Edition) 1990.

Watts, A. *Instant Weather Forecasting.* New York: Dodd Mead & Co, 1968.

Whiter, R. *The Bicycle Manual on Maintenance and Repairs.* Chicago: Contemporary Books, 1972.

Whitt, F R. and D.G. Wilson. *Bicycling Science.* Cambridge, MA: MIT-Press, (2nd. Ed.) 1982.

Wilhelm, T. and G. Wilhelm. *The Bicycle Touring Book.* Emmaus, PA: Rodale Press, 1980.

Zarka, J. *All Terrain Biking.* San Francisco: Bicycle Books, 1991.

Other Titles Available from Bicycle Books

Title	Author	U.S. Price
All Terrain Biking	Jim Zarka	$7.95
The Backroads of Holland	Helen Colijn	$12.95
The Bicycle Commuting Book	Rob van der Plas	$7.95
The Bicycle Fitness Book	Rob van der Plas	$7.95
The Bicycle Repair Book	Rob van der Plas	$9.95
Bicycle Technology	Rob van der Plas	$16.95
Bicycle Touring International	Kameel Nasr	$18.95
The Bicycle Touring Manual	Rob van der Plas	$16.95
Bicycling Fuel	Richard Rafoth	$9.95
Cycling Europe	Nadine Slavinski	$12.95
Cycling France	Jerry Simpson	$12.95
Cycling Kenya	Kathleen Bennett	$12.95
Cycling the San Francisco Bay Area	Carol O'Hare	$12.95
Cycling the U.S. Parks	Jim Clark	$12.95
In High Gear (hardcover)	Samuel Abt	$21.95
In High Gear (paperback)	Samuel Abt	$10.95
The High Performance Heart	Maffetone & Mantell	$9.95
Major Taylor (hardcover)	Andrew Ritchie	$19.95
The Mountain Bike Book	Rob van der Plas	$10.95
Mountain Bike Magic (color)	Rob van der Plas	$14.95
Mountain Bike Maintenance	Rob van der Plas	$9.95
Mountain Bikes: Maint. & Repair*	Stevenson & Richards	$22.50
Mountain Bike Racing (hardcover)*	Burney & Gould	$22.50
The New Bike Book	Jim Langley	$4.95
Roadside Bicycle Repairs	Rob van der Plas	$4.95
Tour of the Forest Bike Race (color)	H. E. Thomson	$9.95
Tour de France (hardcover)	Samuel Abt	$22.95
Tour de France (paperback)	Samuel Abt	$12.95

Buy our books at your local bookstore or bike store.

Bookstores can obtain these titles for you from our book trade distributor (National Book Network for the USA), bike shops directly from us. If you have difficulty obtaining our books elsewhere, we will be pleased to supply them by priority mail, but we must add $3.50 postage and handling (and California Sales Tax if mailed to a California address). Prepayment by check, money order or credit card must be included with your order.

Bicycle Books, Inc.
PO Box 2038
Mill Valley CA 94941
Tel.: (415) 381-0172

In Great Britain: Bicycle Books
463 Ashley Road
Poole, Dorset BH14 0AX
Tel.: (0202) 71 53 49

* Not available from Bicycle Books in the U.K.